THE BATTLE FOR THE RHINELAND

I0879811

THE BATTLE FOR THE RHINELAND

R. W. THOMPSON

WESTHOLME
Yardley

Originally published in 1958 by Hutchinson & Company.
This edition © 2012 Westholme Publishing.

All rights reserved under International and Pan-American Copyright Conventions. No part of this book may be reproduced in any form or by any electronic or mechanical means, including information storage and retrieval systems, without permission in writing from the publisher, except by a reviewer who may quote brief passages in a review.

Westholme Publishing, LLC
904 Edgewood Road
Yardley, Pennsylvania 19067
Visit our Web site at www.westholmepublishing.com

ISBN: 978-1-59416-170-4
Also available as an eBook.

Printed in the United States of America.

TO

LIEUT. "TOBY" STEPHENSON,
KILLED IN ACTION
Scottish Rifles

"*Believe me, nothing except a battle lost, can be half so melancholy as a battle won.*"

The Duke of Wellington
after Waterloo

CONTENTS

ACKNOWLEDGEMENTS

I WISH to record with pleasure and humility my thanks to the Chief of Military History, Department of the Army, Washington, D.C., for his helpful attitude towards my work. I have also to thank most warmly all those busy people who have found time to aid in checking facts, in finding source material, and discussing many aspects of the actions in this campaign. I am again especially grateful to H. A. Cordery, Esq., the Archivist of the Historical Section, for placing at my disposal the relevant War Office records.

I am grateful also to President Eisenhower, William Bradford Huie and Major John North for permitting me to quote from their work, and for replying so courteously and promptly to my letters.

The extracts from *The Supreme Command* by Forrest Pogue, and from *Objective Schmidt* by Charles B. Macdonald in *Three Battles*, are used by permission of the Chief of Military History, Department of the Army, Washington, D.C.; from *Triumph and Tragedy*, vol. VI by Winston S. Churchill by permission of Lord Camrose and Messrs. Cassell & Co. Ltd.; from *North West Europe*, 1944-5 by John North, and *Grand Strategy*, vol. VI by John Ehrman, by permission of Her Majesty's Stationery Office; from *The Execution of Private Slovik* by William Bradford Huie, by permission of the author and Messrs. Jarrolds.

To all those others, some among my friends, others previously unknown to me, others known only by way of correspondence, who have all given me encouragement in various ways through a very difficult time, I offer my warmest thanks. I embarked upon this task because circumstances had combined to give me a unique personal view of these battlefields. I wish I had the talent to do justice to the opportunities I have enjoyed.

FOREWORD

IN *The Eighty-Five Days* I argued my belief that the main line of attack after the break-out from Normandy should have been the Antwerp, Breda, Moerdijk, Rotterdam line, and not Brussels, Nijmegen, Arnhem, Zuider Zee. I thank those professional soldiers and historians to whom this argument seemed valid, and worth stating.

The book was also an attempt to relate major strategy to the lot of the common soldier on the battlefield, to show what happens to "Jones" when, in the conventional phrases of generals, armies are flung across rivers—or flung back. So far as I know it was, and remains, a task not before attempted in this way.

This second volume, *The Battle for The Rhineland*, argues the vital importance of Schmidt in relation to the Rhineland battle, and to the whole front north of the Ardennes. I believe the argument that the front north of the Ardennes should have been one front is unanswerable.

I have not been able to find anyone who has considered Schmidt in this context, and very few soldiers in this country who have heard of Schmidt at all.

In a more ambitious way than in *The Eighty-Five Days* I have attempted to relate major strategy to the soldier on the battlefield, and to reveal in a new perspective the facts behind the long arguments which bedevilled relations between the Allied generals.

It is inevitable in work of this kind, and at this distance, that men should begin to assume a human shape. In the midst of the passions and distortions of war it was not surprising that the real worth of many commanders was obscured. Some of them seemed to cast gigantic shadows, and the shadows were mistaken for the men. It lent courage to ordinary people to see them in such a fashion.

But we were served by men, not Gods—or "Sacred Cows". These men faced tasks of a magnitude far greater than any in that field which had previously confronted human beings, and far beyond anything in the experience of any one of them. It is not surprising that they made so many mistakes, but that they made so few.

In the history of war from Alexander the Great to Mao Tse Tung the world had not produced more than a handful of men of genius capable of commanding armies. The name of Napoleon springs to mind. Hannibal, perhaps. The magnificent "Pippins", Charles Martel and Charlemagne. Marlborough? I doubt it. Such men are not thrown up generation after generation.

It is certain that nothing approaching genius touched the generals who gave of their best in the Allied cause in N.W. Europe in 1944–5. If these men are to have their just dues they must be seen as men, wrestling with giant tasks bravely, and often boldly. Human stature must be restored to them.

Perhaps of them all only George Patton was truly capable of commanding an army. Not one could manage a group of armies.

It would be a travesty to suggest that Field Marshal Montgomery was "commanding" the left wing of his armies engaged in the battle of the Scheldt, and an even greater travesty to suggest that General Bradley's right hand knew much about what his left hand was doing.

It may be true that the very magnitude of the problems confronting these men forced them to think of themselves in outsize terms, lest by realizing their own true stature they might quail. A senior staff officer once remarked to me: "Even generals wet their knickers". I doubt whether that was true of the commanders of armies and army groups.

The Supreme Commander, General Eisenhower, is exempt from these particular criticisms—if they are criticisms. He did not face these tasks. He has been criticized by some, his own countrymen among them, in that he acted as "a Chairman", and did not exercise his powers of command and enforce his will. It is not, I think, a valid criticism. He had to be a chairman. Short of a Napoleon being available that was the very best we could hope for, and we were fortunate to find a man at once so able in that role, and of unimpeachable integrity. The defects of his virtues, if I may say so, have become apparent in his subsequent role as President of the United States of America.

It is not reasonable that men should expect men suddenly

called to such tasks to become gods. It is stupid to continue to insist that they were gods.

In subjecting many battles to critical and detailed analysis certain constant factors in command have become apparent to me. I found that I was not alone in observing that following the promotion of battalion commanders to command brigades the timings of brigade movements were always too fast. The battalion commander, knowing perfectly well in his mind the composition of his new command, could not at a bound span the gulf between the possibilities of movement of a battalion and a brigade.

It was said by Guderian, I think—or it may have been von Manteuffel—that Hitler was never capable of visualizing anything larger than a division. That was the cause of many of his gravest mistakes. I think it is true of almost all generals: the command of a division represents the limit of the abilities of most very able men.

Field Marshal Montgomery, for example, commanded a division extremely well. It is probable that he made a good job of commanding the Eighth Army—I cannot speak with authority, for I have not studied it. He might have been a very good commander of the 2nd Army—and so might General Sir Miles Dempsey.

The Montgomery-Dempsey relationship is interesting to compare with the Bradley-Patton relationship.

I venture to bring up some of these points with great diffidence, not only because of my admiration for men like Montgomery, and for others whose roles made less monumental demands upon them, but also because I am aware that we do not inhabit a world of reason. The sharp division of the world into two harsh spheres has made itself felt right down the scale, perverting and inhibiting all normal criticism and expressions of opinion on a wide variety of subjects. When I wrote *Cry Korea* I was said to be "anti" all those things for which I was prepared to give my life, and for which I have often risked it. On the slender basis of any criticism of the U.S.A. men are said to be "anti-American".

Since these are the kind of epithets experience has led me to expect I deny them in advance, and in my turn brand the users of such terms as evil men and women, among the foremost enemies of mankind. Such people are threatening the vital freedoms of thought and expression which the communists deny openly, and which the West denies under the counter. But these are among the values for which tens of thousands fought and died on the battlefields I attempt to portray. In common with tens of thousands of others I owe a personal debt to my friends, and my companions, who died to preserve, among many other things of greater importance my right to write what I believe to be true.

Unhappily, certain passages in this book have been suppressed. Their loss is not great, save as a symptom of the most pitiful and craven fears afflicting this great Nation. But I add that these passages, relating to U.S. troops, were unquestionably acceptable to the Americans as valid and genuine criticism, without malice. The attitude of the American authorities to historical inquiry is not only beyond all praise, but also not the least of the hopes of mankind in a wider sphere. They are not afraid of the facts of history.

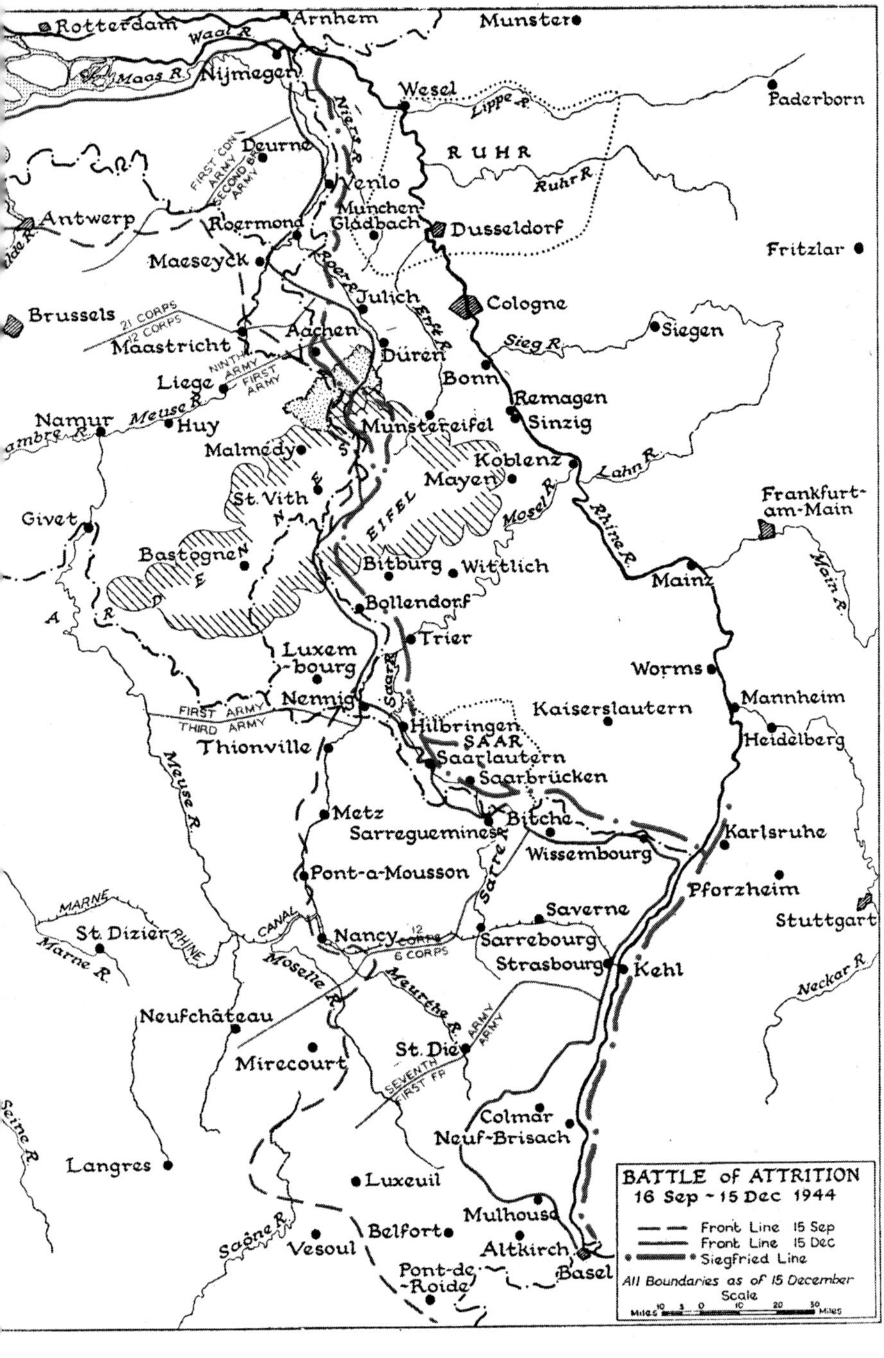
BATTLE of ATTRITION
16 Sep – 15 Dec 1944
Front Line 15 Sep
Front Line 15 Dec
Siegfried Line
All Boundaries as of 15 December
Scale
Miles 10 5 0 10 20 30 Miles
Rotterdam
Arnhem
Munster
Waal R.
Maas R.
Nijmegen
Wesel
Lippe R.
Paderborn
Niers R.
RUHR
Ruhr R.
Deurne
FIRST CDN ARMY
SECOND BR ARMY
Venlo
Antwerp
Munchen-Gladbach
Roermond
Dusseldorf
Fritzlar
Maeseyck
Roer R.
Julich
Erft R.
Cologne
Brussels
21 CORPS
12 CORPS
Aachen
Siegen
Sieg R.
Maastricht
Düren
NINTH ARMY
FIRST ARMY
Liege
Bonn
Remagen
Meuse R.
Namur
Huy
Munstereifel
Sinzig
Malmedy
Koblenz
Lahn R.
Mayen
St. Vith
EIFEL
Mosel R.
Frankfurt-am-Main
Givet
Rhine R.
Bastogne
Bitburg
Wittlich
Main R.
Mainz
Bollendorf
Trier
Luxembourg
Worms
Saar R.
Nennig
Kaiserslautern
Mannheim
FIRST ARMY
THIRD ARMY
Hilbringen
SAAR
Heidelberg
Thionville
Saarlautern
Saarbrücken
Meuse R.
Metz
Bitche
Sarreguemines
Karlsruhe
Wissembourg
Pont-a-Mousson
Pforzheim
Sarre R.
MARNE
Saverne
Stuttgart
St. Dizier
RHINE
CANAL
Nancy
12 CORPS
6 CORPS
Sarrebourg
Marne R.
Strasbourg
Kehl
Moselle R.
Meurthe R.
Neckar R.
Neufchâteau
ARMY
ARMY
St. Dié
Mirecourt
SEVENTH
FIRST FR
Colmar
Neuf-Brisach
Seine R.
Langres
Luxeuil
Mulhouse
Saône R.
Belfort
Vesoul
Altkirch
Basel
Pont-de-Roide

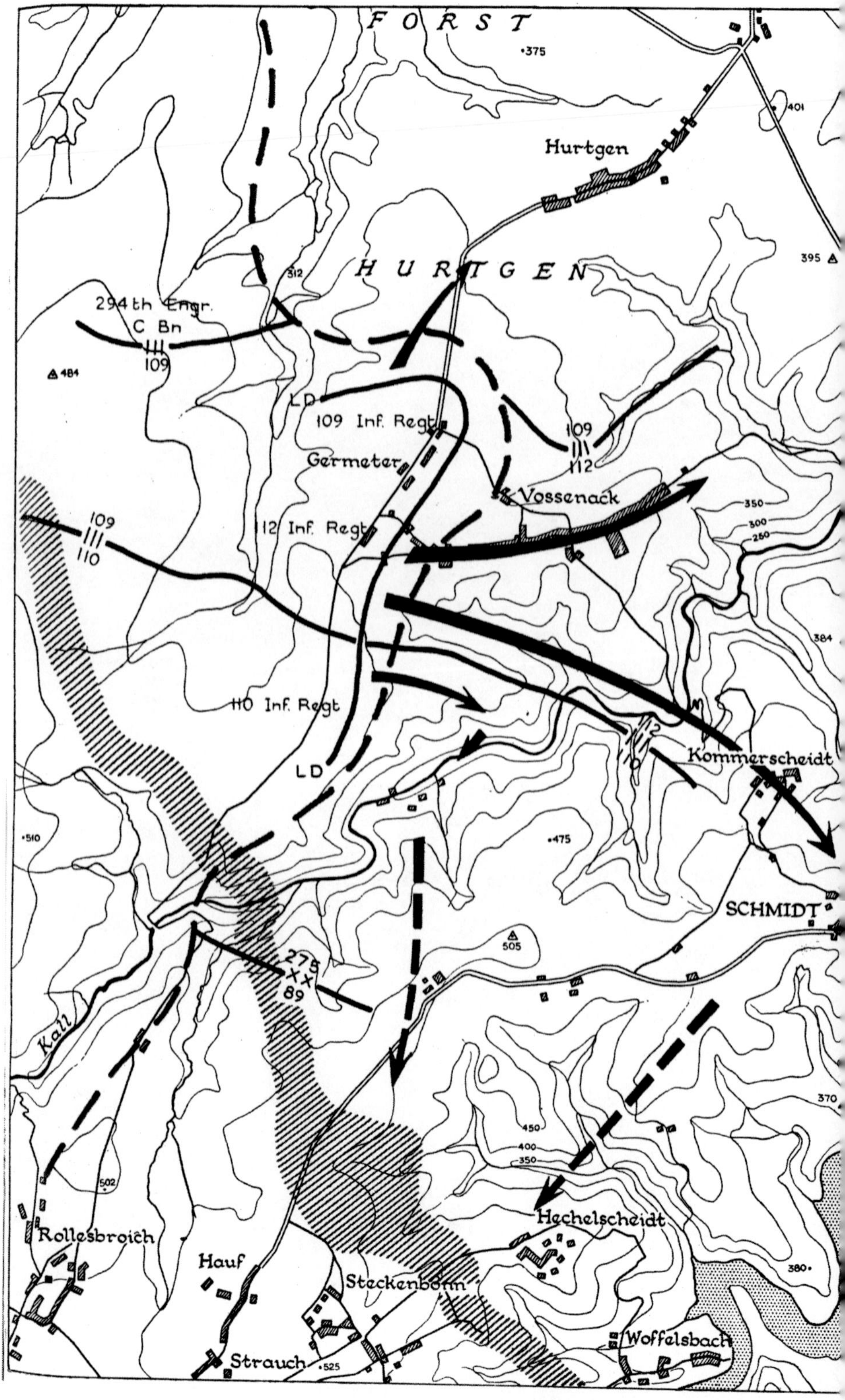

FORST
375
401
Hurtgen
395
HURTGEN
312
294th Engr.
C Bn
109
484
LD
109 Inf. Regt
Germeter
109
112
Vossenack
109
110
112 Inf. Regt
350
300
250
384
110 Inf. Regt
112
110
Kommerscheidt
LD
510
475
SCHMIDT
505
275
XX
89
Kall
370
450
400
350
502
Hechelscheidt
Rollesbroich
Hauf
Steckenborn
380
Woffelsbach
Strauch
525

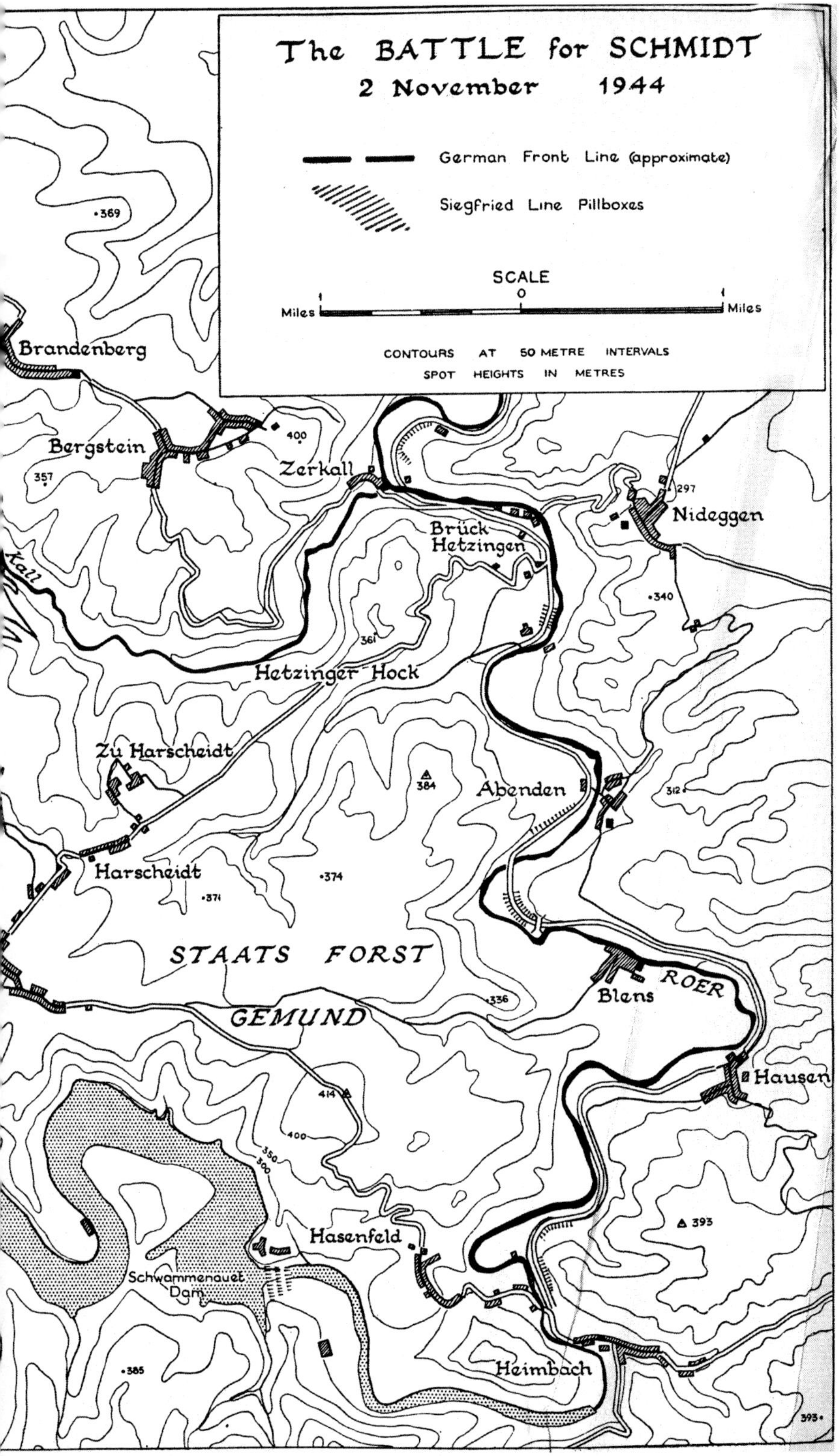

The BATTLE for SCHMIDT
2 November 1944
German Front Line (approximate)
Siegfried Line Pillboxes
SCALE
Miles 1 0 1 Miles
CONTOURS AT 50 METRE INTERVALS
SPOT HEIGHTS IN METRES
369
Brandenberg
Bergstein
357
400
Zerkall
Brück
Hetzingen
Nideggen
297
340
Kall
361
Hetzinger Hock
Zu Harscheidt
384
Abenden
312
Harscheidt
374
371
STAATS FORST
GEMUND
336
Blens
ROER
Hausen
414
400
350
300
393
Hasenfeld
Schwammenauet
Dam
385
Heimbach
393

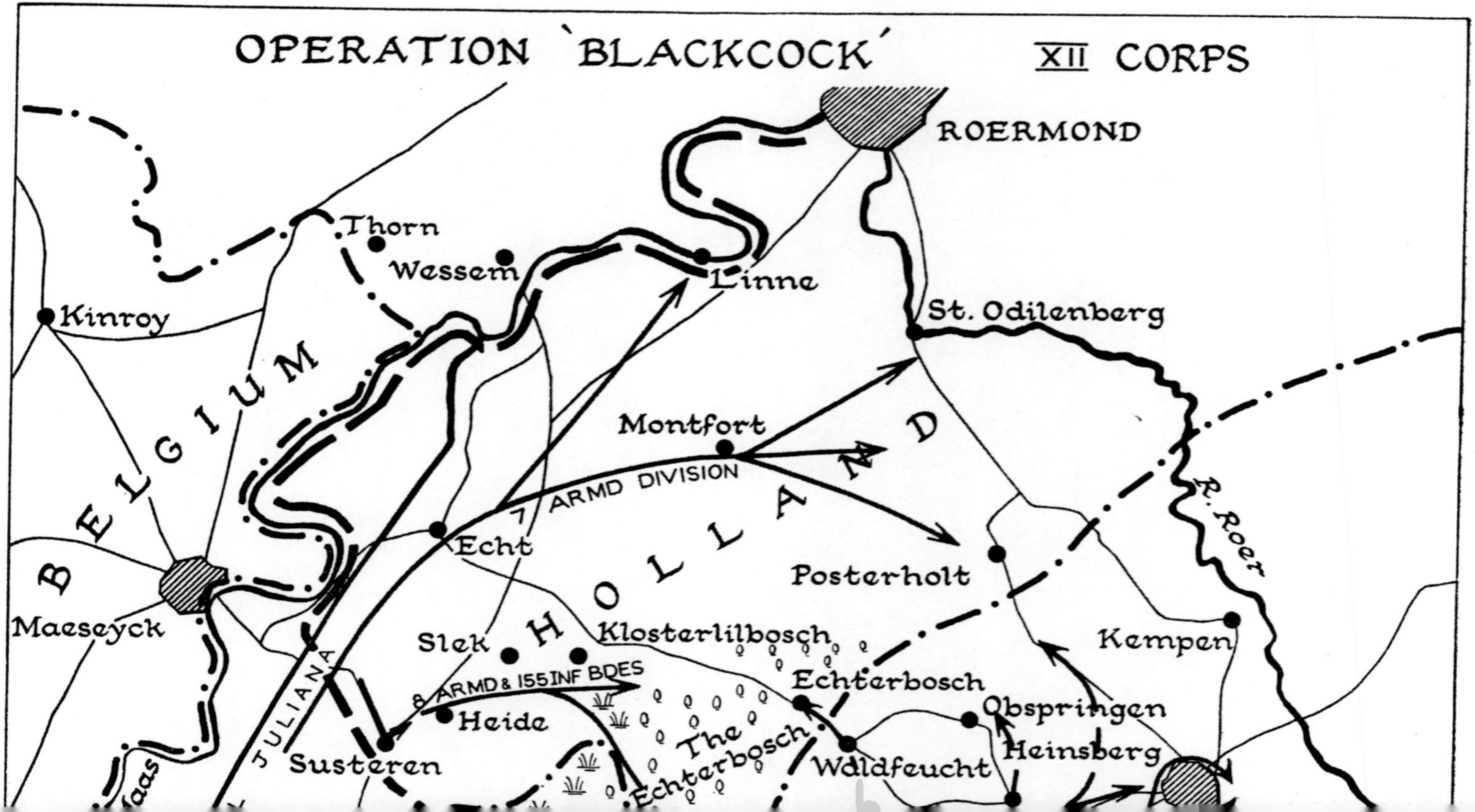
OPERATION 'BLACKCOCK'
XII CORPS
ROERMOND
Thorn
Wessem
Linne
St. Odilenberg
Kinroy
BELGIUM
Montfort
7 ARMD DIVISION
HOLLAND
Echt
R. Roer
Posterholt
Maeseyck
Slek
Klosterlilbosch
Kempen
8 ARMD & 155 INF BDES
Echterbosch
Obspringen
Heide
The Echterbosch
Heinsberg
Waldfeucht
Susteren
JULIANA
Maas

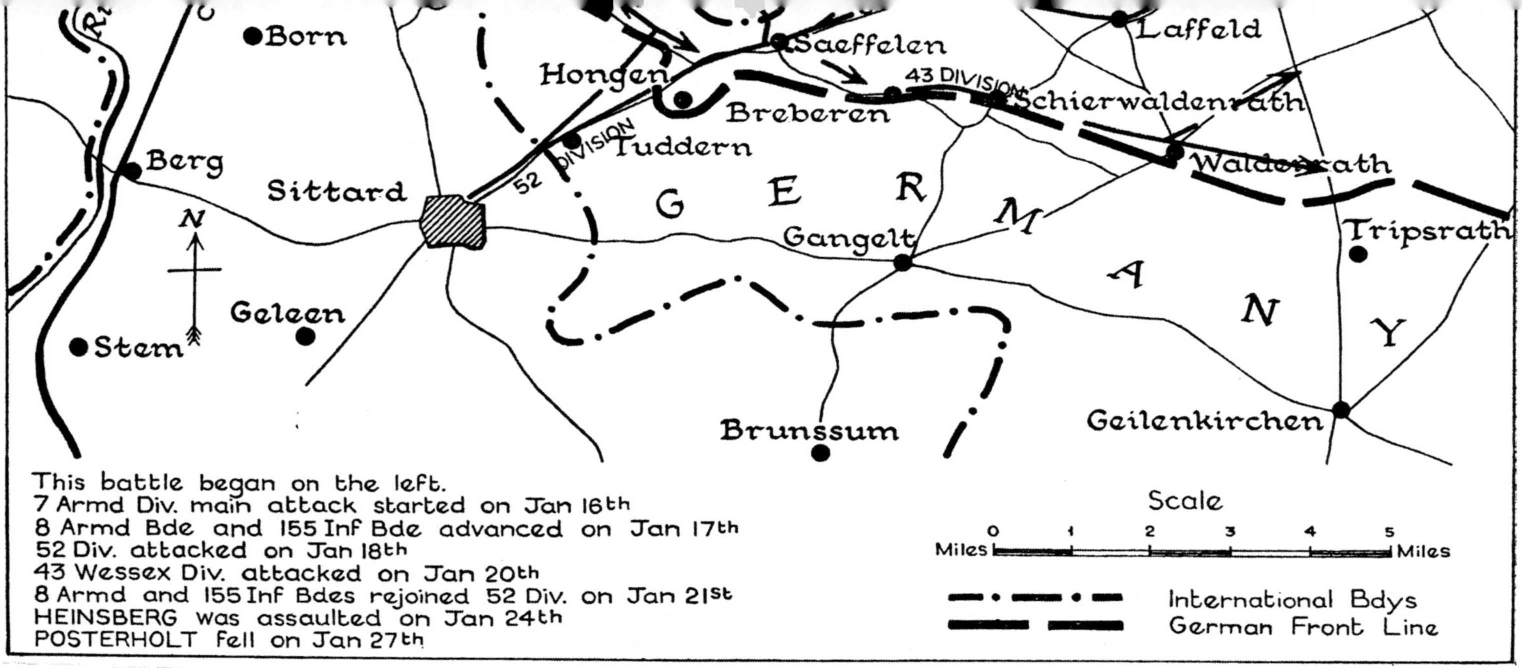
Born
Laffeld
Saeffelen
Hongen
43 DIVISION
Schierwaldenrath
Breberen
52 DIVISION
Tuddern
Berg
Sittard
Waldenrath
G E R M A N Y
N
Gangelt
Tripsrath
Geleen
Stem
Brunssum
Geilenkirchen
This battle began on the left.
7 Armd Div. main attack started on Jan 16th
8 Armd Bde and 155 Inf Bde advanced on Jan 17th
52 Div. attacked on Jan 18th
43 Wessex Div. attacked on Jan 20th
8 Armd and 155 Inf Bdes rejoined 52 Div. on Jan 21st
HEINSBERG was assaulted on Jan 24th
POSTERHOLT fell on Jan 27th
Scale
Miles 0 1 2 3 4 5 Miles
International Bdys
German Front Line

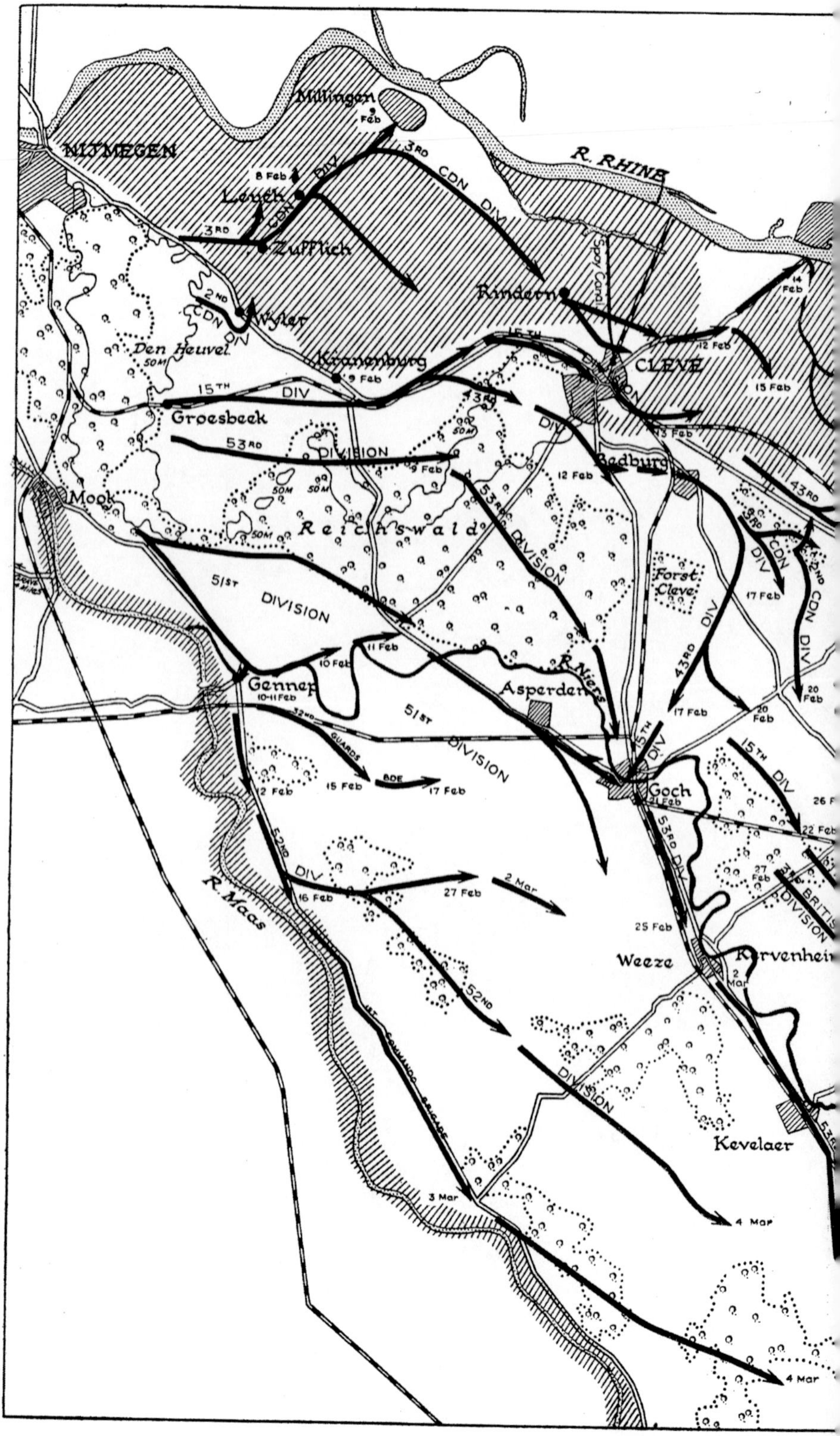

NIJMEGEN
Millingen
9 Feb
R. RHINE
8 Feb
Leuth
3RD CDN DIV
Zyfflich
3RD CDN DIV
Spoy Canal
Rindern
2ND CDN DIV
Wyler
Den Heuvel
50M
Kranenburg
9 Feb
CLEVE
15TH DIV
Groesbeek
43RD DIV
53RD DIVISION
9 Feb
12 Feb
13 Feb
12 Feb
14 Feb
15 Feb
Bedburg
Mook
Reichswald
53RD DIVISION
43RD
3RD CDN DIV
2ND CDN DIV
Forst Cleve
17 Feb
51ST DIVISION
10 Feb
11 Feb
Gennep
10-11 Feb
R. Niers
Asperden
43RD DIV
17 Feb
20 Feb
20 Feb
51ST DIVISION
32ND GUARDS BDE
12 Feb
15 Feb
17 Feb
15TH DIV
Goch
15TH DIV
26 F
22 Feb
21 Feb
53RD DIV
52ND DIV
16 Feb
27 Feb
2 Mar
27 Feb
3RD BRITISH DIVISION
R. Maas
25 Feb
Weeze
Kervenheim
2 Mar
52ND DIVISION
1ST COMMANDO BRIGADE
Kevelaer
3 Mar
4 Mar
4 Mar

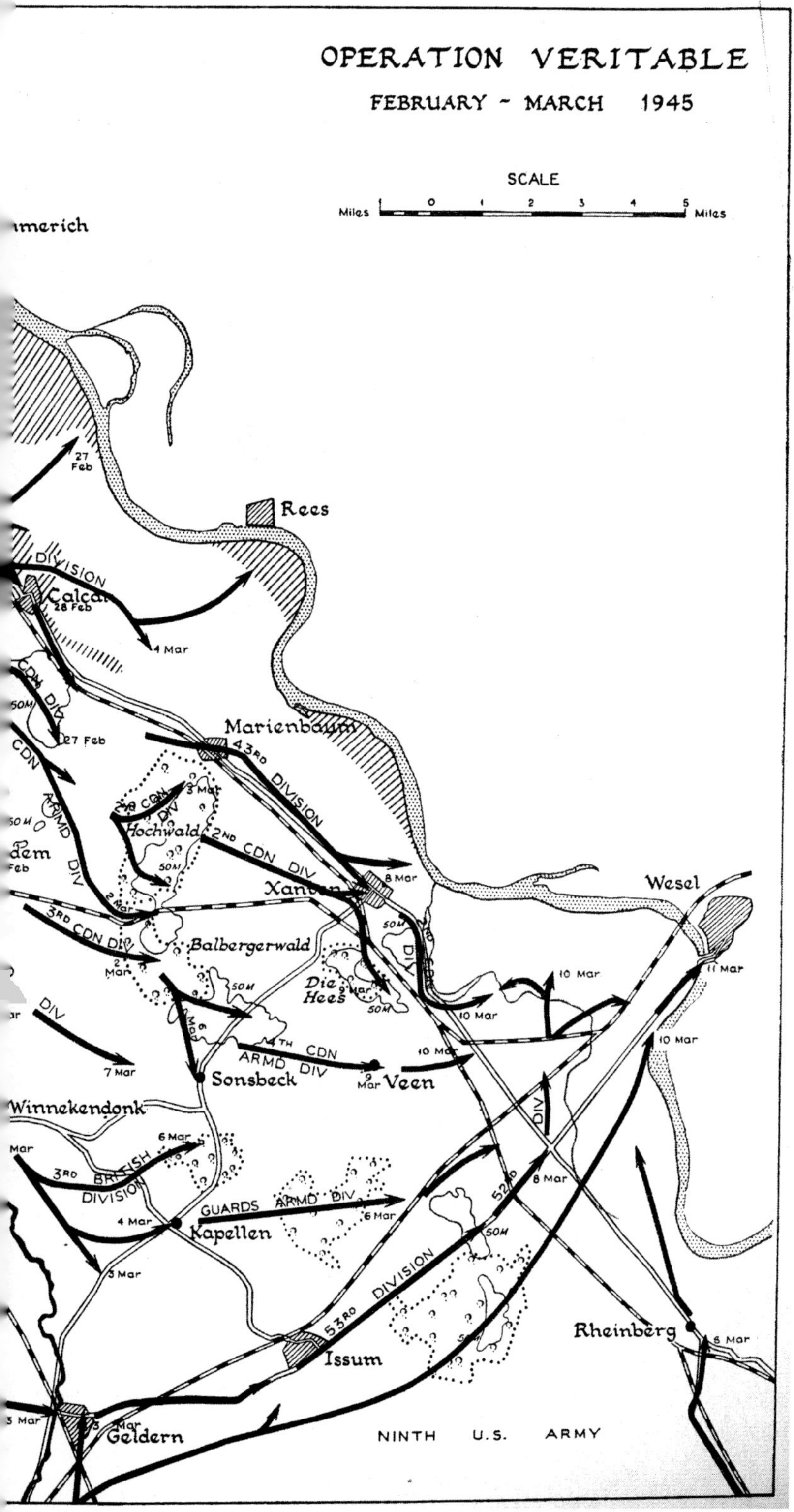

OPERATION VERITABLE
FEBRUARY ~ MARCH 1945
SCALE
Miles 1 0 1 2 3 4 5 Miles
Rees
27 Feb
28 Feb
4 Mar
27 Feb
Marienbaum
43RD DIVISION
3 Mar
Hochwald
2ND CDN DIV
50M
Xanten
8 Mar
Wesel
3RD CDN DIV
2 Mar
Balbergerwald
Die Hees
9 Mar
10 Mar
11 Mar
10 Mar
10 Mar
4TH CDN ARMD DIV
7 Mar
Sonsbeck
9 Mar
Veen
Winnekendonk
6 Mar
3RD BRITISH DIVISION
4 Mar
GUARDS ARMD DIV
6 Mar
Kapellen
52ND
8 Mar
3 Mar
53RD DIVISION
Rheinberg
6 Mar
Issum
3 Mar
Geldern
NINTH U.S. ARMY

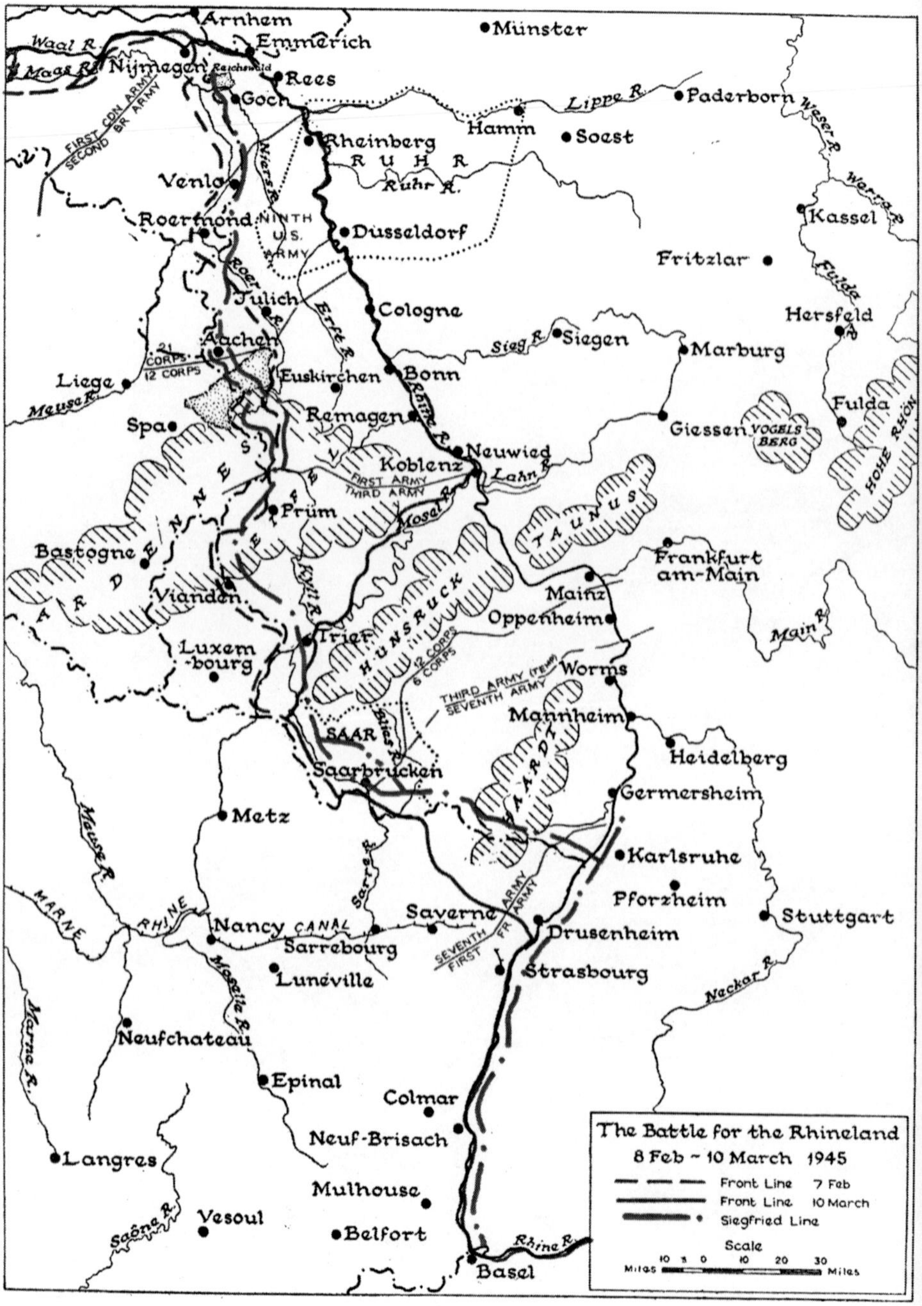
The Battle for the Rhineland
8 Feb ~ 10 March 1945
Front Line 7 Feb
Front Line 10 March
Siegfried Line
Scale
Miles 10 5 0 10 20 30 Miles
Arnhem
Münster
Waal R.
Emmerich
Maas R.
Nijmegen
Reichswald
Rees
Goch
Lippe R.
Paderborn
Weser R.
FIRST CDN ARMY
SECOND BR ARMY
Rheinberg
Hamm
Soest
RUHR
Ruhr R.
Niers R.
Venlo
Werra R.
Roermond
NINTH U.S. ARMY
Kassel
Dusseldorf
Fritzlar
Roer R.
Fulda
Julich
Erft R.
Cologne
Hersfeld
21 CORPS
12 CORPS
Aachen
Sieg R.
Siegen
Marburg
Liege
Euskirchen
Bonn
Meuse R.
Rhine R.
Remagen
Fulda
Spa
Giessen
VOGELS BERG
HOHE RHÖN
Neuwied
Koblenz
Lahn R.
FIRST ARMY
THIRD ARMY
EIFEL
ARDENNES
Prüm
Mosel R.
TAUNUS
Bastogne
Frankfurt am-Main
Mainz
Vianden
Kyll R.
HUNSRUCK
Oppenheim
Main R.
Trier
Luxem-bourg
12 CORPS
6 CORPS
Worms
THIRD ARMY (TEMP)
SEVENTH ARMY
Mannheim
SAAR
Blies R.
HAARDT
Heidelberg
Saarbrucken
Germersheim
Metz
Karlsruhe
Sarre R.
Meuse R.
Pforzheim
MARNE
RHINE
Saverne
FR ARMY
ARMY
Stuttgart
Nancy
CANAL
Drusenheim
Sarrebourg
SEVENTH
FIRST
Luneville
Strasbourg
Moselle R.
Neckar R.
Marne R.
Neufchateau
Epinal
Colmar
Neuf-Brisach
Langres
Mulhouse
Vesoul
Saône R.
Belfort
Basel

PART ONE

THE CHECK

1

THE NATURE OF THE BATTLE

I

AT five o'clock on the morning of 8 February, 1945, the British 30th Corps, two hundred thousand strong and backed by one thousand guns, launched its spearheads out of the narrow throat south-east from the Nijmegen bridgehead against the powerful northern hinge of the Siegfried Line in the Reichswald forest.

The British 30th Corps was under command of the Canadian 1st Army, while headquarters British 2nd Army planned the crossings of the Rhine, which must follow swiftly upon the successful outcome of the battle.

North of the Reichswald forest the Canadians launched infantry in amphibious attack over the floods that had made a vast inland lake of all the country north of the Nijmegen—Cleves road to the Rhine banks opposite Emmerich.

To the south, covering the right flank of the British 30th Corps, seven infantry and three armoured divisions of the U.S. 9th Army, under command of Field Marshal Montgomery's 21st Army Group, faced the river Roer in spate from Julich to Duren, timed and ready to assault on the 10th February, and to converge as the right arm of the embrace crushing the enemy back upon the Rhine at Wesel.

But the enemy, defying all the Allied attempts by land and air through four months, had at the last dynamited the sluices of the Roer dams south of Duren to release a tidal wave which made of the river Roer an impassable barrier flowing at 8 knots and three feet above its banks.

For thirteen days the U.S. 9th Army was forced to watch and wait, and on the 23rd February, with the river Roer still a full eighty yards wide and with a 4 knot current, the leading divisions crossed. On the 28th February the spearhead of the U.S. 9th Army emerged from the bridgehead in the wake of bulldozers heaving through the rubble of the town of Julich, and the way was clear. By that time the Canadians and the British 30th Corps had drawn the bulk of the enemy forces in the north to their challenge. As at Caen in Normandy, now in the Reichswald forest, it fell to British troops to fight the second and last of the great battles of "the hinge", and to open the way.

Farther south the U.S. 1st Army with its 7th Corps covering the flank of the U.S. 9th Army, pressed on with fourteen divisions across the Cologne plain. At last there too the way was open. The reserves covering Cologne and Dusseldorf had been drawn into the British battle of the Rhineland, while only four weak divisions faced the U.S. 9th Army. The whole German army in the north, by accepting the British challenge, had put itself off balance by its own hand.

From the Rhine floods in the extreme north to the Swiss frontier eighty-five German divisions faced an equal number of Allied divisions on the last battlefield in the final struggle that was to destroy the Nazi power west of the Rhine.

This great battle of the Rhineland, encompassing the utter defeat and destruction of the German armies in the west, is the climax of the long winter of discontent, the climax of a long period of anti-climax. In it British troops met the greatest weight of fire and the most resolute enemy they had ever had to face, and were locked in a death struggle for four weeks. Such a struggle cannot be viewed in isolation.

It seems now, in the light of all that is known, that the battle falls naturally into its time and place, something beyond the wills of men, resisting all the stresses of personalities, and above even the unpredictable chances of war. In the end, when it is done, when all the factors are considered and weighed, it seems inevitable, falling into the pattern of destiny.

But, of course, it would have been impossible for any one man, or any body of men, at any time, living in the midst of these stresses and strains, involving the condition, the dreams, the fears of nations, the bigotries and biases of men and peoples, the behaviour of commanders subscribing to different principles, inspired by their own peculiarities of ambition, and their standards of professionalism, to assess the factors, or even to be aware of them.

And above all there was the unpredictable, brooding and sinister figure of Hitler, imposing his will on the pattern of his own destruction and the defeat of his armies. Towards the end, replying to the pleas of von Runstedt, and others of his generals, to withdraw across the Rhine, Hitler stated that he saw no point "in transferring catastrophe from one place to another". The words sounded almost casual, yet in case there might be any doubt about their meaning, Hitler added that any commander yielding a bridge across the Rhine would pay for its loss with his head.

The battle in something like its final pattern was born in the mind of Montgomery in the early autumn of 1944, months before it took place. It was also part of the strategy of the Supreme Commander, General Eisenhower. Yet in the end it was the will of Hitler that prevailed in the manner, time and place of the destruction of the Third Reich. He was the strategist of his own defeat, and not alone in the Battle of the Rhineland. The German people had not proved worthy of his vast and terrible dreams, and the answer must be complete suicide for him and for them.

There are innumerable lesser strands in the pattern leading to the last battle. On the Allied side it was Eisenhower who prevailed, or seemed to prevail. From the outset, backed unfalteringly by the U.S. Chief of Staff, General George Marshall, he clung to his ideas, resisting all the efforts of Montgomery and the British Chiefs of Staff, compelling them to his pace, denying, while never seeming to deny, "the major thrust in the North". In the final result it looked like the fulfilment of all that Eisenhower meant to do, yet this battle was less Eisenhower's than Montgomery's, and Hitler was its main architect.

Through all the winter army group and army commanders pulled and pushed, jockeying for supplies and for position, each one taking advantage of every opportunity to impose, or to carry forward, his own ideas. But the events in which they were caught up were greater than themselves.

In the last count the results were achieved by the masses of individuals, forged into armies in the field, and behind the field, the weapons of the politicians and generals. It was their morale, their readiness to endure, to suffer, to die, that exerted unrelenting pressures, and was the governing factor.

Hitler was constantly aware of this great factor. He pinned his hopes on the probable failure of the Americans to endure, and to British exhaustion. He believed that the Germans themselves would hold until "five minutes past midnight", forgetting that five minutes past midnight is always too late.

The appalling losses suffered by his armies, the exhaustion and ruin of the German people and the country, fashioned Hitler's last desperate strategy. He played for time to the bitter end, and won a great deal of it, convinced that the alliance of the Soviet, the U.S.A. and Britain must break under its stresses . . . . if only he could hold on a little while longer.

Similarly, the manpower, the vast wealth, the huge industrial output and the security of the United States, far from the battlefields, governed the strategy of Eisenhower.

The leaders of Britain had different problems. The long sustained effort of the British people at home and abroad through four years, the inevitable exhaustion of manpower, of productive capacity, the awareness that Britain was scraping the bottom of the barrel in men, women and wealth, was the spur everlastingly driving Montgomery, urging him either to extreme caution or to discover a short cut to victory.

But there was no short cut.

It was a fight to the death. Even such factors as the Unconditional Surrender, the Morgenthau Plan to "turn the Third Reich into a potato patch", were irrelevant. In the very nature of the struggle, and from the very beginning, there could be no other end but total defeat or total victory for either side. It was total war.

II

The Battle of the Rhineland was fought four months after the original planned date, and more than five months after Field Marshal Montgomery had hoped to drive through to victory in the north. In its final shape the original outline was still clear. In a sense it existed as a battle through all the four months of attrition that preceded it, and in this I believe it must be unique in the story of war.

The long delay is the measure of the remarkable recovery of the German armies in the west, and of the failure of the Allied Command to appreciate the situation in early September 1944. This was not due so much to any failure of Intelligence to supply vital information, but rather to political forces and the difficulties of supply.

On the British 21st Army Group front the battles of the Scheldt and Arnhem should have been avoided. In the south Patton should not have been permitted to use up vast quantities of ammunition in abortive actions which resulted in heavy losses in men and materials without compelling the enemy to give ground or to move so much as a reserve division. This behaviour of General Patton, which must be the responsibility of his Army Group Commander, General Bradley, forced the Supreme Commander, General Eisenhower, to startle the Western Allies with an urgent broadcast appeal for increased production of ammunition. That was in November.

At Aachen the U.S. 1st Army was held after a penetration into German territory south of the city on the 13th September, and even two months later the vital importance of the whole Hurtgen forest area was inadequately appreciated.

South of the Ardennes, the U.S. 3rd Army entangled itself for weeks in the wilderness of Metz and its surrounding fortresses, and by the end of November the Germans could claim Arnhem, the Scheldt, Aachen and Metz as defensive victories.

North of the Ardennes, through all the month of November, the U.S. 1st and 9th Armies battered away week after week in mud, flood, ice, snow, and torrential rain, measuring their total gains in yards, and without improvement in their positions. In the region of the Roer dams villages changed hands more than a score of times in bitter fighting, and at Vossenach and Schmidt the U.S. 28th Division suffered the most tragic defeat of the whole campaign in a battle, badly appreciated, carelessly planned, hopelessly organized, and almost unheard of. Four months of hard fighting in appalling conditions were needed to regain the positions which had been gained and should have been held at Schmidt in early November, and which were an essential pre-requisite to the Rhineland battle. It was this failure at Schmidt in the first week of November which held the U.S. 9th Army impotent for two weeks west of the River Roer in February 1945.

But for this continuous and sustained failure to appreciate the extent and nature of the German recovery and strength, the Battle of the Ardennes might not have been launched. Certainly it should not have come as a surprise if the Intelligence reports had been carefully correlated and noted by 12th Army Group and the Supreme Command.

As it was, the failure of the German "All-out gamble" in the Ardennes undoubtedly spelled out very clearly the final doom of the German armies, but this doom had been unescapable from the moment of the Allied success in Normandy. From that time forward Germany was besieged on three sides, and there could be no escape from the final closure of that huge embrace. The Ardennes battle heavily underlined the "strategic reverse", hotly denied by the Supreme Commander, but which had none the less occurred through the autumn of 1944.

But it is the pattern of these months leading to the final denouement that is so infinitely absorbing, for the conclusion is foregone; and one of the most absorbing factors is Field Marshal Montgomery's singleness of vision and purpose from the outset. The way to victory lay in the north, and he was resolved to strike through the Rhineland and north of the Ruhr. There was no other way, not only for his army, but for all the armies; and no other priorities. It blinds him to all else. It is his strength and his weakness.

There can be, I believe, no doubt that it led him at first not to see the battle of the Scheldt, then to avoid it, and finally grossly to underestimate that long drawn out and costly struggle. It led him directly to the Arnhem adventure even when it must have been clear to him that it was already too late, and he did not seem at any time thereafter to appreciate the implications of that failure. He insisted on regarding it as "90% successful". But these two failures, the Scheldt and Arnhem, were felt far beyond the campaign in north-west Europe, the one depriving Mountbatten's South-East Asia Command of urgently needed landing craft, and the other tying up airborne power which could have been better employed in the vital reconquest of Central Burma.

Even when it was certain that Arnhem would not be won Field

Marshal Montgomery continued to hope to launch the Battle of the Rhineland on the 10th October. "By the end of the first week of October I realized that I should not be able to carry out my plans as speedily as I had hoped," he wrote.[1] At that time he was forced to give his attention to the operations progressing slowly to clear the Scheldt estuary and to open up Antwerp to Allied shipping.

Nevertheless at the Brussels conference of the 18th October with the Supreme Commander and General Bradley it was agreed to launch the Rhineland battle in November, and with the U.S. 9th Army under Montgomery's command. Less than ten days later the enemy launched a powerful counter attack against the right flank of the British 2nd Army in the Roermond–Venlo sector. The attack was contained a mile or two short of Helmond, but it was many weeks before the awkward enemy salient in the Heinsberg–Roermond triangle was finally eliminated.

Indeed it was no easy matter even to line up along the Maas and the Roer, and beyond those barriers lay the Ems, the Erft, and a whole complex of waterways which made of the Reichswald forest almost the only dry land between the Maas and the Rhine. Through all this country of water and forest ran the defences of the Siegfried Line. It would be a horrible battlefield. Water, it could be seen, was the enemy's most important ally. Seven dams at the head of the River Roer south of Duren in the Hurtgen forest region controlled one hundred and sixty million cubic metres of water, and the Germans could send "a calamitous flood cascading into the ravine-confined Roer down to Roermond".[2] A complete water barrier would thereby guard the Cologne plain.

In November, if not before, all this was evident, yet General Bradley permitted General Patton to drag the campaign out of shape southward in abortive attacks against the Saar, costly in life, and dangerously costly in ammunition. By the end of the month the Allied armies were virtually bogged down over the whole front, and Montgomery wrote a highly critical letter to the Supreme Commander, stating that none of the objectives outlined in the October directive had been achieved, and that we had suffered a strategic reverse. The Field Marshal then asked for

[1] Normandy to the Baltic.
[2] N.W. Europe 1944-45. John North.

a new plan, and renewed his appeal "for closer ground force co-ordination".[1]

Montgomery's appreciation was justified, but he remained "cock-a-hoop" about his own front, and drew a hot denial of the "strategic reverse" from General Eisenhower. The weather had been terrible, the worst for fifty years, and its promise was no brighter. Roads were inadequate and in appalling condition. Bridging was a nightmare in conditions of alternate freeze and thaw and flood. But Montgomery was pleased with the position of his own armies. He wrote: "On the Allied front north of the Ardennes we were now 'tidy' along the line of the rivers Roer and Meuse except for an enemy salient in the Heinsberg area and virtually the only commitment remaining as a preliminary to major operations between the Rhine and the Meuse was the elimination of this pocket." Antwerp was at last open, and the Canadians, so long involved in that waterlogged battle, had taken over the Nijmegen bridgehead and were responsible for the whole northern flank.

The statement appears to ignore the menace of the Roer dams, still in enemy hands, and on the 2nd December the enemy underlined the general nature of his water ally by breaching the banks of the Neder Rhine west of Arnhem, and confining the Canadians to a small island bridgehead, as well as condemning them to a war of water almost to the bitter end. At least the pattern of the future battlefield of the Rhineland was becoming clear.

On the 7th December Montgomery joined Eisenhower and Bradley at a conference at Maastricht, and again confirmed the plans for the Rhineland battle. The U.S. 9th Army would take over the awkward Heinsberg salient leaving Montgomery free to regroup. At once the British 30th Corps began to move to its positions in the Nijmegen bridgehead ready for the assault against the Rhineland. The U.S. 1st Army had moved up to Duren, and mounted an attack against the Roer dams on the 13th December. In the month from mid-November the 1st Army had suffered over 21,000 casualties in the Hurtgen forest region while the 9th Army had losses of 10,000 men in the very limited improvement of its positions. Yet the line up along the Maas and the Roer was almost complete, but for the dams.

[1]Montgomery to Eisenhower. 28 November.

On the 16th December, with the U.S. 1st Army's attack against the dams in its third day, Field Marshal Montgomery published a directive as follows:

> "The enemy is at present fighting a defensive campaign on all fronts; his situation is such that he cannot stage major offensive operations."

And this was not Montgomery's view alone, for Bradley later wrote that he would have agreed with this estimate. In fact his 12th Army Group stated on 12th December:

> "It is now certain that attrition is steadily sapping the strength of German forces on the western front and that the crust of defences is thinner, more brittle and more vulnerable than it appears on G-2 maps or to troops in the line."[1]

Nevertheless in the cold dawn of the 16th December von Runstedt launched Hitler's last gigantic counter offensive through the Ardennes in an attempt to break through to Antwerp, and the next day the British 30th Corps was rushing south to fling a defensive screen round Brussels.

With that Montgomery's eastern vision faded, and it was clear that Antwerp had been opened just in time. Without it we might have lost it, and there would be a different story to tell.

[1]12th Army Group Summary 18. 12 December, 1944.

2

THE DOGS OF WAR

I

THE whole pattern of the autumn and winter battles in north-west Europe, and all the bitter frustrations and arguments between the Allies, derives from the events of the month of August 1944. It was in August that the unbalance in strength between the U.S.A. and Britain began to assert an overwhelming influence on the campaign. Neither the Chiefs of Staff,[1] nor even the voice of Churchill, could any longer prevail in matters of major strategy or policy. The design, henceforth, was the design of Roosevelt, and of George Marshall, the head, and one might say—shoulders, of the Joint Chiefs of Staff[2] in Washington. In the field Eisenhower was the Supreme Commander, secure in his powerful backers, and beyond challenge.

The immense toll of war, long sustained, had reduced Britain to the role of junior partner even before the production and man-power of the United States had reached their peak, and because of that fact alone it may be that August 1944 not only marked a vital turning point in the campaign in north-west Europe, but also in world history. The shape of things to come was no longer conceived in the mind of Churchill, a mind matured in the political and historical background of Europe, aware instinctively of the subtle balances of power, the nuances of ambition, the underlying hatreds, the national chicaneries, and the genuine aspirations of the European peoples. All this was in his blood, a part of his political heritage, and if it is possible that peace could have followed war, that possibility was more likely to stem from the perceptions, ideas and strategies of Winston Churchill than from any other mind available at that time. Yet all the force of his powerful personality, all his political genius and "nous", all his command of strategical problems, availed

[1]British. [2]American.

nothing against the power of the United States in the councils, and the determination of President Roosevelt. The results of American innocence, naive idealism, bigotry and good intentions, were to be profound.

In the midsummer of 1944, Britain, having withstood the siege and contrived at last the springboard into Europe, was denied the chance to be the architect of the victory she had made possible. I believe that it is legitimate to restate this vital fact in the context of this book, for it was this fact above all that was at once the inspiration of Montgomery's dreams for quick victory, and the reason why they were impossible of attainment. It was difficult to accept that in August 1944, but it was already crystal clear. Indeed, it was more than difficult, it was truly agonizing, for it was certain that the Germans were beyond hope, and might be within days of utter defeat. Victory in 1944 seemed a certainty, and this sudden vision, so soon to fade, was difficult for the British at home and in the field to relinquish. To the Americans it was of much less importance: time, which for Britain was running out, was on their side.

In Britain, awakening suddenly from the long plod of war, the terrific sense of urgency and hope gripped all minds. The peak of production attained in 1943 had been passed and could not be regained. The labour force was declining, and the call up of new age groups could no longer meet the demands of the Army. Five divisions and four armoured brigades would have to be disbanded unless more men could be found without delay.[1] It was no longer possible to do more than make up new brigades, and it was necessary to rob the Navy and the Air Force to keep the Army going.

In March 1944, the numbers in the field had been shared equally by Britain and the United States, but by the beginning of July the disparity had grown to forty-eight American divisions against thirty-eight British divisions. Six months later the gap had widened to seventy-eight American to forty-eight British divisions. The strain could scarcely have been borne by a people less dedicated to prevail at whatever cost.

For the second time within the span of thirty years Britain had given of its blood and treasure, and at last the accumulated wealth

[1]Grand Strategy, Vol. vi, pp. 20-21, John Ehrman, H.M.S.O.

of centuries had been consumed in war. The United States had received the last of our gold, absorbed the last of our great industrial assets within her boundaries, and insisted—with a kind of paternal benevolence—that reserves were no longer necessary, or possible. Only then did Lend-Lease fill the void.

The material losses of Britain throughout the world, within the confines of the Island, and upon the seas, were immense. As an item eleven million tons of our merchant shipping had been sunk, and these the very veins and arteries of the national existence in peace or war. Factories, power plants, schools, houses, in tens of thousands lay in ruins, and the prospect of peace might well have filled Government and people with a dismay no less than the prospect of continuing war.

In spite of this burden Britain continued to dispense material aid on a massive scale to her Allies, and shipped £700 millions of the sinews of war, excluding reverse Lease-Lend to the United States. Of this huge total £312 millions had gone to Soviet Russia. The Russians had used it well, "tearing the guts out of the German army" in Churchill's phrase. In June, July and August 1944, the Germans had sustained the colossal total of 900,000 casualties on the Eastern Front, and in early August, Winston Churchill, surveying the scene in the House of Commons, said:

> " . . . . there was no other force in the world which could have been called into being, except after several more years, that would have been able to maul and break the German army unless it had been subjected to the terrible slaughter and man-handling that has fallen to it through the strength of the Russian Soviet Armies."

In the west in these same months the British and Americans had swollen the huge total by 300,000 Germans, killed, wounded and missing. In addition the enemy had been forced to man her fortresses with 230,000 officers and men, 85,000 of them drawn from the army in the field. All these performed a static role until finally captured. The toll of German commanders was also severe. Rommel, Dollman and von Kluge were dead, Hausser was badly wounded, Eberbach captured, Chevallerie relieved. Even von

Rundstedt and Model were temporary casualties of the unpredictable humours of Hitler.

It seemed impossible that the enemy could sustain such losses and continue to fight. He had lost his last allies in the west, and was alone. The injuries to the German homeland were on a devastating scale. The economy was shattered, and production made possible mainly by the genius and drive of Speer. Oil was running out.

It is not surprising that in early August the scent of victory was overpoweringly strong, demanding a last great effort from the British people, for every week was precious if the wounds of Britain were to be staunched and finally healed. The pulse of the people quickened, and to General Montgomery in the field, at the moment of his great victory in Normandy, it seemed that the hour had struck, and there were very few who thought otherwise.

The SHAEF G-2 summary at the end of August stated:

> "The August battles have done it and the enemy in the West has had it. Two and a half months of bitter fighting have brought the end of the war in Europe within sight, almost within reach."

In the following week the summary gave its opinion that the German army was "no longer a cohesive force but a number of fugitive battle groups, disorganized and even demoralized, short of equipment and arms."

In the first week of September the Combined Intelligence Committee came to the conclusion that German recovery was not possible, and they doubted that organized resistance could continue beyond 1 December, 1944.

That is something of the background situation which made General Montgomery clamour for his "forty divisions", and to drive through in the north to the heart of Germany. But in those last days of August it was the tragedy of the Allies, with the enemy reeling and defeated, that the strength could not be mustered to deliver the last blow. Almost alone Eisenhower sounded a cautious note when, on the 20th August, he warned journalists not to arouse too great hopes. The advance, he stated, had been so rapid and supply lines were so strained that "further movement in large parts of the front even against weak opposition is almost impossible."

This was no less than the sober and unpalatable truth, the "pill" which stuck in the throat of General Montgomery, and led him to the errors of Arnhem and Antwerp.

II

In the light of the tremendous possibilities apparent in August it is understandable that the more sober and reasoned Intelligence summaries went unheeded. Third United States Army G-2 estimate 9 of the 28th August reads as follows:

> "Despite the crippling factors of shattered communications, disorganization and tremendous losses in personnel and equipment, the enemy nevertheless has been able to maintain a sufficiently cohesive front to exercise an overall control of his tactical situation. His withdrawal, though continuing, has not been a rout or mass collapse. Numerous new identifications in contact in recent days have demonstrated clearly that, despite the enormous difficulties under which he is operating, the enemy is still capable of bringing new elements into the battle area and transferring some from other fronts.
>
> It is clear from all indications that the fixed determination of the Nazis is to wage a last-ditch struggle in the field at all costs. It must be constantly kept in mind that fundamentally the enemy is playing for time. Weather will soon be one of his most potent Allies as well as terrain, as we move east to narrowing corridors . . . . But barring internal upheaval in the homeland and the remoter possibility of insurrection with the Wehrmacht, it can be expected that the German armies will continue to fight until destroyed or captured."

It is ironical that Colonel Koch, the author of this remarkably accurate forecast of the shape of things to come, should have been General Patton's Chief of Intelligence, for Patton declared his intention of crossing the German border within ten days, and agreed with the SHAEF view that the German army was no longer a cohesive force. But it is doubtful whether any of the senior commanders took the slightest notice of the first class Intelligence available. From beginning to end of the campaign Intelligence officers were supplying accurate information and estimates, and there were no surprises, not even in the Ardennes attack. One can only conclude that G. Intelligence is one of the most thankless tasks.

The fact is that in August the commanders in the field had made up their minds on the courses they would pursue. The Supreme Commander was resolved to press the enemy all along the line, giving him no rest, and finally destroying him, if possible, west of the Rhine. Montgomery was equally determined to fight for a single powerful thrust to the heart, and believed that this thrust should be in the north. Bradley steered a middle course, leaning heavily in support of Patton's opportunism on his right flank, and thus weakening the offensive position of the northern group of armies. Through all the months of attrition the commanders adhered to their views, and because of this the struggle took on, at least to my imagination, a pattern of the inevitable, unfolding in its own slow tempo.

It is possible that had a sufficient force been available in August, and had it been possible to mount and sustain it for a drive of hundreds of miles through difficult country, over many major water obstacles, into the heart of Germany, victory would have been gained. It is at least equally possible that such a force driving into the heart of the enemy might have been destroyed there. The means, however, were not available. The force Montgomery clamoured for in August was not there, and had it been there the power to set it in swift motion was lacking. One more fact is certain: by the end of August it was too late.

III

The controversies raging round the might-have-beens of August and September 1944, have tended to obscure the great achievements of the Allied armies in the west following immediately upon the break-out from Normandy. For two and a half months the Allies had been locked in mortal combat with an immensely powerful enemy, as resolved not to give ground as the Allies were to gain it. They had been forced to rely for the build-up of their strength and the maintenance of all the complex equipment of war on beach installations of a kind unique in war or peace, and subjected to devastating and unprecedented gales. Nevertheless, within two weeks from the 18th August they had crossed the Seine, cleared all Northern France, Belgium and Luxembourg, and advanced a full 200 miles to the German border. By mid-September most of occupied Western Europe had been swept clear of the enemy. In the south a line was forming from Metz through Epinal and Belfort to the Swiss frontier, and on the 12th September, the U.S. 6th Army Group, which included the 1st French Army, having advanced 300 miles clearing much of southern France on the way, made contact with the right flank of Bradley's 12th Army Group. In the north Montgomery's 21st Army Group had reached the Dutch border, and the Canadian 1st Army had cleared most of the Pas de Calais.

It is difficult to understand how more could have been expected or achieved in the light of all the factors. Hitler, at any rate, realizing the supply problems which must govern the Allied advance, had gauged accurately the possibility, even though he had credited the Allies with 54 divisions instead of the 38, not all of which were mobile, which they disposed. Hitler was playing for time, and his first estimate served him well.

Eastwards then lay the West Wall, the Siegfried Line, the battles of attrition and the long winter of discontent.

By the end of September the hard facts of the German recovery could not be denied. Montgomery's attempt to turn the Siegfried Line in the north had failed, and the harsh facts of Arnhem were inescapable. The long battle which must be fought to open Antwerp and clear the estuary of the Scheldt was becoming increasingly evident. At Aachen the Americans had come hard up against the rigid German defences, and to the south Patton's 3rd Army was meeting fierce counter attacks on the Moselle.

The Allies were slow to recognize two facts: that the check was inevitable, and that Hitler was in supreme command, henceforth controlling the pattern of defeat beyond all argument.

• • • • •

By the end of September Hitler knew that he had staved off defeat for the winter, and believed that the inevitable rift between the eastern and western Allies must come to his rescue.

Early in September 12th Army Group captured the minutes of a meeting held at the German Ministry of Propaganda on the 4th September. These provided early evidence of German thinking, and revealed that the enemy had anticipated the supply and transport difficulties which would halt the Allied advance in the west. The following is one of the first intimations of Hitler's hopes to come into Allied hands:

> "It is certain that the political conflicts will increase with the apparent approach of an Allied victory and some day will cause cracks in the house of our enemy which no longer can be repaired."[1]

This was indeed the only valid hope remaining to the enemy, and John Ehrman discusses Hitler's obsession with this idea.[2] In August the Fuhrer had remarked: "The time will come when the tension between the Allies will become so great that the break will occur." Again in December he stressed to his generals that these "antagonisms" (between the Allies) "grow stronger from hour to hour. If now we can deliver a few more heavy blows, then at any moment this artificially-boasted common front may suddenly collapse with a gigantic clap of thunder."

Later it almost seemed as if the Russian advances in the New Year were a source of increased hope rather than of despair. In January the Fuhrer challenged his advisers:

"Do you think the English can be really enthusiastic about all the Russian developments?"

And in April, when the end was upon him, he said: "Is it not possible that any day—nay, any hour—war may break out between the Bolsheviks and the Anglo Saxons over their prey, Germany?"

But it no longer mattered what he said. In this context Ehrman[3] discusses Hitler's habit of over-simplifying major problems, and

[1] 12th Army Gp. periodic report 106, 19 September.
[2] Grand Strategy, vol. vi. and full quotes of Hitler's statements on this theme.
[3] Grand Strategy, vol. vi. John Ehrman, H.M.S.O. 1956.

suggests that his "Marxist" method of reasoning enabled him to convince himself that the fundamental differences between the aims of Soviet Russia and the western Allies would be certain to break the Alliance. He had hoped that the split would come over the Balkans, and when it did not his hopes were unabated.

Following the abortive attempt on the Fuhrer's life in July and the subsequent dreadful purges of the army Hitler had become the sole focal point of continued German resistance. Hitler was in supreme command, unchallenged and beyond all challenge. Even the commanders in the field had resigned themselves into his hands, and it was this vital fact that the Allies failed to appreciate. They wondered what Rundstedt might do, when all they should have considered was the will of Hitler. In John Ehrman's words: "This one man, and perhaps he alone, held the German people together and impelled it to destruction."[1]

Hitler, therefore, was the sole architect of German strategy at the time of the Allied break through in Normandy, and with his brilliant and energetic henchman, Albert Speer, in charge of production, he commanded the total organization of all that remained of Nazi Germany.

The future had ceased to exist, and there was only now. All that Nazi Germany possessed in life and material could and must be expended. In such circumstances a great nation defeated, even beyond the normal conception of defeat, remains a potent force.

In the sphere of civilian life the production of consumer goods had remained remarkably high. Now there was no further need even for a saucepan. The last material resources must be thrown into the last battle. At the same time the last reserves of manpower were assembled. One hundred fortress battalions of infantry were brought into the battle from the rear areas. Boys of 16 years were drafted at once into the army and swiftly trained. A force of 200,000 workers was rushed to strengthen the defences of the Siegfried Line, and by mid-September the weak points had been reinforced, and the last possibility of successful Allied thrusts had disappeared.

Above all, the major port that might have spelled Germany's doom remained, lamentably, under German control. An army of

[1]Grand Strategy, Vol. vi. John Ehrman. H.M.S.O. 1956.

100,000 men, which should have been trapped beyond all hope in the Pas de Calais, had made an orderly retreat, safeguarding the bulk of its equipment and artillery, and was strongly entrenched to deny the Scheldt estuary to the Allies, perhaps for weeks. The neck of the Beveland isthmus was sealed. The road through to Rotterdam, closed.

In the north the Germans lay in strength along the line of the Nederrijn and Ijssel in time to deny Montgomery his bridgehead, and his hopes of turning the Siegfried Line. The great barrier of the Maas was still virtually intact, and the enemy still held bridgeheads on the west bank.

In the south Hitler had conceived powerful counter-attacks against the long extended flank of the U.S. 3rd Army, and had he been able to bring reinforcements to bear in time he might have prevented the junction of the 3rd and 7th Armies. As it was, impatiently, he committed his forces piecemeal, and delivered them to the Allies. His heavy attacks against Patton's bridgeheads on the Moselle were too long sustained. Indeed, the nature of the German counter-attacks in the south should have convinced the Allied commanders that Hitler himself was ordering the battle.

Yet by the end of September the Germans had given clear proof of their ability to continue in the fight, and the winter was fast approaching. With the failure to take Antwerp, and to go through swiftly on the Breda–Moerdijk–Rotterdam axis, Montgomery had lost his only chance to change the inexorable pattern of the campaign. The chance would not, and could not, recur.

3

THE OCTOBER PATTERN

I

AN intricate and desperately hard series of battles slowly taking shape over the whole area of operations dispelled the optimism prevailing as October opened. The pattern was at first difficult to discern. Whereas the Allied actions in September had been dictated by enemy collapse and restricted predominantly by sheer physical and logistical problems, now the enemy clearly dictated the slow measure of a virtual stale-mate, and imposed a decisive check all along the line. The severity of the check, and the nature of it, was very slowly understood, for it was not until the end of the first week of October that Field Marshal Montgomery realized that his plans must be delayed.[1] Despite the knowledge gained from the Arnhem failure, and with the U.S. 1st Army heavily engaged and checked on the approaches to Aachen, while the U.S. 3rd Army had been forced on the defensive in the south, Montgomery still hoped to launch his Rhineland battle on or about 10th October. This is some measure of the blinding nature of his vision.

But it must be understood that the attack in the north aimed at the Ruhr, and thence through to the heart, was the pre D-day concept for the main line of advance of the Allied armies. It remained so with varying degrees of emphasis through all the vicissitudes of battle, and all the arguments of the commanders in the field. The Ruhr was the most vital area of Germany in the west, the area he must defend at all costs, and it was, therefore, Montgomery's target from the outset, the decisive role of the group of armies under his command. This knowledge, coupled with his acute awareness of his lack of strength, may well have added to his anxiety and fixation. He was always dependent upon American support. He could never move alone. The fulfilment of all his plans

[1]Normandy to the Baltic, p. 151.

must depend upon his ability to gain the co-operation of Bradley, and to have at least one of Bradley's armies under his own command.

Montgomery's anxiety is apparent in his first cable to the War Office in mid-August, when he had tried to gain Bradley's support for a powerful drive to the north "so strong as to fear nothing". It is a *cri de coeur*. His inability to act alone is at the root of all his frustrations. He was never reconciled to it.

Nevertheless in the final assessment the failure to grasp the opportunities, if they were there, is not his. The failure is inherent in the original plans, for "in hardly any respect (wrote Forrest Pogue)[1] were the Allies prepared to take advantage of the great opportunity offered them to destroy the German forces before the winter . . . . virtually the whole intricate military machine was geared to a slower rate of advance than that required in late August. Unfortunately the period of the great opportunity lasted only a few weeks and there was not sufficient time, however vast the effort, to make the necessary readjustments in the logistical machinery which would ensure speedy victory."

By the end of the first week of October Field Marshal Montgomery began to realize the untidy nature of his front, and many of its unhappy possibilities. He saw clearly that the Nijmegen bridgehead must be consolidated and made ready as a springboard for the northern attack; that the line of the Maas must be made good, and that the Scheldt estuary must be cleared and Antwerp opened. But he underestimated all these tasks. He thought that days, or at most two or three weeks, would see him ready to mount his Rhineland battle, and he revised the date to 10th November. His reluctance to look west is astonishing. The Canadian 1st Army lay from the Channel coast at Zeebrugge on a line along the Leopold Canal to Antwerp. South-west Holland was still in enemy hands, and the whole country west of s'Hertogenbosch and south of the Maas was wide open. The line-up west of the Maas loomed as a hideous winter operation, difficult to assess. The 30th Corps was consolidating the Nijmegen bridgehead, and with little room to move. The 8th Corps, reinforced by the U.S. 7th Armoured Division, was beginning to move up-stream from Grave to probe the enemy bridgehead in all

[1]The Supreme Command.

that watery region. The U.S. 9th Army was moving up to fill the right flank of the 21st Army Group.

The brief Indian summer of September had swiftly given way to bitter winter, and the menace of a veritable avalanche of water to flood the Cologne plain and the whole valley of the Roer was ever present while the enemy controlled the great dams south of Duren. In that region of hill and forest, hidden village, narrow gorge and torrent, threaded with the bastions of the Siegfried Line, the U.S. 1st Army was having its first taste of experiences which it is not extravagant to describe as hideous. In the north, too, it was clear that there was the probability of extensive floods.

All these operations extending from the Channel coast to Nijmegen and from Nijmegen south to the Roer dams in the Hurtgen forest, involving scores of major and minor actions against a powerful enemy in strong defensive positions backed by good artillery, and reinforced by water and threats of water, were the essential prologue to the battle of the Rhineland. And behind the whole front Antwerp would be vital to the final mounting of an all-out offensive.

This is the broad framework containing the winter ordeal of the Allied armies, and which seemed to grow so unexpectedly out of the moment of victory. It is a period of limbo, of an almost shapeless struggle, barely recorded and most bitterly remembered.[1]

In these dismal circumstances the October battles began to take shape in the north, as though dragon's teeth sprang to life in a score of unexpected places, and names like Overloon, Venraij, Venlo and Roermond became indelibly imprinted upon the minds of soldiers. In that sodden region, called by the Dutch "de Peel", roads were few, and incapable of bearing heavy transport, and every "field" was a lake enclosed by dykes. Eastward from Helmond the main railway line traverses "de Peel" to cross the Maas at Venlo into enemy territory. Opposite Venlo on the west bank of the Maas there is a place called Blerick. It was the hard core of the enemy bridgehead which extended south to Roermond and covered a powerful defensive area eastward between the Maas and the Roer and bounded by Heinsberg. This was the "Roermond triangle",

[1]The pattern of the western battles is covered in "The Eighty-five Days". The nature of the struggle may be read in Regimental records.

the thorn in the flank of the British 2nd Army, and which became an abscess most difficult to cut out. On 12th October the British 8th Corps launched its main attack upon the village of Overloon with the intention of driving on through to capture the road junction of Venraij. On the right wing of the salient pressure was developing steadily from the area of Weert and Meijel to force the enemy to contract upon Venlo and Roermond. A direct thrust would come in from Deurne, and it was hoped then to pass the 11th Armoured Division through Venraij upon Venlo.

The first task was given to the U.S. 7th Armoured Division under command of the British 8th Corps, and they set about it in characteristic fashion. Wave after wave of Thunderbolts hurled high explosive upon the small straggling village of Overloon, and in the aftermath of these fierce air attacks the armour attempted to advance, at first confidently, then with misgiving. Immediate opposition from 88's, mines, and an enemy showing himself unbowed and a master of mobile defence, halted the American armour almost literally in its tracks. Again and again the Americans "turned on the heat" in the unvarying pattern of their offensive tactics, and three days later the U.S. 7th Armoured Division was still on its start line. The enemy had not budged a yard out of the smouldering ruin of Overloon.

After that there were few illusions about the battle of the "Maas pocket". It was a job for infantry advancing through skilfully planned minefields covered by fire of such intensity and variety that the troops said that the enemy flung everything at them including "the kitchen stove". It was one of the first solid and unmistakable assurances on this front after Arnhem that the nature of the enemy recovery was solid. All this region was defended by paratroops of the highest quality, masters of defensive tactics, resourceful in using the diabolical nature of the country, and resolved to fight for every yard.

At noon on the 15th October infantry of the British 3rd Division took over from the armour and began to move close up under a barrage. It was bleak open moorland flanked by thin belts of saplings. A tall screen of trees masked the village of Overloon, and in the tracks of flail tanks beating the mines out of the sandy loam, and behind Churchill tanks of the 6th Guards Armoured Brigade on the flanks, the infantry went in. The earth pulsated with dull explosions and all the air above shuddered with the invisible weight of shells. The sun was faintly luminous like a pale cheese as the Typhoons plunged down upon Overloon out of the scudding clouds of that October sky. It was heavy going, but the troops moved steadily as though carried forward on the surge of the fire power supporting them. When men fell it seemed like accident, for all that could be seen through the smoke pall was a smouldering line of ruin stabbed with flame.

On the very heels of the barrage, as it lifted, the infantry went in, smothering the weight of fire that rose, flickered from the waste ahead, and went out. By nightfall the leading companies lay uncomfortably under accurate fire, glad of the dug-outs under the husks of the little houses, cottages and workshops that had been a prosperous village. More than one hundred enemy paratroops lay dead, and a hundred more were prisoners. In the cellars men squatted bandaging minor wounds with their field dressings, and glad of mugs of hot sweet tea. By candlelight company commanders studied maps of the frightful no-man's-land ahead, and waited anxiously for news of their patrols, probing out into the darkness.

Shortly before dusk a church tower a mile or two ahead had seemed to explode in the fading light as the gunners first bracketed it, opened a hole with A.P., and followed through with high explosive. With that the forward eyes of the enemy gunners had been closed. That was a relief. But all round, in the saplings, behind the dykes, knowing well the minefields, the enemy swarmed, invisible, menacing, and Venraij was still a long way ahead.

Two days later, on 17th October, the U.S. 7th Armoured Division advanced on Venraij from Deurne while the British 3rd Division pressed on hard and grimly from Overloon, deprived of their supporting tanks, which they saw floundering and hopelessly bogged. It was going to be an infantryman's war.

That night the road junction of Venraij was occupied, and for the time being that was almost all. The intention to pass the 11th Armoured Division through to attack Venlo "evaporated in face of an enemy who seemed to possess unlimited quantities of mines and was determined to fight every yard."[1]

[1]North-West Europe 1944-45. John North, H.M.S.O.

The outer husk of the enemy defences had been most painfully peeled off. The hard nut remained. The small unrecorded battle of Overloon marked the beginning, and the nature, of the long winter struggle in the north.

II

The main business at the Brussels conference of 18th October was to make a sober re-appraisal, and decide on the immediate possibilities in the light of the enemy recovery, and the delay in the opening of the port of Antwerp. The Deputy Supreme Commander, Air Chief Marshal Sir Arthur Tedder, attended with his chief to confer with Montgomery and Bradley.

At long last all that could be spared of the offensive power of the British 2nd Army had been ordered west to clear south-west Holland, and thereby to aid the Canadian 1st Army in its tedious operations on both banks of the long Scheldt estuary. On the 20th October the British 1st Corps, under Canadian Army Command, would launch its attack on the Canadian right, and two days later the British 12th Corps would be ready to move on s'Hertogenbosch and Tilburg from a line Oss–Veghel–St. Oudenrode.

With the British 30th Corps in the Nijmegen bridgehead and 8th Corps becoming fully engaged in the watery maze of the Maas pocket, major offensive operations were clearly beyond the power of 21st Army Group. Inevitably, and for the first time since August the main thrust was given to the U.S. forces and the emphasis moved south.

The possibility of quick victory had gone.[1] Every task all along the front from the Channel to Metz had been grossly underestimated, and an unrealistic optimism still prevailed. It was recognized that any major offensive must wait upon the opening of Antwerp, and the effects of this could not be felt on the battlefield before December. At that time U.S. reinforcements would also be coming into the line. In view of these factors it was Eisenhower's purpose to keep the enemy stretched as fully as possible everywhere, and to prevent

[1]The Combined Chiefs of Staff in Washington discussed the possibility of ending the war in 1944 at a Conference on 20th October. Immense considerations of air attack and new weapons came into it.

him from further strengthening his defensive positions. Finally the Supreme Commander wished to close up to the Rhine over as wide a front as possible.

Field Marshal Montgomery left the conference hoping to launch 30th Corps south-east out of the Nijmegen bridgehead on 10th November, but this thrust would be subsidiary to the main thrusts of Bradley's 1st and 9th Armies aimed through the Aachen gap at Cologne and Bonn. The 9th Army would swing north-east across the Roer upon Dusseldorf and Krefeld. With this plan the main thrust was moved for the first time to the south of the Ruhr, and the British 2nd Army's role would be to fight down between the rivers to link up with the Americans.

Before these plans could be implemented, and before even the results of the conference were promulgated on 28th October,[1] the Germans, counter attacking strongly out of the Maas pocket, had knocked the northern armies off balance at the point of contact between the British and Americans. The effect of this attack at this point, at this time, was far reaching, a miracle of fortuitous timing.

The attack itself, launched by the 15th Panzer Grenadier Division and the 9th Panzer Division in addition to the paratroops holding the salient, hit the U.S. 7th Armoured Division head on, swiftly crossed the Noorer canal and the Deurne canal, captured Meijel, and was finally halted a mile or two short of Helmond. Fortunately the operations of 12th Corps south of the Maas were moving to a close, and the 15th Scottish Division was hurried in to contain and repulse the enemy. A day later the 51st Highland Division was able to reinforce, and by the end of the month the position had been restored. But the repercussions were far reaching.

The attack had, of course, emphasized the strength of the Maas pocket, and the enemy determination to hold it, and it had also forced the postponement of Montgomery's part in the offensive planned for 10th November. These were the immediate and obvious local effects, but the U.S. 1st and 9th Armies were also unbalanced by the dangerous situation on their left flank, and it seemed that the start of their own operations must be postponed.

No effort was made by the 12th Army Group Commander, General Bradley, to restore the situation. Instead he felt confirmed

[1]See "Grand Strategy", vol. vi.

in his inclination to give equal weight to the role of Patton's 3rd Army south of the Ardennes. The relevant paragraph in the Supreme Commander's directive of 28th October reads:

> "To conduct operations so as to destroy the enemy in the Saar, to secure crossings over the Rhine, and to be prepared to advance from the Saar later in accordance with the situation then prevailing. All of these operations are to be timed so as best to support the main effort to which they are subsidiary."

There is no possible warrant in this paragraph for Bradley's translation. The clearly stated subsidiary role for the 3rd Army had not pleased him. It had pleased Patton even less, and he was quick to see and to seize his opportunity.

Throughout October Patton had grown increasingly restless, meeting formidable opposition in his attacks against the fortifications surrounding Metz. His forces had become virtually bogged down, and he had been forced to withdraw from Fort Driant on 12th October. Thereafter his army had been confined to "aggressive patrolling". Now, as October ended, and it was clear that the northern plan must suffer a check, he hastened to assure Bradley that an attack against the Saar would succeed in three days, and that he would breach the West Wall. He had managed to hoard considerable stocks of fuel and ammunition, and outnumbered the enemy by as much as three to one. The argument that the enemy would be forced to move reserves from the north was a potent one, and Bradley was readily susceptible.

The situation in the centre was far from promising. The U.S. 1st Army had suffered a severe check throughout October. The mission to take Dueren and Cologne had been thwarted by the resolute enemy defence of Aachen, and it was not until the 21st October that the city had finally surrendered. There remained the nagging problem of the Roer river and its dams high in the inaccessible forest country south-east of Aachen, and in the midst of the enemy's main defences. It was an unescapable fact that the capture of the dams was a prerequisite for any advance across the Roer, and upon Cologne. Until the dams were captured and the Roer crossed the battle of the Rhineland could not take place. Yet the fact and the factor of the Roer and its dams seems to have been "escaped". The immense difficulties were never adequately assessed.

Despite the capture of Aachen the targets of Cologne and Dueren remained almost as far off as ever. Aachen was but the outer gateway. The "moat" of the Roer and the fortress shielding the dams had yet to be forced.

It was in these circumstances that Bradley agreed to Patton's demands, and authorized a full-scale attack against the Saar by the 3rd Army as soon as weather permitted. There were other more personal considerations, noted particularly by Chester Wilmot,[1] for Bradley could not forget that Patton had been his senior, and he preferred him to the diffident General Hodges commanding the U.S. 1st Army.

Inevitably the weight of effort was dragged to the south to the immediate and lasting detriment of the centre,[2] and the balance could not be easily restored. The directive of 28th October confirming the October Conference had become waste paper before the ink was dry.

On 2nd November Eisenhower recognized the new position in the north by ordering 21st Army Group to confine itself to operations west of the Maas and to conform to the movements of the U.S. 1st Army. 2nd November is one of those days that mark decisive change. It is, I believe, the blackest date in the whole calendar of the campaign in north-west Europe, and it marked also the beginning of the most bitter month of the struggle.

III

In the north as November opened Montgomery was able at last to gather his armies together, to re-group and to face east, and to tidy up the battle map. All south-west Holland was clear, and

[1]The Struggle for Europe.

[2]I use centre to mean the centre of the Northern Groups of armies. Patton's Army south of the Ardennes is the centre of the front as a whole, and the southern extremity of the Rhineland struggle as it bears directly upon my story.

the successful final assault on Walcheren Island on 1st November promised the opening of Antwerp by the end of the month. The immediate task was to close up along the line of the Maas, eliminating the awkward pocket covering Venlo and Roermond, and to strengthen the flank between the British 2nd and the U.S. 9th Armies.

These were modest possibilities, yet in their realization there would also be a modest satisfaction. The battlefield of the Rhineland lay ahead with the Maas and Roer rivers in between.

Looking back from the 9th November when the Canadian 1st Army took over in the Nijmegen bridgehead, and prepared for its watery northern role, the hopes of September and October are seen as extravagant fantasies, arising perhaps out of Montgomery's great anxieties. Yet there is, I believe, strong justification. In late August as his armies prepared to burst out across the Seine it had not been unreasonable to hope for a miracle. But the Field Marshal had hoped for two miracles; a miracle on the left at Antwerp, and a miracle on the right at Arnhem. When he was faced with grim reality perhaps he bluffed—even himself—for if once he let slip his tenacious vision of the Rhineland and the Ruhr Eisenhower might deny it also. Had he permitted himself to admit the impossibility of mounting the Rhineland battle in October it would have been difficult to gain Eisenhower's consent for it in November. And it had to be fought. Without Montgomery's continuous insistence the weight might have shifted south for good. Governing all the Field Marshal's thinking and actions was the belief that the Rhineland and the Ruhr were the right road for the conquest of Germany, and the foreordained tasks of his armies. He could not act alone. If there could not be a single ground force commander he must have one of Bradley's armies under command, and the certain co-operation of the U.S. 12th Army Group on his right. Patton's 3rd Army must be curbed. That, I believe, is the basis of Montgomery's long struggle, and the basis of his nightmare. If he admitted the weakness of his position it would become true. He feared constantly that if the weight was once thrown to the centre it would be an irreparable mistake, a strategic blunder of the first magnitude. In the last resort he would yield the command of "his" battle; but it must be fought.

But the battle was not only in the field. Vast political issues loomed as victory came in sight. The New World was fighting to destroy the German armies: the Old World is fighting to win a political victory, to make Europe a safe place to live in.

There is a point where these aims diverge, for war is not so much a political instrument to the Americans as an act of retribution. My purpose here is simply to draw attention to these factors, not to discuss them. An awareness that such factors exist may be helpful in the contemplation of the campaign in the field.

IV

It was ironical that in the first week of November when Montgomery had his feet firmly on the ground for the first time since August that Bradley should choose to shift the strategic centre of gravity southward. There was no satisfaction for Bradley or for Patton in the change of plan, and their misfortunes were upon their own heads.

November opened with the worst weather for fifty years all along the line, and set the tone for the winter. The Supreme Commander toured the 1st and 9th Armies, visiting formations down to division level. The weather disconcerted him less than the shortage of supplies, for U.S. 1st Army was short of almost everything, and ammunition stocks were barely adequate for a limited offensive. It was following this early November tour that General Eisenhower made his alarming broadcast for increased industrial production, and especially for ammunition.

It seems a great misfortune that the Supreme Commander was unable in the first week of November to visit his 3rd Army, and especially the 12th Corps commanded by Major-General Manton S. Eddy. His presence at a crucial moment might—it is the merest chance—have averted an attack that was to prove costly in men and ammunition, to serve no strategic purpose, to strengthen the morale of the enemy, and gravely to limit the offensive ability of the U.S. 1st Army.

On the evening of the 7th November, the eve of the attack, General Eddy pleaded with his commander, General Patton, for delay. It had rained in torrents for three days. The Seille river on

Eddy's immediate front was swollen to two and a half times its size, and flowing fast. Behind him the Moselle was in spate, and with the bridges down except at Pont-a-Mousson midway between Metz and Nancy. The whole country was a morass in which it was madness to imagine that armour could fight. In these conditions Eddy believed that it would be impossible to make much headway.

Patton's answer was characteristic: it was to tell him to get on or to get out—"to name his successor". Eddy did not name his successor, nor did he tell Patton to do so. He "got on". It is rarely possible to pin-point such a moment, and it is a coincidence that in that same week another general had been told "to get on or get out".[1] It may be a measure of the anxieties and pressures of that week.

On the 18th November the 12th Corps attack went in north-east from Nancy upon the Saar line. Twenty-four hours later the 20th Corps moved to encircle Metz. Deprived by the weather of the considerable air support, alert but grounded, and unable to find a way through for his armour, Eddy's infantry struggled on bravely and hopelessly through drenching rain and flood. Before them the enemy with defence in depth backed by the West Wall, absorbed the attacks, and fell back at his own speed, selling ground he could afford and maintaining an unbroken line. At no single point was a great weight brought against the enemy, and at the end of the first week the 12th Corps was no better off than at the beginning. It had gained up to fifteen miles of ground, strategically worthless, and at great cost.

General Walton Walker's 20th Corps was at the same time having a hard struggle in its attempts to envelop Metz, and it was not until the 23rd November that the city, a smouldering wilderness of iron and steel which seemed to writhe under the leaden sky in a tortured Gorgonesque confusion, was finally won. Eighty days earlier, on 6th September, General Walton Walker had first issued his orders to advance to Mainz on the Rhine, to seize crossings of the Moselle and the Saare, and if "Metz did not fall like a ripe plum" the armour was to by-pass the city.[2] Now in November Patton's engineers were seeing their Moselle bridges swept away by the

[1]The Eighty-Five Days.
[2]20th Corps G-3 journal, Sept. 1944.

torrent and themselves "sitting down in the mud and bawling like babies".[1] Mainz and the Rhine were still a long way ahead, but even then, in November, bitter experience had not inclined the generals to appreciate just how far, or even to take serious notice of the first class intelligence reports with which they were unfailingly supplied.

The Siegfried defences of the Saar withstood all Patton's assaults until the end. The immensely superior forces at his disposal would have enabled him, even in early November, to strike in overwhelming strength at any chosen point. Instead he failed to concentrate his massive artillery strength and frittered it away, while attempting to advance all along the line.

By mid-November huge stocks of ammunition and supplies had been consumed to no purpose. The offensive had failed even to force the movement of reserves away from the U.S. 1st Army front.

I have summarised the November actions of the 3rd Army at this point because of their effect on the Rhineland battlefield. The Saar attack must be condemned as among the most irresponsible actions in the history of the campaign. The alternative to the attack north of the Ruhr could only be an attack by the U.S. 1st Army south of the Ruhr. The whole weight of 12th Army Group resources behind the U.S. 1st Army at this time might have achieved success, and by such a success the tempo and pattern of the campaign could have been changed greatly in the Allied favour.

For this, then, the plans of the October Conference had been sacrificed by the Commander of the U.S. 12th Army Group, and, it must be stated, with the tacit consent of the Supreme Commander.

Perhaps because of this the events of the week beginning on the 2nd November have escaped notice, and have never been assessed in their context. On the 2nd November the 112th Regiment of the U.S. 28th Infantry Division of the U.S. 1st Army advanced in a fog of ignorance upon Schmidt, and there suffered one of the most tragic disasters ever to befall American arms.

[1]War as I knew it, by General George S. Patton.

4

SCHMIDT

I

EARLY in November the U.S. 1st Army planned to launch its main offensive with the 7th Corps south and south-east of Aachen upon Dueren, and thence across the Roer river to the Rhine at Bonn. On the left the U.S. 9th Army would launch an assault against the Roer with the British 30th Corps driving through to breach the Siegfried Line at Geilenkirchen. A massive air bombardment would precede the offensive.

As a preliminary the 5th Corps on the right of the 1st Army would launch a flank attack with the main purpose of protecting the flank of the 7th Corps from counter attack, and to force the movement of enemy reserves away from the main 1st Army thrust. The objective of the 5th Corps attack was a small town called Schmidt. From thence the intention was to drive south-westwards to take in the rear the strong enemy defences of Monschau in conjunction with a frontal assault by the 5th Armoured Division.

The task of taking Schmidt and of advancing subsequently upon Monschau was given to the U.S. 28th Infantry Division. The division moved into the line east of Rotgen to take over from the U.S. 9th Infantry Division on the 26th October. It was an unhappy experience. The 9th had had a hard time and showed it. The troops were unkempt, dirty, unshaven and unutterably weary. Above all they showed signs of prolonged strain, dull eyed, morose, nervous. They had been badly shaken. The sight of them had a depressing effect upon their successors, and so also had the ground. Behind them and in front of them, surrounding them on all sides, they saw dark rain-saturated forest. It had the feel of some nether region, foul with the offal of war. The broken muddied trails were pockmarked and heavily cratered by shells and mines. The splintered trees added to the sense of ruin. Rotting, sodden garments clung to hideous scraps of green flesh that yet bore an obscene resemblance to the living. Tins, helmets, boots, tools, spent cartridges and old mines lay about in that dark and muddied confusion. In it there seemed the breath of despair.

The forest rose steeply to heights of more than one thousand feet, embracing closely narrow belts of open field round the villages and small townships which, here and there, lay upon the high plateaux and in the deep folds. The heavily wooded and precipitous gorges were threaded with fast running streams and small torrents, emptying the one into the other, and many of them into the Kall river gorge which joined its waters to the main stream of the Roer at a point some five miles due east of the American forward positions.

Such was the first prospect of the Hurtgen forest. In the area of the U.S. 28th Division it comprised also the forests of Rotgen and Gemund, part of a thickly wooded mass of high ground extending south-east from Eschweiler to join with the Ardennes. Simply as a strip of difficult country nullifying American superiority in armour and in the air it was of great value to the enemy.

The U.S. 9th Division had breached the outer defences of the Siegfried Line at Rotgen and had penetrated into the Hurtgen forest proper, but by holding Aachen for a month the Germans had gained time to strengthen their main belt of defences running through the whole forest and north through Dueren to Geilenkirchen on the right flank of the British 2nd Army.

The whole forest area was thickly studded with powerful pill boxes and strong points, sown with mines and booby traps, and covered by mortar fire. Artillery, well sited on ridges both east and west of the Roer river, dominated important objectives and road junctions.

Through all October it had been the scene of bitter and desperate fighting, ending in a virtual stalemate. Isolated villages had become heaps of muddied ruins, losing identity, changing hands from day to day, even from hour to hour, in that battered no-man's-land on the fringe of the German main defensive line.

The U.S. 28th Division took up its positions with its leading companies just forward of the road, Wittscheide–Germeter–Richelskaul–Raffelsbrand. The 109th Regiment on the left, the 112th Regiment in the centre, and the 110th Regiment on the right.

These dispositions and the roles of the regiments were dictated by 5th Corps. In the centre the 112th Regiment would attack and take Schmidt. On the left the 109th Regiment would attack to the north to secure the dangerous flank and shield against the heavy counter-attacks which must be expected out of the Hurtgen forest. On the right the 110th Regiment, less one battalion held as divisional reserve, would move south-east through thick forest to seize the enemy strong point at Simonskall, and secure the road from Schmidt to Strauch.

For this task the 28th Division was reinforced by battalions of tanks, self-propelled guns, 4.2 in. mortars, and an Engineer Combat Group. Field artillery battalions of 4.5 in., 105 mm., 155 mm., and 8 in. guns of the 5th and 7th Corps would reinforce the divisional artillery, and fire the most extensive programme the slender supplies of ammunition would allow. The attack was timed to go in on the 31st October.

The appalling weather conditions allied to the natural difficulties of terrain and the close proximity of the enemy inhibited patrol activity. The divisional headquarters staff studied 1/25,000 maps, and disliked what they saw. Air photographs added very little to their knowledge, for the trees and the narrow gorges masked the important trails.

Immediately ahead of the 112th Regiment lay the village of Vossenach, served by a hard road out of Germeter and approached over a narrow belt of open fields enclosed by the forest. Forward of the village the ridge looked bare and exposed to the enemy batteries sited on the Brandenburg–Bernstein ridge overlooking the position. No troops could be spared by the 5th Corps for an attack on the German batteries, but they would have to be neutralized.

Vossenach was the first objective of the 112th Regiment in its assault on Schmidt, and as soon as the village was taken the main assault must go through. A road ran south out of Vossenach to cross the Kall river gorge and to link the village with Kommerscheidt, and Schmidt immediately beyond. A road ran north-south at the foot of the gorge, but nothing could be seen of the trail leading down the steep and thickly wooded slopes, across the Kall river, and up again on the other side. But that was the only way to Kommerscheidt and Schmidt, and there could be no other until the road from Strauch might be won and opened.

The task and responsibility of establishing and maintaining a line of communications over the Kall river gorge would be a heavy one. It would be the one possible life line, the one possible channel for supplies to reach those who might get across, the one possible way of retreat. This vital task was assigned to the 20th Engineer Combat Battalion, and its grave importance emphasized.

The responsibility of 28th Division headquarters was limited to the details of the plan, for the 5th Corps had dictated the roles of the troops, the attack missions having been dictated by U.S. 12th Army Group and U.S. 1st Army. It had been arranged that the 9th Tactical Air Command of the 9th Air Force should isolate the battlefield, but this would be a task of great difficulty, largely governed by the weather.

Fog and rain forced the postponement of the operation, but there was little margin of time to spare, and on the cold and misty morning of the 2nd November the leading troops of the 28th Division, in a state of innocence most terrible to contemplate, and beset by vague fears, advanced out of their positions under fire.

Even with his very limited knowledge of the battlefield, and in profound ignorance of the true position, Major-General Norman D. Cota, commanding the 28th Division, considered that the operation had no more than "a gambler's chance". In fact, it had no chance at all.

II

The township of Schmidt lies within one mile of the great Schwammenauel dam, the principal dam controlling the flood waters of the Roer river. This was the most vital and sensitive point in the German defences, probably over the whole front from the Swiss border to the North Sea. It controlled the gateway to the Cologne plain, and while the dam remained in German hands it was not militarily practical to cross the Roer river. The Rhine itself could not be a reasonable target south of Dusseldorf.

While the dams remained under German control troops crossing the Roer could be isolated piecemeal, and destroyed. Bores could be sent roaring down the river to wash away all bridges, and render the river impassable for some days. In the event of threatened disaster the Germans could release an immense torrent to flood the whole Cologne plain, thereby meeting disaster with disaster. The Schwammenauel dam was therefore the essential—and obvious—pre-requisite to the offensive of the U.S. 1st and 9th Armies.

The great importance of the strongly held enemy pocket of the Maas at Venlo, and in the Roermond–Heinsberg triangle is evident, and easily understood, in relation to Schmidt, for it is at this point that the effective defensive potential of the Roer comes to an end. It is the second gateway to force in order to open the way for the battle of the Rhineland.

All this topography had been the subject of intensive scrutiny over many weeks, yet the 112th Regiment launched its attack on the 2nd November without any knowledge of the Roer dams. Colonel Carl I. Peterson, commanding the regiment, stated categorically that the "Roer dams never entered the picture". It is equally certain that all his battalion commanders were equally unaware.[1]

This is a startling fact, yet it is even more startling that the dams are not mentioned in 5th Corps orders or in 28th Division orders for the battle. The Intelligence estimate of 28th Division reveals no awareness of the real importance of Schmidt "fundamental in the German scheme for preventing an Allied break-through to the Rhine".

In a footnote to "Objective: Schmidt" Charles B. Macdonald comments, "Just when the American command fully realized the importance of the dams is not clear." But in the U.S. 1st Army operational report covering the period August 1944, to February 1945, there is a passage referring to a plan by 5th Corps "to seize the two large dams on the Roer river".

[1]It is probable that no single action in the history of war has been subjected to an investigation as thorough and meticulous as that which followed the battle of Schmidt. Almost every survivor, from generals to G.I.s, was interviewed and carefully questioned. The war diaries and Intelligence summaries of 12th Army Group, 1st Army, 5th Corps, 28th Division, of the regiments and all supporting arms and services involved, have been carefully examined.

See: THREE BATTLES, Office of Chief of Military History, Dept. of the Army, Washington, D.C.

Throughout all October the enemy had reacted with the utmost violence to all attacks in the sensitive Hurtgen forest area, immediately to the north, and had observed all Allied dispositions and troop movements in the Rotgen area with great care. The arrival of the 28th Division had been noted, and the expected attack had been confirmed to the enemy by U.S. artillery preparation. The Germans believed that the attack could have no other purpose but the taking of the dams.

In those few days between the arrival of the 28th Division and its attack on Schmidt the position had taken on an even greater importance for the enemy. It was not only the linch pin of the Rhineland defences, it had become also the vital point on the northern flank of Hitler's planned offensive to drive through the Ardennes, to cross the Meuse, and thence on to Brussels and Antwerp. With the defences of Schmidt and Monschau in Allied hands such an attack would be prejudiced before it began. At that stage also the dislike of von Rundstedt and von Manteuffel for the Ardennes plan had led them to suggest an alternative which would involve pinching out the Americans in the whole Aachen salient. This secondary plan enhanced the value of Schmidt.

The Allies knew nothing of these things at the end of October, but they did know—or they should have known—everything about the Roer dams.

These facts, I believe, justify the statement that the 112th Regiment advanced out of Germeter in a state of innocence most terrible to contemplate, and to meet the worst disaster on a divisional level to befall U.S. troops in the campaign in north-west Europe.

III

The morning of the 2nd November dawned cold and clammy with mist under a dirty sky like the inside of a rough iron casting. There might be snow, or sleet, or bitter cold rain. The temperature was within a degree or two of freezing point. The woods were thick with mist, curling round the trees, hanging heavily. At eight o'clock the whole of the 5th Corps front erupted with the stabbing flame and thunder of guns, and the men of the 28th Division lay under that harsh turbulence, waiting and listening. At fifteen minutes to nine o'clock the barrage came down on close targets, and the change in the pattern registered instantly in the ears. There were fifteen minutes to zero.

In the hours before dawn engineers had cleared lanes through their own defensive minefields. At nine o'clock the 2nd Battalion of the 112th Regiment began to advance out of its outposts and into the wilderness of mist and smoke. On the flanks the 109th and 110th Regiments were going into action, but in the centre they, the 2nd Battalion, moved out alone to prepare the way for the main attack of the regiment. Most of them did not know this; many of them did not know their regiment; too many had been rejected a year before as unfit for "combat" service. They went into battle. Seven tanks supported the left hand company, and three tanks moved forward with the right hand company. The centre company would move up as soon as the right flanking company had cleared a distance of three hundred yards, and mop up the little township of Vossenach which lay dead ahead. The gaunt skeleton of the church steeple stood up above the tower out of the mist. The map showed that it stood at the cross-roads, facing west, a massive bastion barring the way to the main street of Vossenach.

The men moved close up behind the tanks, keeping in their tracks for safety against mines. But safety was gone. Upon the instant, as the barrage lifted, the enemy artillery came down upon the forward positions all along the line, accurate and deadly, killing and maiming men as they rose up from cover to go forward.

On the left the lanes through the minefields were poorly marked, and at the outset one of the tanks leading G Company hit a mine and lost a track. Almost at once a second tank bogged down. The going was bad, soft and sludgy in patches over open fields. The command tank moved forward to take the lead. The five remaining tanks went on steadily, shielding the riflemen, firing steadily and concentrating on the tower of Vossenach church. The fire of supporting machine guns crashed into the fringe of the woods to the north. 81 mm. mortars put down a creeping curtain of high explosive one hundred yards ahead.

The enemy in Vossenach had sustained an immense weight of artillery fire, but had not been silenced. Mortars, automatic weapons and small arms fire sought out the men as they moved through the minefield. The short delays at the loss of the tanks had been costly. One man stepped on a booby trap, and a second man moving to pick him up stepped on another, touching off a chain of five anti-personnel mines. Twelve men of the headquarters group were killed or wounded in the minefield within four hundred yards of the start. The leaders of the machine gun platoon were casualties. The riflemen paid a steady toll, but the attack went doggedly on.

Sergeants took over as lieutenants fell, corporals led in place of sergeants. There was no cover, but after its initial difficulties G Company made good progress, harassed by enemy artillery, mortar and small arms fire. Its role was to skirt the township of Vossenach and to take up positions on the bald nose of the ridge forward, and close up to the forest line.

On the right F Company had a more complex role. Advancing astride the Richelskaul–Vossenach road, it met direct enemy resistance from machine gun posts and anti-tank guns. The bulk of the enemy had withdrawn from Vossenach, but strong pockets remained, ready to hold their fire, to let the leading platoon pass, and to take those who followed by surprise. Nevertheless by early afternoon F Company occupied most of the township, and had established itself at the eastern end. The men of G Company no longer felt so alone in their foxholes on the bare eastern ridge.

By half past three o'clock the mopping up company had come up through the centre of Vossenach, blasting small groups of enemy out of houses with grenades, and consolidating the gains of F Company. But in its experiences there had been ominous undertones. The company had met with delay at the outset, owing to the failure of F Company's reserve platoon to move out. The platoon had not been called upon, and awaited orders. The mopping up company assembled too soon, and in those minutes of doubt on the start line the men stood exposed to the enemy artillery fire, and suffered casualties.

The main body of the company then moved forward behind a platoon of tanks and with an attached section of machine guns. The first platoon got away well in advance of the main body, and with the role of protecting the right flank, but it took the wrong line out of Richelskaul, and came at once under heavy machine gun fire from the forward edge of the woods to the south. Enemy mortars at once concentrated on the men where they lay. Brave individual attempts to go forward in rushes failed. Finally the few survivors managed to withdraw, and to go into Vossenach behind their company.

Nevertheless this opening phase of the action designed to clear the way for the main attack of the 28th Division against Kommerscheidt and Schmidt, had progressed swiftly and successfully, despite severe casualties. With Vossenach held, the northern flank was secure, and the immediate route opened to the crossing of the Kall river gorge.

At noon, H plus three hours, the 1st and 3rd Battalions mounted the main attack of the 112th Regiment, the 1st Battalion leading in column of companies to cross the Kall river gorge and seize Kommerscheidt, the 3rd Battalion to pass through and take Schmidt. Both battalions would then prepare to attack towards Steckenborn and Strauch. Schmidt was the objective, not the object.

The 1st Battalion advanced out of Richelskaul on time intending to take a line through the wooded slopes to the south of Vossenach. A rough track leads out of the village to join with the Simonskall road at a point about one quarter of a mile out of Richelskaul. At that point the leading platoon ran head on into concentrated fire from automatic weapons and small arms, losing its platoon commander. It went no farther. A concentration of fire from the 81 mm. mortars failed to dislodge the enemy. A second platoon tried to move forward, and failed despite brave efforts by its severely wounded platoon commander.

No other company was committed and the main attack was called off. Under cover of darkness the company withdrew.

The attacks of the 109th and 110th Regiments on the flanks had also failed. The 109th, with the role of gaining a start line for an attack against Hurtgen, and of protecting the northern flank, was halted mainly by minefields within five hundred yards, and there finally had to "button up" for the night. The 110th came up against the powerful pill box and concrete defences built into the hillsides, covering the vital area of Steckenborn and the rear of Monschau. The 110th Regiment suffered heavy casualties. No progress was made towards the Schmidt–Strauch road.

The attack of the 28th Division on this opening and vital day "had been pushed with a surprising lack of vigor . . . . it had set back considerably the hour by which Schmidt might be taken."[1]

The weather had greatly hampered the hoped-for air support, but this failure could not have contributed to the failure of the 28th Division to press home its main attack. The first aircraft were unable to leave the ground until well after noon. Only one mission out of five succeeded, fighter bombers attacking the Bergstein ridge and targets on the Roer. One squadron bombed U.S. artillery at Rotgen causing twenty-four casualties, including seven killed.

The night of the 2nd November was quiet and bitter cold.

IV

The 112th Regiment revised its plan of attack during the night, and at seven o'clock in the morning the 3rd Battalion moved out of Germeter in column of companies into Vossenach. On the right the company of the 1st Battalion which had bloodied its nose on the enemy strong point athwart the original line through the woods, put in a diversionary attack, hoping to mask the new line of approach. The 1st Battalion was timed to follow up through to conform with the progress of the leading battalion.

Sunrise was at thirty-two minutes past seven that morning, but the event had long since lost its happy promise. At seven o'clock it was still dark, even in the east. The night mist was heavy, indistinguishable from drizzling rain, and seeming to seep steadily through clothing to chill the bones. Again the temperature was a degree or two above freezing.

Behind the lines in Germeter, Richelskaul, Wittscheide, petrol stoves were roaring, and cooks were boiling up coffee. That was another world.

The men strung out at five yard intervals, companies echeloned three hundred yards apart, signals, machine gun and headquarters jeeps, keeping position, the thin steel rods of their aerials curving like the thin masts of dhows seen afar off, the antennae of the troops,

[1]"Objective: Schmidt", Charles B. Macdonald.

radio sets squawking with muffled voices. Supporting tanks and heavy vehicles churned the sodden earth to a morass.

But for intermittent harassing fire the artillery was silent, so that the noises of men and vehicles on the move over the sludgy ground, the dull clank of arms and accoutrements, and the squelch of feet, became predominant. The enemy guns were silent. They had been silent through most of the night.

At half past seven o'clock the leading company of the 3rd Battalion reached the road junction at Vossenach church, and prepared at once to move out south on the Kall river trail to the woods. One company of supporting tanks moved forward to the bare ridge where the advance company of the 2nd Battalion had watched out the night, huddled in their foxholes and bitterly cold.

The first platoon of tanks reached its position safely, but the leading tank of the second platoon struck a mine three hundred yards east of Vossenach church. It seemed to spark off a chain explosion, for almost at that precise moment the enemy guns opened up from the Brandenburg–Bergstein ridge to bring down a fierce concentration of fire upon the battalion assembly point, forcing the men to scatter for cover. The armour moving into its position opened fire on the woodland line to the south-east.

The enemy fire lifted as suddenly as it had begun, and the leading company of the 3rd Battalion assembled swiftly and moved off sharply to gain the woods. The sky looked like mud. The saturating mist lay in the trees as thick as wool. Sporadic fire came down upon the men in the open, but they moved steadily on into the woods, over the rough Kall trail, slithering down, slipping on the outcropping rocks. Their supporting tanks lifted their fire to concentrate with their hull guns on Kommerscheidt across the gorge.

Harassed constantly by tree bursts the leading company negotiated the steep trail. Snipers caught the signal line layers, and brought death to stragglers. The forward scouts met a small enemy pocket at the Kall river crossing, and blasted it out of the way. At nine o'clock the forward platoon of the 3rd Battalion forded the river at a point to the south of a water mill, Mestrenger Muhle. There was a stone bridge, probably capable of bearing tanks. The bridge must be tested by the engineers. The water was bitter cold, but safer. The bottom was hard rock.

It is a steep climb up to the 420 metre contour line, the crest of the Kommerscheidt ridge, but lower than the high point south-west of Schmidt itself. The men went up the trail in silence, saving their breath, listening to the gunfire of their supporting tanks fluffing overhead from Vossenach.

When they reached the ridge, and came out of the woods they saw their shells falling on Kommerscheidt. A short burst of small arms fire challenged them across the open fields in front of the township, but the scouts deployed, moving fast at the double. The tank fire lifted, and within half an hour the leading company of the 3rd Battalion was in Kommerscheidt, almost unopposed.

Schmidt sprawled on the eastern slopes a thousand yards ahead, and to the forward company it appeared to hold little of menace. They could see the houses straggling away to join with Harscheidt to the east, and along the Hasenfeld road to the south. A small group of cottages lay between them and their objective at a curve of the dirt road. The dark woods enclosed the broad high clearing on all sides, with narrow spears and bulges of woodland thrusting inwards marking the re-entrants.

On the left the second company of the battalion was already in position, having crossed the Kall river gorge at a point some three hundred yards north of the stone bridge, and keeping pace with the leading company, it had gone up to come into Kommerscheidt from the east. The third company had also made good progress. At noon the 1st Battalion had moved out of Germeter to follow up through Vossenach and over the trail.

All companies and supporting arms had sustained casualties from enemy shelling and mortaring, especially moving out of Vossenach. Tree bursts continued over the trail all day, and the woods had an ominous feel. An occasional sniper's bullet testified to the eyes of the enemy. That was all.

A heavy concentration of enemy artillery forced the leading company to take cover as it prepared to move out of Kommerscheidt, warning them that their presence was known. An hour later Schmidt was taken. A score or so of enemy had been surprised, some eating and drinking, one or two riding bicycles casually down the main street, seemingly unaware of danger threatening. A few shots came from of isolated houses, and were quickly silenced. A machine gun opened fire from a small group of houses along the Hasenfeld road. By dusk the battalion had organized all-round defence for the night. There had been too little time, but they had done the best they could. Mines had been placed out on the roads in full view, but covered by bazookas. The mortar men and the machine gunners, toiling over the trail, humping their heavy weapons, had had an exhausting day. It was dark before they could set up their weapons.

The 1st Battalion in Kommerscheidt gave a solid feeling to their backs. All along the Kall trail and all through the night a battalion of engineers would be working against time to open a supply route from Germeter through Vossenach to Schmidt. Above all it was vital to move armour over that steep and narrow trail.

Long after dusk machine gunners and mortar men continued to hump their heavy weapons forward to the Kommerscheidt–Schmidt ridge, to wait for the dawn.

V

The difficulties and extreme vulnerability of the Kall river gorge had not been sufficiently appreciated. In the planning phases of the action the opening, maintenance and defence of the supply route, had been allotted to the Engineer Combat Group, and the security emphasized. But the emphasis had been lost in the break-down of the plan. The Engineer plan issued on 30th October failed to allot the defence precautions to any of its units, and merely observed that *local* security would be required. The plan with this wording was seen and approved by 28th Division. The 20th Engineer Combat Battalion moved off to its task of opening up and maintaining the trail, unaware that it needed to do more than keep a sharp look-out. North and south along the main gorge road, and through all the thick woods, the enemy could move at will.

Through the first night of intense and ferocious endeavour, with jeeps, weasels, trailers, slewing, slithering off the trail, with medical officers, supply officers, and many other striving to reconnoitre routes for their vehicles and services, the work of three men in particular was outstanding. These were Lieut. Muglia, a medical officer, 1st Lieut. William George, the 3rd Battalion motor officer, and 1st Lieut. Raymond Fleig, a tank platoon commander. The names of these three men weave a bold and coherent pattern through seven days and nights of growing disaster. They were not only brave, but resourceful and tireless. In all the broken strands these three strands hold.

Muglia had gone ahead with the leading troops, and had found a dug-out built into the rock and reinforced with logs. There he gathered medical supplies and established his main aid station on the trail.

By midnight on the night of the 3rd-4th, Lieut. George had wrestled a supply train of three weasels over the trail, and dumped the stores safely in Kommerscheidt. He had then made the return journey with wounded, and again returned with anti-tank ammunition. By then it was nearing dawn, and armour blocked the trail.

The task of coaxing Sherman tanks over the Kall trail cannot be exaggerated. It would have been dismissed as impossible by many, but it had to be possible. The track was nine feet wide, a shelving out of the rock wall and with open shoulders from which the woods fell away steeply. Rocks outcropped in dangerous patches, a menace above all to armour, which could easily belly down upon them. Hairpin bends turned angles of 180 degrees and were too shallow even for weasels to turn without shunting. Trailers had to be manhandled. At such points the rock wall bulged to lessen the usable width of the trail. In places it was precipitous. It was mined, booby-trapped, sniped, and shelled constantly with tree bursts.

At dusk on the afternoon of the 3rd two tank captains went forward to make a reconnaissance. At one point a weasel blocked the trail. This was Lieut. Muglia's weasel. He had been forced to abandon the vehicle and hump his medical supplies forward with the help of his orderly. Engineers were getting down to hard labour, sweeping for mines, assembling tools, and trying to blast away the rock bulges with German Teller mines. The trail was the exact width of a Sherman tank, with not an inch to spare. Wherever the rock wall bulged even slightly the heavy armoured vehicles would be forced out on the open shoulder.

Mines and shell fire had accounted for three tanks out of sixteen in Vossenach during the day, and the remaining thirteen of the company assembled ready to attempt the crossing of the Kall. Their presence had given some comfort to the riflemen on Vossenach ridge, but not much. The men had found that any attempt to leave their foxholes in the hours of daylight brought down heavy concentrations of fire upon them. They were cramped. The damp cold gripped their bones. They lay sleepless, a few dozing fitfully, but without rest through the second night, awaiting their third day.

In contrast, across the Kall gorge, the men of the 3rd Battalion in Schmidt were in good spirits, buoyant after their easy victory, confident of success.

Soon after midnight Lieut. Fleig led his platoon of Sherman tanks onto the trail. His tank hit a mine missed by the engineers in the first two hundred yards, and blew a track. Using the towing cable of the damaged tank, and the tank itself as a pivot the platoon sergeant Spooner contrived to winch his tank round Fleig's, and winch it back again onto the trail. The armour was blocking the life line, and deeply aware of it, yet a moment of impatience might have cost hours, and brought disaster. Behind them enemy shelling was making it uncomfortable for all those who waited.

As soon as the platoon sergeant's tank was well on the trail Lieut. Fleig took over and went on. He had a picture of men without armour in his mind, and he was resolved to beat the dawn. Behind him on the trail the tank crews winched, towed, side-slipped off the crumbling shoulder, lost tracks, re-fitted, and fought their way by inches down to the gorge, and all the cavalcade piled up through Vossenach into Germeter, the signal wires and all the air sizzling with urgency.

Fleig went steadily on, talking to his driver softly, guiding, never faltering. He knew that his outer track was crumbling the open shoulder, but he judged vehicles would manage. In any case he had to get through. The stone bridge across the river was sound. Fleig coaxed his driver and the heavy vehicle, rocking blind up and down switchbacks, and as the first light came into the leaden sky Fleig's Sherman roared up over the last ridge into Kommerscheidt. At that precise moment a hail of enemy shell fire hit Schmidt, crashing into the American positions, traversing the town from end to end, weaving a pattern of fire from which it seemed there could be no escape.

Communications were already bad, and they were swiftly worse. Enemy shell fire constantly clipped the signal wires back from Vossenach to Germeter. Communications were also bad forward. The companies in Schmidt kept contact with their perimeter defence platoons by runners, but runners had very short lives.

In the fringes of the woodland the men in the forward foxholes thought they saw movement, the milling of many men, preparing to attack. They were sitting athwart the enemy's main line of communications to his powerful defences at Steckenborn and behind Monschau. Knowing as little as they did about Schmidt, the battalion commanders and company commanders knew that, and it seemed to them enough. No man doubted that the enemy shelling heralded the assault.

As the dawn broke the 3rd Battalion in Schmidt braced itself for battle while behind them over the Kall river trail two tanks of Lieut. Fleig's platoon were steadily gaining ground, and a host of men toiled without rest to keep the pulse of supplies beating. Far behind on the trail the second platoon of armour met Fleig's abandoned tank on the trail. Believing that the tank must have been by-passed, and not realizing that the leading platoon had winched its tanks, the second platoon slid off the trail. Enemy shelling killed the men as they left the leading tank to investigate. Five tanks in all were disabled on the trail, and behind them four others waited, unable to move.

5

COUNTER-ATTACK

I

THE news of the advance on Vossenach, and the start of an attack by the U.S. 28th Division, was brought to the notice of Field Marshal Model, commanding Army Group B, while in the course of a 'map study' conference with his commanders at Schlenderhan Castle, near Quadrath on the Urft. The Commander of the German 74th Corps returned at once to his command while the U.S. attack and its probable developments became the subject of study for the generals. A real problem had fortuitously replaced a hypothetical one.

The task of appreciating the U.S. intention appeared to present little difficulty. The intention must be to take the Schwammenauel dam, to open the way for an offensive across the Roer into the Cologne plain, and to outflank, and to cut the communications of, the Monschau–Steckenborn defences. None of this could be tolerated.

The U.S. attack was expected, but in the early stages the method was obscure. Nor did it become less obscure at any time. With ample forces at his disposal the enemy awaited developments before committing his main striking power to counter-attack.

The 275th Infantry Division was responsible for the defence of the Hurtgen area, with the 12th Volks-grenadier Division on its right, and the 89th Infantry Division on the left. The presence of Field Marshal Model at the map conference probably accelerated the movement of a Kampgruffe of the 116th Panzer Division from Army Group B reserve near Muenchen Gladbach.

The German principal intention, which was to remain throughout, was to cut off the enemy along his base line, the Hurtgen–Germeter road. For this reason the attack of the 109th Regiment on the American left towards Hurtgen was at once held, while the Vossenach attack and its later developments were followed closely.

The weather favoured the enemy, and unless an unlooked-for break occurred U.S. air power would be unable to exert a major influence. The whole area of Vossenach, Kall river, Schmidt lay under the German guns.

Holding both ends of the north-south Kall gorge road, and with many concealed positions in the woods lining the gorge, with powerful defences covering Steckenborn and Strauch, the enemy's first task was to hold the flank attacks, and to observe the 112th Regiment as it climbed steadily out onto the long slender limb, from which it appeared there could be no going forward and no going back. It was obvious that unless powerful forces could be brought in behind the 112th Regiment no further move could be made, and yet there was no way for such forces, nor did they appear to be available.

It was impossible for the enemy to grasp the intention of the 3rd Battalion, isolated in Schmidt, without armour, with a line of communications that was at best precarious in the extreme. Indeed, if things were as they seemed, the enemy did not doubt his ability to cut the Kall trail, annihilate the engineer groups working there, and deal with the forces in Schmidt and Kommerscheidt at will.

Even if the Germans had realized the failure of the U.S. command to grasp the obvious importance of the Roer dams, it would still have been difficult, if not impossible, to understand the tactics of the 28th Division. General Cota himself, commanding the 28th Division, knew that he could not possibly move his battalions out of Schmidt and Kommerscheidt, either towards Strauch–Steckenborn, or anywhere else, without strong support. If he moved on Schmidt, and Kommerscheidt would be empty, the rear would be wide open. Of his ability to remain in Schmidt and Kommerscheidt he was soon in little doubt.

But in the German mind many possibilities could not be too swiftly discarded. The development of a powerful U.S. attack against the Brandenburg–Bergstein ridge must be expected, and whatever the appearances the Roer dams must be the target. It was enough, therefore, in the early stages to hold the flank attacks of the 109th and 110th Regiments, and to watch and wait, and to harass incessantly with shell fire.

The forward companies of the 2nd Battalion on the exposed Vossenach ridge were a sitting target, whose least movement might be observed. German patrols in the Kall gorge woods watched constantly alert for any development of a major threat, while their artillery and mortars made the narrow trail deadly. The lack of defensive developments in the Kall gorge was bewildering, for unless the Kall trail was secured there could be no hope for the battalions in Schmidt and Kommerscheidt. Indeed, even in terms of a reconnaisance in strength, an attempt to probe the dam defences prior to a major attack, or a feint to mask an alternative approach, it was impossible in enemy eyes to see any sane meaning in the remarkable situation.

But the presence of U.S. troops in Schmidt, even if it could not be understood, could not be tolerated. The rest, even Kommerscheidt, could wait.

II

It seemed to the men of the 3rd Battalion manning their perimeter defensive positions at Schmidt that the enemy shell fire burst upon them from all sides, and from all angles, and with less warning than the fall of an avalanche. In fact, the shelling came in from three sides. As the sky slowly lightened to the dirty brown of a new day the men forward covering the Hasenfeld, Harscheidt and Strauch roads with bazookas felt as naked and exposed as their mines, outcropping on the roads in full view.

As the morning barrage lifted small groups of enemy infantry burst from cover to race across open ground to gain the shelter of houses. A machine gun suddenly opened fire from a building less than fifty yards from the forward foxholes on the south east, and at that Sergeant Ripperdam charged with two other men.

The enemy attack developed slowly, it seemed, almost tentatively. A small group of infantry were seen advancing from the direction of Harscheidt, a large group appeared from the direction of Hasenfeld. The forward platoons of the 3rd Battalion met them with bursts of automatic fire, but all at once enemy infantry, grey in the grey brown light, oozed towards Schmidt like an enveloping blanket, coming in from all sides save only the north, the road back to Kommerscheidt.

For nearly an hour the harsh din of machine guns, small arms and mortars emptied out of the smoking ruins of Schmidt, and into it, so that all the high open ground held within the dark belt of woods had become a chaos of smoke and flame through which men moved, stumbled, screamed, cursed and died like shadows under the crimson lid of sky that was like a low roof upon them.

At ten minutes to nine o'clock corps and divisional artillery answered the urgent calls for fire from the hard pressed battalion, and for nearly half an hour the grey encroaching blanket of enemy was held. Then suddenly a new and ominous note came to the ears of those still manning the foxholes forward on the road verges. From Hasenfeld and from Harscheidt the rumbling of armour grew to a dull roar as enemy mark IV and mark V tanks led columns of infantry. The armour came on steadily, five tanks leading from Harscheidt and five from Hasenfeld, raking the American defences with fire, moving off the roads to avoid the mines so hastily and uselessly laid.

A direct hit on the lead tank from a bazooka on the Hasenfeld road made the tank swerve momentarily at the shock, but it came on. Those forward were unnerved. The 3rd Battalion began to break, slowly at first round the edges. Here and there men began to run, infecting others. Officers and N.C.O.s roared orders, striving at first to halt the men, and then, when that was hopeless, to direct orderly withdrawal into Schmidt. Many ran for the woods and into the arms of the enemy. Those who were holding saw others breaking on their flanks.

Captain Rokey, a company commander, one of the first to sight the enemy, Sergeant Ripperdam, who had charged the enemy machine gun position, and others fought to rally men to their sides, but the tide was rising to the flood. In the northern outskirts of Schmidt the 81 mm. mortars were still firing. Machine gunners still manned their weapons. But there was nothing now to halt the enemy infiltrating into Schmidt in the wake of their armour.

Two company headquarters groups formed a line at the heart of the smoking wilderness of Schmidt, but nothing could stand against the confusion of fear that had gripped the 3rd Battalion. A single cry of withdraw from any mouth was enough to send those who faltered streaming back. The cries passed from mouth to mouth, withdraw, withdraw, "the word spread quickly, and none questioned its source".[1]

By ten o'clock Schmidt "with or without orders" was being abandoned. Only a handful of medical men remained, striving to ease the wounded. The dead lay where they had fallen.

At that hour a junior staff officer reached Kommerscheidt on his way to Schmidt with a regimental order to the 3rd Battalion to hold temporarily in Schmidt while the 110th Infantry Regiment continued its assault on the flanks. The staff officer was in time to see the first stragglers running back with shouts of "They're throwing everything they've got at us".

III

From the moment of Lieut. Fleig's arrival in his Sherman tank the 1st Battalion in Kommerscheidt had been under light artillery and mortar fire. The din of war enveloping Schmidt was ominous, warning of danger imminent. Urgently the officers of the 1st Battalion looked to their defences, and prayed for more armour. By mid morning the frightened stragglers coming back from Schmidt in ones and twos had grown to the proportions of "a demoralized mob", impervious to orders, appeals, threats.

Here and there in that disorderly stream officers and N.C.O.s, tossed about like driftwood, fought to halt the flight, to find men steady enough to form groups to strengthen the 1st Battalion for the impending ordeal.

Sergeant Ripperdam had built a group of twenty-six men round his own indomitable figure, and with these he took up a position to the north-west of Kommerscheidt, there to be joined by a small group from 3rd Battalion headquarters. Two company commanders had salvaged each a handful of men and three machine guns. In the woods a platoon commander organized two under strength

[1]Quotes are from "Objective Schmidt", U.S. Army in World War II. Dept. of the Army, Washington, D.C.

platoons from the remnants of a company. If it would not go forward at least it might rally to fight on the Kall trail.

The Kall trail was thick with men resolved only on getting back, each one carrying his burden of fear, along the trail through Vossenach and into Germeter. Less than one hundred men in the final count out of a battalion rallied to fight with the 1st Battalion.

All of this was no more than a confused blur in regimental headquarters and division remained totally unaware of impending disaster. Only communications with artillery seemed to be effective, for the American guns were giving more and better support as the day progressed, harassing the Germans re-grouping in Schmidt almost as much as the enemy was harassing the 1st Battalion and the remnant of the 3rd in Kommerscheidt.

To Lieut. Fleig, joined by mid morning by two of his sergeants with their tanks, and manoeuvring carefully to discover points of vantage for his small armoured force, things looked very dirty, but the feel of battle stimulated him. Schmidt lay on a ridge commanding Kommerscheidt, and the enemy armour could dominate the American positions. It did not daunt Fleig.

At half past twelve o'clock P.47s swooped down upon Schmidt and came in bombing so close to Kommerscheidt that the defenders put out identification symbols. It was not until two o'clock in the afternoon that five German Panther tanks[1] led a group of infantry in not more than company strength from a bulge of the woods to the east. At once the American field artillery answered the radio calls of the 1st Battalion with accurate fire. Forward, Fleig led his three Shermans to a slight rise in the ground, and opened fire, stopping two enemy tanks with his first rounds. A few minutes later, manoeuvring his tank to a new position to give heart to the defenders on the flank, Fleig saw a Panther approaching obliquely at a distance of two hundred yards. Opening fire at once he hit the enemy twice with high explosive, but without noticeable effect. He realized then that all his armour piercing ammunition was in the sponson rack. Scoring another direct hit with high explosive Fleig saw the German crew leaving their tank, probably fearing a brew up. Taking his chance he leapt out of his Sherman with his gunner, retrieved the

[1]Survivors state definitely that Tiger tanks came against them, but there were no Tiger tanks on the strength of 116 Panzer Division at that time.

armour piercing shells under heavy fire, and regained his tank almost at the same moment as the enemy regained theirs. Fleig's first round cut the barrel of the Panther's gun, and his next tore through the hull. Two more rounds sent up a great billow of black smoke to mark the end.

Through all that day of the 4th November, and again through repeated attacks on the 5th and 6th, the 1st Battalion held on desperately in Kommerscheidt. Engineers, tanks, tank destroyers, medical men and supply columns, battled incessantly along the Kall trail, constantly infiltrated by enemy, incessantly harassed by mortars, shell fire and machine guns. By nightfall on the 6th November the Kall trail was virtually in enemy control, and at least one company of Combat Engineers had been annihilated.

The almost total lack of security precautions caused anxiety to the enemy, just as an open door might cause a burglar to feel suspicion, and to proceed warily. Constantly ambushed, at times with squads of men wiped out by bursts of fire, the Americans simply continued doggedly to try to force their way through and back. The medical men worked on, Lieut. Muglia among them, organizing, tending, and evacuating the wounded from the log cabin dug-out, ignoring the enemy, unaware it seemed of everything except their mission. Even when Muglia found German sentries guarding his dug-out he paid no heed, for at times they were there, and at times they were not, in that strange confused struggle on the Kall Gorge trail.

One of those who knew exactly what he was doing and why was Lieut. George, fighting his way through with supply trains alongside others who pressed grimly forward through the tattered ranks of those who floundered back.

IV

On the morning of the 5th November it was clear to company commanders and N.C.O.s in Vossenach that their position was critical. The men stood up badly to the enemy shelling. One company commander stated that all his men should be evacuated as unfit to carry on. The battalion commander was himself a virtual casualty with combat exhaustion. Indeed, combat exhaustion was spreading through the battalion, a blight, a canker gnawing away at the human spirit.

On the morning of the 5th, platoon commanders and N.C.O.s tried to force many of their men to eat, to take notice. But for the shelling there was no visible enemy movement, no signs of attack.

By that time the 112th Regiment had become little more than a collection of isolated groups without cohesion, and almost entirely lacking in effective communications. Even the 2nd Battalion in Vossenach was out of touch with its regimental headquarters.

At dusk on the evening of the 5th November a sudden burst of enemy shelling killed six men of G Company in their foxholes on the ridge, and at once set off a reaction that grew, slowly at first, to become an enveloping wave of fear. Ignoring the orders, and all the efforts of their officers, men got up, many weeping, and stumbled from their positions back to the shelter of the houses of Vossenach.

Company commanders urgently reported the situation to battalion, battalion reported to regiment, but there was no relief. The situation report of the 112th Regiment for that day reported the "combat condition" of its entire command as "excellent". Yet a colonel of engineers, returning from a mission on the Kall trail, was "so concerned" at the state of affairs in Vossenach that he reported it personally to regimental rear headquarters.[1]

On that day the commanders of the U.S. 1st Army and the 5th Corps visited General Cota at 28th Division headquarters. Their ignorance of the true position remained profound. It was the eve of the last phase of the hopeless ordeal.

Through the night of the 5th-6th the men crouched in their foxholes, many digging down like moles in their efforts to find some warmth against the bitter cold of the night. Many were without greatcoats or adequate clothing for winter. At Vossenach and Kommerscheidt the 112th Regiment awaited the dawn with a mixture of hope and fear.

After three days and nights of effort five more tanks and nine tank destroyers had finally crawled over the Kall trail, many of

[1]Letter from Col. Daley to Hist. Division, U.S. Army.

them literally yard by yard, shedding their tracks, bull-dozed, towed, winched, and constantly under fire. Crews, repair units and engineers all suffered heavy casualties in the task. A machine gun platoon and a rifle platoon had also struggled up through from Richelskaul, and "a decimated battalion" of the 110th Infantry Regiment, hastily organized and supported by light tanks and tank destroyers, was on its way forward with the mission of retaking Schmidt. No such wild illusion presented itself to the weary and harassed men who still clung to their Kommerscheidt positions, and knew themselves to be nearing the end.

By the morning of the 6th the Germans had again mined the Kall trail and regained control of the bridge and the main crossing points of the river. Yet serious as were the prospects of the new day in Kommerscheidt, the situation in Vossenach was more dangerous. A platoon of tanks and a platoon of tank destroyers patrolled Vossenach ridge, and as the night paled slowly to dawn a third platoon of tanks moved forward to join them. Two platoons of engineers and three 57 mm. anti-tank guns strengthened the forces in the town. The two rifle companies still manned their original positions on the ridge, and outwardly the position of the 2nd Battalion remained as strong as on that morning, three days and four nights earlier, when it had moved out behind its tanks to take possession. Only the officers and N.C.O.s in constant contact with their men knew the subtle and deadly sickness in the blood and nerves that was steadily sapping the strength of the battalion.[1]

The official record reads: "As daylight came the men of company G, in the most exposed positions of all on the northern portion of the ridge became suspicious of a strange silence."[2] This silence seemed more ominous to the men than the usual barrage of the morning, and in that silence men were the more acutely aware of the gaps in their ranks, and the wide gap in the centre deserted by their comrades. Through the night in ones and twos others had crawled back into Vossenach.

A short burst of small arms fire from an unknown source broke the silence. There was a "piercing scream", and again silence. When the enemy shelling began half an hour after daylight panic gripped

[1]It did not occur to anyone to rotate the battalion companies.
[2]"Objective Schmidt." U.S. Dept. of the Army.

the men forward. Grabbing wildly at their equipment they began to run for the rear, and those few who might have held, finding themselves abandoned, joined in the flight. For a few minutes it seemed that the second company forward on the right of the ridge might hold. Platoon leaders tried desperately to force their men to orderly withdrawal, "but there was no control".

Back in the centre of the town command groups strove to halt the tide of men surging in wild confusion, trampling upon those who fell, but nothing could stand in the face of the panic-stricken mob, believing itself attacked, and coherent only in its resolve to go back.

Forward on the ridge the armour waited, alert for the least sign of enemy movement in the woods beyond, but there was no attack, nor were enemy observed.[1] In Vossenach officers and N.C.O.s stood firm with a remnant of the battalion to form a line of defence forward of the church to hold the eastern approaches. It was at this stage that a colonel of engineers resolved that his men should fight as infantry, and while the two engineer platoons held fast, more were swiftly armed with infantry weapons. Slow to realize the situation the enemy did not begin to infiltrate into Vossenach until noon. By that time the engineers were ready.

V

In Kommerscheidt and along the northern fringe of the woods line the 3rd Battalion with the remnant of the 1st suffered the ordeal of the 6th November sustained by the best artillery and armoured support they had known. From their commanding positions on the higher Schmidt ridge enemy tanks brought down accurate fire pinning the men to their foxholes and raking the shattered buildings of the township. Utterly weary and bitterly cold, unable to move in daylight, the forward troops were forced to foul their foxholes, while some used K ration tins for their excrement. The incessant din of fire from the Kall trail in the rear could mean only that they were surrounded. The strength of the 1st Battalion was slowly but steadily ebbing as men began to desert their posts.

[1]It has been established that there was no attack.

At about noon the relief force designed for the task of re-taking Schmidt had fought its way through the Kall trail to reach the northern woods line. There they dug in to give some security to the rear of Kommerscheidt. Two officers and fifteen men had been lost at the river crossing. Again the enemy tanks opened fire from Schmidt, and by this time even the sound of a tank engine roaring was enough to send men running for the rear.[1]

In an effort to give heart to the men Lieut. Fleig led out his tanks to draw the enemy fire while the tank destroyers attempted to work round on the opposite flank. Fleig fought his tanks, giving as good as he got, but the destroyers bellied down on the stumps of a hedgerow and were ineffective.

Before dawn on the 6th, Lieut. George had again got through to Kommerscheidt with supplies, and at three o'clock on the morning of the 7th three weasels out of a convoy of nine fought through led by Capt. Rumbaugh in a jeep. An hour later, at four o'clock on the morning of the 7th, Lieut. George formed a convoy of two two-and-a-half ton trucks and five weasels, loaded up the big trucks with wounded, and led off in driving heavy rain in his jeep down the Kall trail. The darkness was almost opaque. A shell burst killed George's driver, but he pressed on. In the heavy trucks, lumbering blind over the battered trail, severely wounded men groaned in agony.

The situation all along the trail was one of utter confusion. American and German medical men had negotiated truces between themselves to evacuate wounded. A column of obvious wounded was reasonably safe from direct attack, but tree bursts and mortar fire were deadly in the shambles of the forest.

Almost within sight of the end of the trail Lieut. George was forced to abandon the heavy trucks at a blocked point. At the same time his convoy came under fire from small arms. Transferring the wounded to the weasels, George ordered every man who could hold a gun "to fire like Hell", and with that the lieutenant raced his convoy over the ridge, skirting Vossenach, skidding over the slippery ground to reach Richelskaul in safety.

That was the last convoy out of Kommerscheidt, and at first light on the 7th a terrific enemy barrage came down upon the last

[1]"Three Battles", p. 350.

defenders of the town. With their armour reduced to a single tank and three tank destroyers the position was beyond hope. Colonel Ripple, commanding the relief force, tried to get a company to move forward from the woods line to strengthen those who still held on precariously forward, but the company would not move. Forward the commander of the 3rd Battalion, Major Hazlett, went constantly among his men, exhorting, striving to give heart by his example. Long before noon the remnants of two battalions with their reinforcements and supporting groups, less than four hundred men in all, withdrew into the northern woods line, while all along the trail men staggered back, dazed and dying, mumbling, impervious to pain.

On the Kommerscheidt woods line the few officers left alive held the men together, resolved somehow to achieve an orderly withdrawal, or to die where they were. "But for the fine artillery support we shouldn't have held the woods line for twenty minutes," said a colonel.

Unknown to these men almost at the end of their tether looking out from the bleak fringes of the woods over the smoking blackened ruin of Kommerscheidt a whole battalion had lost its way in an attempt to reach them. On the morning of the 8th November the 3rd Battalion of the 109th Regiment was advancing to give flank protection, to open up a line of withdrawal and to lead the way out. At dusk the survivors called for a last barrage to mask their movements. The colonel commanding the relief column had taken command. The crippled tanks and destroyers were rendered useless to the enemy, and every man stripped himself down to essentials. Litters were improvised from saplings and clothing, and soon after dusk a column of wounded set off down the trail, unarmed and trusting to luck to get them through. On the trail and in all the woods about, colonels and G.I.s, unrecognizable in their filth, and crippled with wounds, crawled and fought, and in the gorge small groups of engineers fought on.

Under cover of the darkness the last defenders of Kommerscheidt began their withdrawal. Each man had a hand on the shoulder of the man in front, and thus in the pitch darkness, through the shattered, shell-holed forest, without even a compass, the weary men struggled on, many losing contact before the bitter icy rain turned to snow in the dawn. Between three hundred and three hundred and fifty men of all those who had gone forward so hopefully came back into Germeter and Richelskaul.

VI

On the 8th November, 515 replacements joined the 2nd Battalion, but numbers alone do not fit a battalion for battle, and the 112th Regiment was at once relieved.

The enemy meanwhile, having dealt the 112th Regiment a decisive blow, held the 109th Regiment in its attempts to strengthen the flank of the U.S. 7th Corps, and having inflicted heavy casualties on the 110th Regiment in its abortive efforts to advance on Strauch, at once re-grouped and renewed his attacks designed to cut off the Americans along the base line of the Hurtgen–Germeter road.

The battle of Schmidt had not only been lost in the field, it had been lost also from the records, and might never be assessed in its context. U.S. 1st Army and 5th Corps had maintained constant contact with 28th Division headquarters through all phases of the battle, and were at all times unaware of the true situation. Even had the G-3 reports[1] of the 28th Division been available for study by visitors little could have been gleaned.

Charles B. Macdonald quotes the 28th Division G-3 journal, 6th November, 1944, as follows: "2nd Battalion received very heavy and concentrated artillery fire, withdrew to reorganize and then regained their original position."

This was the day of the disaster at Vossenach, and Macdonald comments: "Actually the 2nd Battalion had been routed, recovered none of the ground it had lost, and had been destroyed as a fighting unit."[2]

By the 19th November the 28th Division had been relieved of further responsibility in the sector, and moved into the quiet 8th Corps area of the Ardennes to recover. It had failed to achieve any of its objectives, including the movement of enemy reserves away from the 7th Corps front. Its losses had been severe, and in their nature, startling. The division had suffered an estimated 6,184

[1]Operations. [2]"Three Battles." U.S. Army in World War II.

casualties in this one assault, and of these the 112th Regiment had lost 2,093 officers and men. A distressing feature of the casualties was the very high proportion of 544 officers and men listed as "non battle casualties". Combat exhaustion was becoming endemic in the U.S. Army, and General Cota, commanding the 28th Division, although assured that the situation was as bad in other units, expressed some alarm.

William Bradford Huie stated, particularly in regard to this front in November 1944: "A commander could go up at night expecting to find two hundred men in the line and be lucky to find seventy. There was an epidemic of 'combat fatigue', and division commanders swore at psychiatrists."[1]

Material losses were also heavy, including thirty-one out of fifty medium tanks, sixteen out of twenty-four tank destroyers, and large numbers of weasels, trucks, bull-dozers and weapons.

Students of war may be grateful for the meticulous and brave post mortem carried out on Schmidt. The post mortem examined all the organs of the division to discover the why and wherefore, but it did not put the battle of Schmidt into its context in the struggle for the Rhineland. That was not the function of the researchers. The result is that no historian striving to pick up the strands from the war diaries of army groups, armies, corps, divisions, regiments and brigades could hope to discover it. It is not there.

If I have laboured the point, I hope I may be forgiven, for

[1]In an analysis of American manpower *William Bradford Huie* states: " . . . . one youth out of every eight was excused from military service for reasons other than physical . . . . their number was 1,532,500—the temperamentally unstable, the maladjusted, the sexually perverted, and the overly nervous . . . . Of the 10,110,103 who were inducted only 2,670,000 were trained for actual ground combat; and of these a very large number, believed to be as high as a million men, soon managed to escape combat by such devices as bad-conduct discharges, or self-inflicted wounds, or by being excused by psychiatrists for some form of mental insufficiency . . . . Among those who evaded combat were about forty thousand who were believed to have 'taken off' or 'bugged off' or 'deserted before the enemy'."

See: "The Execution of Private Slovik".

Author's note: These facts had a profound effect on American tactics and strategy, and may be considered as one of the principal factors in changing the nature of war. The massive base in manpower needed to sustain one man in the front line was also growing with the weight of organization.

properly to have appreciated the importance of Schmidt in October-November 1944, to have planned and mounted an attack to take and to hold that vital area and its menacing dams, would have changed the course of the campaign. But that attack was never conceived, never planned, and never mounted, and in the final upshot the irresponsible attack on and brief occupation of Schmidt in November 1944, should not be assessed as "a chance lost", and which took three and a half months of bitter fighting to regain. The chance was never understood.

The vital significance of Schmidt is that it is one of the missing pieces in the puzzle of the Rhineland battle.

PART TWO

THE STRATEGIC REVERSE

6

THE NOVEMBER REALITIES

I

FIELD Marshal Montgomery was quick to grasp the November realities. The vision of a major thrust through to the heart of Germany, which had haunted him since mid-August, was at last killed.

When General Bradley took advantage of the German counter-attack out of the Maas pocket to throw his weight behind Patton in his ill-timed, ill-judged and abortive Saar offensive, Montgomery realised that the planned November offensive of the 1st and 9th Armies to burst out through the Aachen Gap into the Cologne plain was gravely prejudiced. The 21st Army Group must rely on its own unaided efforts to put its house in order. The hopes of the autumn were in ruins.

On the evening of the 1st November the news of the successful assaults against the fortress of Walcheren guarding the mouth of the Scheldt, promised the port of Antwerp by the end of the month, and finally released the Canadian 1st Army, with the British 1st Corps, from the long and dreary struggle to free the estuary. With that the Field Marshal could re-group to face east and begin the operations which he referred to as "Preparations for the Battle of the Rhineland".[1]

By the 9th November the Canadian army with the British 1st Corps had taken over in the Nijmegen bridgehead from the 30th Corps, and released also the two U.S. Airborne divisions which had supported the 30th Corps since Arnhem. These two divisions together with the U.S. 7th Armoured Division and the 104th Infantry Division, which had supported the 2nd Army, returned to United States command.

The Canadians with 1st Corps would guard the whole left flank

[1]"Normandy to the Baltic", by F.M. Montgomery.

from Oss to the sea, and prepare for their major role in the great battle which lay ahead. They had exchanged one water-logged landscape for another, and the patient Dutch in their great cities north of the Maas, in Amsterdam, Rotterdam, Utrecht and The Hague, resigned themselves to a diet of tulip bulbs throughout the long winter, their last hopes of liberation indefinitely postponed.

The 21st Army Group lined up along the Maas with the 30th Corps on the right flank, the 12th Corps in the centre, and the 8th Corps in the north, at long last facing east.

The main task facing the 2nd Army was the elimination of the strong enemy bridgehead west of the Maas, and based solidly on Venlo and Roermond. The operations in mid-October against Overloon and Venraij, and the fierce enemy counter-attack of the 27th October, had revealed the strength of the pocket and the importance attached to it by the Germans. Nevertheless the Battle of the Maas pocket was regarded as a matter of routine clearance. But it was far more than that. It should have been clear not later than the middle of October that there were only three sectors of major threat to the enemy over the whole northern front in the depths of winter, and these were the Nijmegen bridgehead, the Maas pocket, with its deep hard roots east of the river in the Heinsberg triangle, and the Roer and Urft river dams. These were all interdependent if a major offensive into the Rhineland was contemplated. The Maas pocket and the Heinsberg triangle was, therefore, the "Schmidt–Hurtgen" on the 2nd Army front.

On the 14th November General Dempsey launched his attack with the 8th Corps on the left and the 12th Corps on the right, and men and machines began to move over that nightmare landscape of the Peel country, and which no man wishes to revisit or to remember. Even in a normal winter this "land", embraced by the Wessem and Deurne canals and innumerable lesser cuttings and waterways, is flooded. In that November of 1944, hail, sleet, snow and ice had added abundant miseries.

On the opening day of the Battle of the Pocket, Field Marshal Montgomery visited his old division, the 3rd British Infantry Division, at Oploo, a tiny Dutch village at the northern end of the enemy salient. The division had fought the unpleasant battle of Overloon, and had been engaged on the perimeter of the enemy defences ever since, fighting at Venraij and down through Deurne to contain the counter-attack on the Leisel–Meijel road. For a month the infantry had dug themselves in, while the tank men, with an immense distaste for this impossible country, had been even more uncomfortable above ground. In that month, from mid-October to mid-November, the enemy shelling and mortaring at close range had been regular and accurate. The only reasonably safe place to be through certain hours of each day, and particularly of each evening, was in a deep hole, or in a house with a tank drawn close up alongside as a bulwark.

The 14th November would not have differed greatly from any other day for the 3rd British Infantry Division but for the Field Marshal's visit. The purpose was to pin up some medals. But for my purpose the visit is notable because of a speech the Field Marshal made to junior officers and men.

His speech is memorable in this context for one passage in particular. He was speaking of the German mistake in counter-attacking in Normandy instead of retreating to fight behind the Seine. He said:

> "Why did the Germans make that big mistake? They have the same general in charge of the battle now as they had in Normandy, Field-Marshal von Rundstedt. The reason was that von Rundstedt was not allowed to do what he wanted to do because Hitler was running the war. It is very interesting to note what is happening now. A general gets the feel of what the other chap is doing when he is fighting a battle, can tell whether he has got a good grip on the battle or not. It is my view that the German battle to-day is being fought very well by the same man who fought badly in Normandy, by von Rundstedt, so I think it's obvious that the German generals, having seen Hitler off, are running the war in the way they want, and they are running it very well."

That was the cardinal mistake not only of Montgomery, but of all the generals, and it led the Allies to terrible errors.

In the light of it Field Marshal Montgomery's final passage is interesting.

> "You want to know," he said, "how long the war is going to last. I have some money on it myself. The Germans fought the battle for France on our side of the Seine. Will the battle for Germany be fought on our side of the Rhine? If the answer to that question is 'Yes', then I say 'That's easy'."

The Field Marshal did not commit himself, but I think it is clear from all his actions that he did think that the battle for Germany would be fought on "our" side of the Rhine. If that is so he must have believed that von Rundstedt would make the same mistake as Hitler, for surely if the "generals are running the show", as Montgomery said, the battle would be fought east of the Rhine, not west?

II

On the morning of the 14th November the enemy-held pocket west of the Maas described an arc from the Wessem canal north of Maeseyck in the south to Mashees in the north, through a point slightly east of Weert and embracing Meijel. The whole area within this "bubble" was flat and water-logged, a maze of canals, cuttings, dykes, and flooded fields, and through it three roads converged on Venlo. It was more like an elaborately mined water system than a battlefield, and without the remarkable array of armoured fighting vehicles provided by the 79th Armoured Division progress must have been next to impossible and casualties severe.

With its right flank on the Maas above Maeseyck the 12th Corps crossed the Wessem canal, the 7th Armoured Division seizing the lock gates at Panheel while the 51st Highland Division from its watery positions round Weert crossed the Noorer canal which traverses the Wessem at right angles at Nederweert. On the right the 53rd Division pressed on towards Roermond. From the north the 8th Corps attacked south towards Horst and Sevenum from Venraij, and east across the Deurne canal on Meijel. It was tedious in the extreme. A great engineering effort had been necessary to make the only three available roads possible for traffic. The weather was a bitter enemy, washing out all possible features from a featureless landscape, and never had junior officers studied their 1 in 25,000 maps with more dismay. It was a battle for navigators.

Slowly and steadily the right flank of the 12th Corps crawled along the west bank of the Maas, and the compression bore in upon the enemy, crushing him back across the river foot by foot. The whole tempo of the campaign had changed. The advances were over, and the long winter of attrition was setting in. Not only the troops and the generals, but the vast audience hungry for news and "spectacle", must adapt to it.

There was no doubt that Field Marshal Montgomery had adapted to it, and it may be that he watched the opening of the offensive of the U.S. 1st and 9th Armies on his right flank with a sombre satisfaction.

On the 16th November, two days after the opening of the modest offensive to close the Maas, General Bradley launched the 1st and 9th Armies into the attack with the intention of advancing across the Cologne plain to the Rhine. To make up for a shortage of ammunition, bombers of the U.S. 8th Air Force and the R.A.F. dropped 9,700 tons of high explosive in the greatest "air-ground co-operative effort yet undertaken by the Allied air forces," and tore the heart out of the ancient town of Dueren, and reduced Eschweiler, Julich and Linnich, and scores of lesser places to heaps of rubble.

In the wake of that ferocious effort 8 U.S. divisions began to advance into the waste land of the Roer valley through driving rain, sleet and snow. It was early afternoon. The enemy, dazed but undaunted, retreated from his outposts behind his main defences, confident in the barrier of the Roer river. From the Hurtgen forest to Geilenkirchen the Germans met the United States divisions head on. Complex minefields covered the most powerful defensive system of strong points on the whole western front, and the Americans quickly learned that even the terrific bombardment the enemy had sustained from the air was no substitute for the ground artillery support they lacked. In the south General Patton was still squandering vast quantities of ammunition against the defences of Metz at the expense of the U.S. 1st Army.

But even had sufficient ammunition been available to the 1st and 9th Armies it is unlikely that the results would have been substantially improved, and there was no hope that Bradley could "bulldoze" his way through. The attack had been foredoomed to failure. At best it could hope to do no more than close the Roer from Dueren to Linnich in the same tedious fashion as Montgomery was closing the Maas. Cologne was never more than a hopeless dream, and indeed, with the Roer dams still in enemy hands, invulnerable to the heavy air attacks of the R.A.F., which now concentrated upon them, it is difficult to believe that Cologne was the object.

Above all the attack lacked imagination. The enemy was ready for it in strength with five infantry and two panzer divisions prepared to fight yard by yard through a maze of linked strong points in an industrial wilderness in depth. Every minefield was covered by mortar and artillery fire.

"The enemy, knowing how the attack must come, had only to block it head-on and inflict the maximum casualties," wrote the historian of the U.S. 9th Army.

Bogged down in mud, water and snow and faced by an uncrossable river, the U.S. 1st and 9th Armies paid the bitter price of Bradley's generalship. With that one counter-attack of the 27th October against the right flank of the 2nd Army the enemy had reaped this rich reward, postponing indefinitely the battle of the Rhineland, and bringing about a stalemate which only the capture of Schmidt and the Roer dams could have prevented.

III

There was very little sugar on the bitter pill of the November operations, but what little there was the 30th Corps, with the U.S. 84th Infantry Division under command, provided. Preceded by an artillery barrage which poured twenty thousand shells into the little German town of Geilenkirchen, and with sustained and accurate artillery support, the 30th Corps attacked into Germany on the left flank of the U.S. 9th Army.

The U.S. 9th Army, supporting the main drive of the 1st Army, made slow but steady progress in the first few days, but it had no illusions that it could do more than reach the Roer. On the morning of the 18th November, when the 30th Corps went in on the flank, an American staff colonel said: "We are pushing slowly, but there is a lot in front of us to push."

The purpose of the British attack was limited to the protection of the flank, but there were new names to attempt to conjure with and new vistas. Within two miles of the pretty Dutch village of Sittard the armour rumbled into Germany through a deserted, but rich countryside, through the empty villages of Wehr and Gangelt, knowing these villages, these fields, these shattered homes and stricken beasts, not Dutch, nor French, nor Belgian, but at last the homeland of the enemy. And the enemy was very close, pressing in from the left, hidden in the bronze belts of woodland, and in the folds of the hills, as solid as a rock, for this was the outer bastion of that Heinsberg triangle destined to be a thorn in the flesh of the 2nd Army and to live in many memories for many weeks.

The intention of the 30th Corps was to take the town of Geilenkirchen, and to thrust north-east along the valley of the river Wurm to the ever elusive Roer. At the outset the going was deceptively easy, save for the ever present menace on the left. On the 20th the 43rd Division enveloped the smoking ruin of Geilenkirchen, and battered on with the petard tanks and flame throwers of the 79th Armoured Division into a harsh wilderness of strong points, of stone dwellings seeming to outcrop from the hillsides, of slag heaps, and tall chimneys, some blackened stumps, others like wilting candles pointing obscene fingers to the brown sky. This was the beginning of industrial Germany and the massive defences of the Siegfried Line.

In Geilenkirchen not one citizen of the 9,000 inhabitants could be found. The shop fronts had burst open to strew their wares over the cobbles down to the Wurm, raging in spate like some subterranean torrent amidst the smoke and rubble and ruin.

There was something deeply impressive about the dead husk of this first German town to be entered by British troops, and utterly abandoned. An old top hat sat on a child's mattress, reams of paper and pots and pans, littered the narrow ways. It was a mark of the grim struggle ahead. Immediately in the wake of the troops the Military Government and Civil Affairs officers came in, finding nothing to administer, no citizens to instruct, and to ask themselves, would this be the way of it? To the bitter end.

But to the infantrymen plodding steadily on it was not only Germany but the first "dry land" they had known for weeks, a land of hills and valleys and dark skylines, of fir plantations, and everlasting menace. But that it was "dry" even though the unrelenting rain poured out of the November sky, was a compensation. There were no friendly people to enliven a brief halt, but there were no inhibitions in the way of roasting a goose or eating the masses of bottled fruits that seemed to furnish every larder.

For three days armour and infantry, flail tanks, petards and flame throwing crocodiles, churned the ground to mud as they strove to carve a path along the Wurm valley, enfiladed at every point, unable to gain a yard to the eastward. In that inferno of shot and shell in all the region of Suggerath and Beeck and Tripsrapth the walls of houses seemed to go in and out like concertinas to the unending concussion. A signpost at a cross-roads pointed to Dusseldorf 70 km. and Koln 65 km., but even one kilometre through that maze of concrete and guns was a long way. Remorselessly the armour strove to break a way through, and remorselessly the enemy counter-attacked. Every strong point had to be assaulted, blasted with petards, seared with flame, only to add its rubble and stone to the confusion. And as the rain teemed down unabated it became impossible for armour to manoeuvre.

On the 24th November the brief sortie into the enemy homeland had to be abandoned, and it would have been necessary to travel south to Alsace before finding a gain of more than the odd mile or two over the whole Allied front. The U.S. 84th Division returned to U.S. 9th Army command, and the northern armies of the U.S. 12th Army Group hung on in their impossible task, resolved at the worst to close the Roer river.

On the 2nd Army front the pocket had become a series of small bubbles of enemy, forced out of basements to the first floors of houses by the rising floods, and retreating doggedly behind the broad Maas. By the end of the month all that remained to the enemy on the west bank of the river was a small but powerful bridgehead at Blerick, opposite Venlo.

From the Hurtgen forest to the Nijmegen bridgehead the whole land had reached saturation point, and the weather, almost as much as the enemy, called a halt. Thus had the high hopes of autumn vanished in the November slush. It was a situation demanding a re-appraisal, and arousing forebodings not alone in the mind of Montgomery, but in the minds of the Combined Chiefs of Staff, and of Churchill.

7

BEFORE THE STORM

I

THE events of November revived the command crisis of the early autumn, and revealed differences not only between the Commanders in the field, but on the highest levels in Britain and the United States.

Throughout November, Field Marshal Montgomery had viewed the developing situation over the whole battlefield north of the Ardennes with a growing unease. He saw—and I think absolutely rightly—the battlefield north of the Ardennes as one battlefield, and believed that it should have one ground force commander. But the events of November revealed the bankruptcy of Allied strategy.

In the south the French had smashed a hole through at Saverne to open the way to Strasbourg and the Rhine. Allied eyes could look out across the river to the Black Forest, and tantalize their owners with the apparent imminence of victory. But the enemy had reacted violently against French advances to the Rhine further south, and Hitler had ordered Himmler to take command and hold a bridgehead in the Colmar pocket at all costs. The U.S. 7th Army was engaged in fierce fighting in the difficult country north of Strasbourg on the right of Patton, and steadily closing up to the Saar river. Metz had fallen, but the strongest of the forts still held out, and by the end of November Patton was bogged down. " . . . . the Allied operations south of the Ardennes had failed by that time to relieve the *impasse* to the north," wrote John Ehrman.[1]

On the 25th November Churchill cabled a report of all these things to Stalin, and referred to the northern front as follows:

[1]"Grand Strategy", Vol. vi, by John Ehrman, p. 34.

"In a week or ten days it should be possible to estimate whether the German armies will be beaten decisively west of the Rhine. If they are we can go on in spite of the weather. Otherwise there may be some lull during the severity of the winter, after which one more major onslaught should break the organised German resistance in the west."[1]

The succeeding days had failed to provide an answer, and as the month ended it was clear that the Allied armies had bogged down completely all along the line.

In early autumn when Montgomery had expressed himself constantly and strongly against Allied strategy, his own alternative strategy had not been realistic. But on the 28th November the news of the first convoy sailing up the Scheldt to dock safely in Antwerp promised the sinews of war at last behind the armies in the north, and with the lines of communication cut to a fraction. In addition, but for a small set-piece battle to clear the enemy from their last small bridgehead west of the Maas at Blerick, his own front was "tidy", as he expressed it. It was, therefore, on the 28th November that Montgomery visited the Supreme Commander to express his views, and his grave uneasiness.

General Eisenhower, patient and attentive as always, was unsympathetic, and it is likely that Montgomery was too sweeping in his criticisms to appeal to the Supreme Commander. In Montgomery's opinion Eisenhower's failure to "implement his directive of 28th October was responsible for the situation".[2] The directive had ordered the main effort to be made in the north to bring about the decisive defeat of the enemy west of the Rhine, and the establishment of bridgeheads over the Rhine and Ijssel rivers. "We have achieved none of this," the Field Marshal said, "and we have no hope of doing so. We have therefore failed; and we have suffered a strategic reverse."[3]

This statement, in my view, fails to take into account that the October directive was impossible, and could not have been achieved even had Bradley played his part. Nevertheless much of Montgomery's statement was justified, and on the 30th November he

[1] "Triumph and Tragedy", Vol. vi. Churchill Memoirs, p. 223.
[2] "The Supreme Command", by Forrest Pogue, p. 312.
[3] Ibid.

put his views in writing to the Supreme Commander,[1] stating categorically:

> "We now require a new plan. And this time *we must not fail.* The need to get the German war finished early is vital, in view of other factors. The new plan *must not fail.*
>
> In the new plan we must get away from the doctrine of attacking in so many places that nowhere are we strong enough to get decisive results. We must concentrate such strength on the main selected thrust that success will be certain. It is in this respect that we failed badly in the present operations."

In the next paragraph Montgomery renewed his appeal for a change in command: "The theatre divides itself naturally into two fronts; one north of the Ardennes and one south of the Ardennes. We want one commander in full operational control north of the Ardennes, and one south."

The Field Marshal ended with the remark: " . . . . and if you decide that I should do that work—that is O.K. by me."

The Supreme Commander reacted with indignation and flatly contradicted the Field Marshal. In fact, I believe that Eisenhower chose to misunderstand the message, and to take it as a condemnation in the broadest possible terms. In his reply he embarked upon a defence of the Allied total achievement since Normandy, but the real point at issue was Montgomery's fear that the emphasis of attack was shifting away from the north. The British Chiefs of Staff shared his view that this was the fundamental of Allied strategy, and to which SHAEF was fully committed. "To get involved in operations which led away from that direction he (Montgomery) considered faulty strategy," wrote Forrest Pogue, "and to drive in the wrong direction, particularly without reaching the Rhine, was 'a strategic reverse'."[2]

Eisenhower's full reply is very long, but since it is not anywhere quoted in English sources, perhaps extracts will not be out of place here.

"I am not quite sure I know exactly what you mean by strategic

[1]Diary Office C in C. Italics in original.
[2]Pogue.

reverse; certainly to date we have failed to achieve all that we had hoped to by this time, which hopes and plans were based upon conditions as we knew them or estimated them when the plans were made. The Ruhr is an important place, but let us never forget for one second that our primary objective is to defeat the Germans who are barring our way into Germany. The Ruhr itself was always given as a geographical objective, not only for its importance to Germany, but because it was believed that in that region the *German forces* would be largely concentrated to meet our attacks."

The Supreme Commander then agreed that:

"a. We must determine how much profit there is in the continuation of our current attacks in the 12th Army Group area, and whether they give real promise of reaching the Rhine.

b. We must recast our future general plans in the light of the conditions as they now exist.

c. We must choose the best line of attack to assure success, including the maintenance of deception lines."

General Eisenhower then wrote: "I do not agree that things have gone badly since Normandy, merely because we have not gained all we had hoped to gain. Our line as late as D plus 60 was not greatly different than what we had hoped to hold in the first week, but I never looked upon the situation then existing as a strategic reverse, even though out of the circumstances of our long confinement in the narrow beach-head have developed some of our greatest difficulties . . . .

Moreover, I do not agree that more strength could have been thrown to the north than was actually maintained there during early September. Lines of communication in the north were so stretched that even delivery of five hundred tons to you at Brussels cost Bradley three divisions, the possession of which might have easily placed him on the Rhine in the Worms area.

. . . . I have no intention of stopping Devers' and Patton's operations as long as they are cleaning up our right flank and giving us *capability of concentration*. On the other hand I do no intend to push these attacks senselessly."

This message did nothing to relieve Montgomery's disquiet, and served only to emphasize his fears. It confirmed also the growing fears of the Chiefs of Staff and the Prime Minister, for in this message the fundamental difference between American and British aims may be seen. In a word, the Americans were fighting to destroy the German army, and the British were fighting to gain a political victory. To the British geography was of paramount importance, and to the Americans it was not. The northern route, to give us control of Bremen and Hamburg, and finally Berlin, was, therefore, vital in British thinking.

In his immediate reply to the Supreme Commander, Field Marshal Montgomery pointed out that he had not intended to suggest for one moment that the campaign had been a failure since Normandy, but had intended to state that the directive of 28th October had not been carried out. To this General Eisenhower sent his "prompt and abject apologies" for misunderstanding. A meeting was arranged at Maastricht for 7th December at which Air Marshal Tedder and General Bradley would be present. Meanwhile the Germans again reminded the generals, as they had reminded them on 27th October, that they also had a say in the matter.

II

On the 2nd December the Germans breached the dykes of the Neder Rhine south of Arnhem, and relieved the 1st Canadian Army of all further preoccupation with the task of planning an attack to the north. At the same time they emphasized the third of the three major sensitive points of the northern battlefield, and produced a huge inland lake north of the Nijmegen–Cleves road to Emmerich. The Canadians had not been without expectation of some such move, and the British 49th Division was ready for the heavy attack by German paratroops, which came in on the 4th with the intention of driving them back across the Waal. But the 49th stood firm, and the reduced Nijmegen bridgehead, essential in the battle of the Rhineland, was swiftly consolidated. On the "island" south of Elst the troops looked forward, dubiously, to a watery Christmas, patrolling in small boats, and regarding the local geese with hungry eyes.

The German move, admirably timed, underlined the "strategic reverse", and might have drawn attention to the possibility that the still powerful German army might still seek to impose a pattern upon the future. Montgomery was not perturbed. On the 3rd December the 15th Scottish, aided by flails, bridging tanks, and troop-carrying kangaroos of the 79th Armoured Division, put in a "set-piece" attack against Blerick, the last enemy strong point west of the Maas, and enabled the Field Marshal to record that "we were now 'tidy' along the line of the rivers Roer and Meuse except for an enemy salient in the Heinsberg area."[1] All that now stood between the Field Marshal and his battle was the clearance of that difficult pocket.

The difficult pocket was, in fact, the central linch pin between Schmidt and Nijmegen, and almost as important to the enemy as Schmidt itself. Unyielding defence coupled with an appalling saturation of the ground compelled the postponement of operations, and the deep abscess between the flanks of the 2nd and 9th Armies continued to fester. Along the base of that Heinsberg triangle our troops had the doubtful pleasure of observing the enemy in Venlo and Roermond across the broad Maas.

In the first week of December the U.S. 9th Army, aided, as it readily agreed, by British artillery support, had closed up to the Roer to look across the unpromising brown swirling flood upon the rubble of Linnich and Julich. The slow dismal action had cost nearly 10,000 casualties, and the U.S. 1st Army on their right was suffering at least twice as heavily and moving twice as slowly in the bitter fight through the Hurtgen forest. The village of Hurtgen, which had changed hands a score of times, was at last behind them, and from Eschweiler and down the Grosshau road they drew in steadily upon Dueren. The Roer was at last in sight, but beyond it, in a wide arc covering Cologne, the enemy had drawn up an impressive array backed by the 6th Panzer Army.

It was a sober outlook when the commanders met at Maastricht on the 7th December. Eisenhower, as Chester Wilmot records, travelled through the Ardennes on his way to the meeting, and was

[1] "Normandy to the Baltic."

disturbed at the absence of troops, transport, installations, and indeed almost a sign that the area was defended. It might be "a nasty little Kasserine",[1] he remarked to Bradley, but General Bradley, somewhat irritably aware of this broad gap in his long front, and minimizing it whenever his attention was drawn to it, had other things on his mind. He had gravely weakened the 1st Army to give Patton priority, and the total achievement after nearly six weeks of bitter fighting could not have given him much cause for pleasure. Attrition all along the line had an unpleasant two-way meaning. Three divisions of the 1st Army had been mauled in the Hurtgen forest to the extent of suffering 21,000 casualties, and at last he was fully aware of "Schmidt", the Roer dams, and all that they meant.

Even in the air the outlook was gloomy. In mid-November Lt.-General Doolittle had said that the Eighth Air Force might have to give priority to the task of reconquering the German Air Force instead of strategic bombing.

The Maastricht conference was conducted amicably, in spite of the very strong feelings, but it served only to accentuate the differences, not only between General Eisenhower and Field Marshal Montgomery, but also in the American and British approaches to war. Only General Bradley in all these exchanges seems to have shown bitterness, but Eisenhower and Montgomery were devoid of malice, sharing a quality of innocence, which was their strength. Old ideas were re-affirmed, but it was agreed—as it had been agreed at Brussels—that the major attack should be in the north early in the New Year. Ten U.S. divisions would be made available under 21st Army Group command for the right hook north-east from the Roer. But the secondary attacks would also be mounted in the south. Eisenhower stated flatly that he would not check Patton while he could make progress, and revealed his long liking for the Frankfurt area.

None of this suited Montgomery. He wanted the full available strength of the Allies to attack north of the Ruhr and all the rest to hold. He felt sure that two attacks would rob each other of the vital punch, and suspected Eisenhower of continuing to pursue a policy of opportunism. The Field Marshal pressed his strong argument for

[1]Reference to the defeat of the Americans at Kasserine, Tunisia, by Rommel.

one ground force commander north of the Ardennes, but Eisenhower argued that the Ruhr was the natural dividing line.

The profound disagreement underlying these issues was masked by the Supreme Commander's insistence that there was no real disagreement. "Believing that he had sufficient forces to support the northern thrust adequately and still mount a subsidiary attack," wrote Forrest Pogue, "he saw no difference between his concept and that of the 21st Army Group commander. But to Field Marshal Montgomery, who believed that experiences of the past few months demonstrated the lack of sufficient resources for both attacks, the difference was between success and failure—and therefore fundamental."[1]

The differences are mainly a matter of emphasis, and to understand them fully it is necessary to follow and to digest the whole long argument, waged often with acrimony, henceforth to the war's end.

It was an argument the Americans were bound to win, on whatever level, for Eisenhower, as Pogue remarks, "was in a position to make his view prevail. For this reason, if for no other, there was never a deadlock between the two commanders-in-chief." The same applied between Roosevelt and Churchill, between the Chiefs of Staff and the Joint Chiefs of Staff. Britain was—by now overwhelmingly—the weak partner.

Nevertheless Field Marshal Montgomery left the Maastricht Conference in high spirits to set about the immediate task of regrouping his forces for the Rhineland battle. He had passed on his "differences of opinion" to a higher level, and was ready to face up to the task in hand with characteristic thoroughness and fervour, and with no thought of failure. Such was his resilience that he now appeared to view the whole situation with great optimism. The U.S. 9th Army agreed to take over the 30th Corps commitment in the Heinsberg salient, and with that Montgomery ordered the 30th Corps to move north into the Nijmegen bridgehead to mount the main attack under command of the 1st Canadian Army, while the 2nd Army headquarters got down to the intricate task of planning the final crossing of the Rhine.

The way, it seemed, was as clear ahead as it could be. As soon

[1]"The Supreme Command."

as the Roer dams were taken the U.S. 9th Army would prepare for its role across the Roer, and to deliver the right hook up through Krefeld. The Canadians and 30th Corps with the bulk of the 2nd Army would navigate the northern floods to sail round the flank of the Siegfried Line and smash through the defences of the Reichswald forest. In the 2nd Army headquarters they had begun, tentatively, to hum a little tune, "Pop goes the *Wesel*", for Wesel was the target for the beginning of the end.

III

The British Chiefs of Staff and the Prime Minister shared Field Marshal Montgomery's fears in regard to the future offensive on the northern front, and felt uneasy at the "apparent disappearance of a master plan". Churchill had at once cabled his friend, Field Marshal Smuts, a full account of the situation:

> "In spite of Metz and Strasbourg and other successes, we have of course sustained a strategic reverse on the Western Front .... I imagine some readjustments will be made giving back Montgomery some of the scope taken from him after the victory he gained in Normandy. You must remember however that our armies are only about one-half the size of the American and will soon be little more than one third .... it is not so easy as it used to be for me to get things done."[1]

This message was dated the 3rd December, and there was still room to hope for some successful outcome of the Maastricht conference. On the 6th December, without waiting for a further report from Montgomery, the Prime Minister cabled Roosevelt:

> "As we are unable to meet, I feel that the time has come for me to place before you the serious and disappointing war situation which faces us at the close of this year. Although many fine tactical victories have been gained on the Western Front and Metz and Strasbourg are trophies, the fact remains that we have definitely failed to achieve the strategic object

[1]"Triumph and Tragedy", Vol. vi. Churchill Memoirs.

which we gave our armies five weeks ago. We have not yet reached the Rhine in the northern part and most important sector of the front, and we shall have to continue the great battle for many weeks before we can hope to reach the Rhine and establish our bridgeheads. After that, again, we have to advance through Germany."

The President's reply was unsatisfactory in the extreme. He had "bicycled over the terrain in the old days", and had formed the impression that it would be "a very stiff job" to close up to the left bank of the Rhine. "However our agreed broad strategy is developing according to plan . . . . "

This was the kind of message to make the British tear their hair. Nothing could have been more disturbing, and on the 12th December General Eisenhower and his Deputy, Air Marshal Tedder, met the British Chiefs of Staff and the Prime Minister in London. There was very little headway. The Supreme Commander was prepared to concede that an advance on Frankfurt should be secondary to the thrust in the north, but he was looking at the whole strategical picture from a different angle than the British. Summing up Eisenhower's views at that conference, John Ehrman wrote:[1]

"While admitting that the current operations in all sectors would not prove immediately decisive, he (Eisenhower) claimed that they were fulfilling his ultimate purpose by wearing down the Germans continuously along an extended line—a process which, thanks to their lack of mobility, they could not hope to check. To halt these operations in favour of those suggested by Montgomery, might on the other hand allow them to reinforce one sector and to reorganize in others . . . . "

British fears were gravely enhanced, and the Chiefs of Staff prepared an immediate memorandum for the Prime Minister. In the spring they estimated that Allied strength would be 80-85 divisions, and felt that this would not suffice for the two offensives contemplated by the Supreme Commander. They proposed to press their views. The situation was beginning to have unpleasant undertones, for if these differences were pressed to the limits it would amount

[1]"Grand Strategy", Vol. vi. John Ehrman.

to setting up one commander against the other, and there would be a "showdown". Nothing would have been more disastrous, for each man possessed unique and valuable qualities, and the loss of either one of them would have been far more grave than a continued disagreement. For it has not been sufficiently understood that, despite all his protests, Field Marshal Montgomery always carried out Eisenhower's orders not only with thoroughness and integrity, but with enthusiasm.

Genral Bradley, on the other hand, seldom argued. Immediately following the Maastricht conference he had ordered General Patton to prepare to mount an offensive against the Saar on the 19th December, and to reach the Rhine by Christmas. Eisenhower warned Bradley that unless the offensive was successful beyond a doubt in the first week it would have to be called off. SHAEF also emphasised that the intention of Patton's offensive was to aid the main effort in the north, "and that any crossing of the Rhine south of the Moselle was to be restricted until the success of operations in the north was assured".

Nothing could have underlined British fears more forcefully, or revealed more strongly Eisenhower's liking for the south. Moreover, there were few illusions now about Patton's technique of "Rock Soup", as he called it, his method of committing his troops in such a way that they would have to be reinforced. The order to "Go" was good enough for him. At this time also it began to be feared that Bradley's influence with the Supreme Commander was very great, and that he and Patton had teamed up to win the war their way. The British in the field certainly believed that "Bradley had the inside track to Eisenhower".

On Patton's right flank the U.S. 7th Army was driving northward between the Sarre and the Rhine, and had elements of all its divisions on the German frontier. Nothing succeeds like success, and on the face of it, the whole front north of the Ardennes looked far less promising. Nevertheless there can be no possible shadow of doubt that to risk compromising the offensive in the north in favour of the south was a strategical blunder of the first magnitude, and it was fortunate that the Germans had decided to call the tune, and to lose the war on a battlefield of their own choosing.

IV

The tactical burden of General Bradley's uncompromising support of General Patton's 3rd Army fell constantly upon the unfortunate shoulders of Lt.-General Hodges, and the U.S. 1st Army. From the end of October Hodges had been forced to fight the battles of Hurtgen forest and the Roer in piecemeal fashion, undermanned, under-supplied, and denied artillery support above a minimum scale. No army faced a more powerful and determined enemy backed by a greater weight of reserves. No sector of the whole Allied front from Switzerland to Arnhem held the terrors and difficulties of terrain of the Hurtgen area, and I would argue that no sector had a greater tactical importance than this key region to the Cologne plain and the northern Rhineland. The enemy held that view.

By mid-December when Bradley ordered Hodges to mount an offensive to take the Roer dams, the 1st Army and its commander were showing signs of strain. The 7th Corps had had a heavy battering in its struggle to reach Dueren; the 5th Corps on the right of the 7th had had a scarcely less severe strain, and in the Ardennes the weak 8th Corps was strung out over a very wide front, counting the battered 28th Division among its effectives.

First Army intelligence reports had been disturbing since mid-November, revealing movement of enemy reserves threatening the army front, and seeming to be aimed at first north of Aachen, but with a marked tendency to shift the balance southward. As a result Hodges had asked Bradley for two more divisions, and had been refused.

On 10th December the 1st Army chief of intelligence said:

> "The restoration of the West Wall is still a probable strategic objective . . . . The enemy has let his situation in both the upper Rhine and south of the Moselle deteriorate while still conserving reserves between Dusseldorf and Koeln. Von Rundstedt apparently is accepting defeats in the south rather than compromise his hope of a decisive success in the north. This would appear to be the keynote of his strategy in the defense of the Reich west of the Rhine. During the past month there has been a definite

pattern for the seasoning of newly-formed divisions in the comparatively quiet sector opposite VIII corps prior to their despatch to more active fronts. The enemy is well aware of the tactical 'ace' which he holds in the Roer River dams. Our recent attempts to breach the dam walls by air bombardment, as yet unsuccessful, have served to emphasize our own concern with the flooding of the Roer valley. The enemy has reacted by building up his forces on the route of approach to the Schwammenauel and the Urfttalsperre, the key dams in this system of barrages.

Besides the divisions in the Sixth Panzer Army, the enemy has 2 Pz. and 116 Pz. Divs. conditionally available for local counter-attacks in the defense of the dams, in addition to at least two Volks-grenadier divisions which are available from the VIII corps sector."

This intelligence report seems immensely revealing, and it is not surprising that the 1st Army G-2 should be inclined to concentrate on the Roer dams. Forrest Pogue comments: "The importance of the Roer dams to both the Allies and the enemy seems to have outweighed other factors when the First Army intelligence chief drew his conclusions as to possible enemy capabilities."

For more than a month the enemy had not yielded a foot of ground without fighting stubbornly along the whole 1st Army front. The morale of prisoners was very high, and there were many other indications of danger ahead. 12th Army Group, however, were not impressed, and there is no doubt that relations between the two staffs were not good.[1]

On the 13th December Lt.-General Hodges, perforce, ordered Lt.-General Gerow, commanding the 5th Corps, to take Schmidt and the Roer dams, and 5th Corps began to move.

In the light of these events it seems clear that either General Bradley was incapable of commanding an Army Group operating on such an extended front both north and south of the Ardennes, or that Field Marshal Montgomery was quite right in insisting that

[1]Forrest Pogue discussed this question with all concerned after the war. He wrote: "While some effort was made by the principals to discount the effect of personalities involved, there seems little doubt that some personality conflicts, and sometimes a tendency to question the validity of predictions, existed between the 12th Army Group and First Army G-2s."

the Ardennes made the natural division of ground force command. Bradley often complained of the length of his front, and said that he had no time to examine essential reports.

It is inevitable, also, that the relationships existing between Generals Bradley, Patton and Hodges, should have been remembered. Patton had been Bradley's senior until the "slap in the face" incident had caused Eisenhower to judge Bradley to be more "emotionally stable". Bradley was deputy commander of the 2nd Corps under Patton, and had later commanded that corps in Patton's 7th Army. Hodges had served as Bradley's deputy commander of the 1st Army, and had moved up to command when Bradley had been promoted to 12th Army Group. It seems at least possible that Bradley may have been conscious—or sub-conscious—of Patton's superiority, not only to Hodges, but to himself. But, in fact, Hodges was the veteran of them all, a soldier of World War I, an infantryman, aware of battle, and one of the very few American generals with any war experience.

Chester Wilmot noted: "Yet Bradley was forever conscious that Patton was not only his senior in rank, but also his superior in tactical skill and experience."[1]

But with the exception of the strong currents of uneasiness in the 1st Army headquarters there was a general sense of well being all along the line in mid-December. On the 21st Army Group front the advance units of the 30th Corps were already moving to take up their new positions in the Nijmegen bridgehead to prepare for the Rhineland battle. On the 15th December General de Guingand, the 21st Army Group Chief of Staff, went on leave to England, and Field Marshal Montgomery asked Eisenhower if he could be spared to visit home the following week. The Field Marshal expressed himself as optimistic about the whole front, and his directive of the 16th December said so categorically.

At that time the Supreme Commander was giving special attention to the situation in the Colmar pocket. The enemy were keeping eight Allied divisions fully engaged, and Eisenhower ordered Devers to postpone "Operation Independence" against the enemy garrisons still holding out on the Atlantic coast of France, and put all the force he could muster in against Colmar.

[1]The Struggle for Europe

Strangest of all, on the morning of the 15th December the SHAEF G-3 (Operations) briefing officer stated that there was nothing to report on the Ardennes sector. This could only mean that SHAEF operations and intelligence were out of contact, or that the statement was deliberately misleading.

All, in fact, was far from quiet on the western front.

8

"ES GEHT UMS GANZE"

I

LONG before the dawn of the 16th December enemy storm troops, moving rapidly out of the Eifel forest under artificial moonlight and evading contact or combat, had infiltrated the loosely held American forward positions in the Ardennes. Behind them in the south and centre three Army corps of the 5th Panzer Army under General von Manteuffel, advanced on a thirty mile front from Prum to Wilz, imminently to threaten St. Vith and Bastogne. Advancing from Echternach the German 7th Army covered the southern flank.

At the same hour the 6th Panzer Army under General Dietrich began to advance on a fifteen mile front upon Monschau and Malmedy.

When the Americans awoke that morning it was to the thunder of two thousand guns laying the heaviest barrage the Germans had fired in the campaign, while overhead shoals of V.1s, speeding upon Liege and Antwerp, laid their fiery trails across the heavy sky. In the upper air, unseen and unheard, V.2s carried their cargoes of high explosive to Antwerp.

In the north it had been snowing for a week, and soon it would be snowing in the Ardennes. It was bitter cold, and the enemy came like wraiths out of the morning mist, exultant, believing in victory. The men in the thinly held forward line had no chance.

The intention of the Germans was to seize crossings over the Meuse between Liege and Huy, and to sweep through to Antwerp with the 6th Panzer Army on the right, while on the left the 5th Panzer Army, matching its speed to the main thrust, took Liege and went through to Brussels. Thus, in one last great effort Hitler hoped to drive a wedge between the Allied armies and force a Dutch Dunkirk upon the British.

It was, as the 69-year-old Field Marshal von Rundstedt had said —a man by all his training and experience not given to the loose or extravagant use of words—"Es geht ums ganse", literally "It goes for all", colloquially "all or nothing".

Perhaps not least among the fundamental weaknesses of this last all-out offensive effort of the enemy on the Western Front was the lack of faith in it of its commanders. Von Rundstedt himself thought it madness. Field Marshal Model and the young General von Manteuffel, the only two men who dared, or were able with any effect, to argue with the Fuhrer, strove to dissuade him from the venture. The corps and divisional commanders did not learn of their tasks more than three days in advance, too late properly to plan. Dietrich, the "Butcher Boy" protégé of Hitler, commander designate of the 6th Panzer Army with the major role of the right hand punch through to Antwerp, was equally ignorant. Such security precautions may have been necessary, but they weighed heavily against success. Enemy junior officers and troops had been led to believe the offensive would be aimed at Aachen, and this certainly had helped to mislead the Allies.

The Battle of the Ardennes still awaits a full assessment,[1] but that it was doomed to failure there can be little doubt. The very conditions essential to its possibility, the bad weather to prevent Allied air observation and attack, mitigated against success, hampering the swift movement of the armoured columns, and holding them to a slow tempo in the steep muddied defiles that would soon be deep in snow. To succeed, the Meuse had to be reached and crossed by the third day at the latest. Even faced with the most meagre token resistance that task, in the mid-winter conditions, would have been severe. Above all fuel was short, and fuel dumps would have to be over-run.

The Germans knew well the forces against them, but their appreciation of the American resistance was faulty. They must have counted on complete disruption and confusion, and the precipitate evacuation of the key road centres of Bastogne and St. Vith, the overwhelming of Monschau, and the opening of the way through to Eupen and Verviers. Disruption and confusion there were, but

[1]"The Ardennes", Hugh M. Cole. In preparation. U.S. Dept. of the Army, Washington.

as the early fog of battle began to clear hard cores of resolute resistance became evident. The battered and unlucky 28th Division, with the wounds of the Hurtgen forest scarcely healed, and with many raw replacements in their ranks, streamed back through Bastogne warning 8th Corps headquarters of disaster. One regiment of that division stood and fought, barring the road long enough for the reinforcements rushing up from Luxembourg and from Rheims.

Long before the shape of the battle was clear to commanders in the field reinforcements were moving to key points; the U.S. 7th Armoured Division speeding down from north of Aachen, picking up stragglers on its way, reached St. Vith, and brilliantly commanded by Brigadier-General Hasbrouck, revealed that not only could it advance at lightning speed, but it could also fight a withdrawing action, disciplined and tight as a drum.

On the enemy right flank Dietrich's Panzer army blunted its nose on two divisions of Gerow's 5th Corps as they moved against the Roer dams on a line Butgenbach–Monschau. Thus at the outset vital impetus had been lost.

Meanwhile the enemy had organized a special American-speaking force in jeeps and tanks to rush through like a Trojan horse, and this force, coupled with rumours of large parachute drops in the rear, added to the confusion. In fact, the enemy-planned air drop of 1,000 picked men under Col. von der Heydte with the role of sitting astride the Eupen–Verviers road junction, had failed dismally.[1] Dropping by night from aircraft manned by unskilled crews, many were killed and injured in the drop and far from the target area. In the end von der Heydte collected 200 men, and with these he did his best, until he was captured, to disrupt communications and hamper troop movements.

It is not my purpose here to describe, beyond this brief survey, the course of the Battle of the Ardennes;[2] but to attempt to consider it in the context of my story, primarily its effects on the higher command, and on the Battle of the Rhineland. Its effects on the Battle

[1]"The Other Side of the Hill", by B. H. Liddell Hart.

[2]Excellent summaries may be read in:
"North-West Europe, 1944-45", by John North. H.M.S.O.
"The Struggle for Europe", by Chester Wilmot. Collins.

of the Rhineland were, of course, profound, and Field Marshal Montgomery showed himself a master of "maintenance of the objective", for not for one moment did he lose sight of the battle he was resolved to fight, and which must be fought, in the Rhineland in the furtherance of Allied strategy.

In the last count, it may be that Hitler's offensive in the Ardennes was lost not so much in the west as on the Vistula, for at the outset the renewed threat of Russian pressure compelled Hitler to call off complementary thrusts in the north.

The main thing wrong with the Ardennes offensive was expressed in von Runstedt's words, "all or nothing", and Hitler's point blank refusal, as in Normandy, to withdraw, to adopt alternative and secondary objectives when the main targets were clearly beyond reach. Because of this it was "all or nothing", and since it could not be all it had to be nothing, if nothing can be said to bear the meaning of catastrophe. Indeed, it may be argued that in the Ardennes the war in the west was finally lost militarily by the Germans and politically by the Western Allies. There was the graveyard of great hopes.

Before dusk on the dark day of 16th December the Germans had cut the communications of the 12th Army Group and isolated General Bradley's headquarters in Luxembourg from effective control of his 1st and 9th Armies in the north. That night neither General Bradley, nor General Hodges commanding the U.S. 1st Army, knew very much about the battle, and were gravely underestimating its potential. Only Lt.-General Gerow, commanding the 5th Corps, appreciated the drive of the German 6th Panzer Army, but his urgent request to Hodges to be permitted to call off his attack against the Roer dams was refused.

Through the night the German armour was rumbling over the battered roads, forced to by-pass Bastogne and to take Houffalize and Wilz in the south, split into twin streams by the defence of St. Vith in the centre, and forced south of Malmedy in the north by Gerow, encroaching upon Stavelot, and soon to alarm 1st Army headquarters in Spa.

It took General Bradley two days to awaken to the full threat, while in the extreme north Field Marshal Montgomery reacted swiftly, halting the northward movement of the 30th Corps, and moving to cover his southern flank. By the night of the 19th December British units were 'fielding long-stop' on the battlefield of Waterloo, covering the road to Brussels, and the Meuse line was secured.

II

On the 21st December, while the Battle of the Ardennes was still in its early stages, the Supreme Commander recommended General Bradley's promotion to General Marshall. The 12th Army Group Commander, Eisenhower stated, "kept his head magnificently and . . . . proceeded methodically and energetically to meet the situation. In no quarter is there any tendency to place any blame upon Bradley."[1]

It was too early to apportion blame, nevertheless in defending Bradley in advance the Supreme Commander reveals, perhaps, an expectation for the future. It was, in fact, a bad moment in the Allied camp, and with passions fully aroused by the appointment on the 19th December of Field Marshal Montgomery to command the U.S. 1st and 9th Armies in the battle.

A full assessment of the Intelligence reports and summaries, followed by interviews and correspondence with the heads of Intelligence concerned, induced Forrest Pogue to write:

> " . . . . one may well ask what additional information the Allies would have needed to predict the 16th December attack. In many ways their information was highly accurate. Most of the units which made up the panzer armies had been spotted days and even weeks before the attack. Air reconnaissance, while hampered at times by bad weather, had marked the steady stream of men and supplies westward across the Rhine. Despite the clever deceptive measures of the enemy, the Allied intelligence experts had correctly analyzed most of the German dispositions and, in the closing hours before the counteroffensive, were aware of shifts towards the Ardennes area and of the arrival of new units in the zone of VIII corps."[2]

[1] Eisenhower to Marshall. 21 Dec. in personal file.
[2] "The Supreme Command."

Major-General K. W. D. Strong, the SHAEF Chief of Intelligence, consistently expressed his uneasiness and drew attention daily to the possibilities open to the enemy "for at least a fortnight before the attack".[1] In his appreciation of the uses the Germans might make of the panzer army, General Strong emphasized three main courses, (a) to go to Russia; (b) to counter-attack an Allied penetration; (c) to stage a relieving attack through the Ardennes.

General Strong went further. He stated that the German attack through the Ardennes would come whenever the enemy had a prediction of six days of bad weather. General Walter Bedell Smith, the SHAEF Chief of Staff, confirmed these views, and was so greatly impressed with the possibility of course (c) that he asked General Strong if he was sure General Bradley was aware of the possibility. "I replied in the affirmative," wrote General Strong, "but nevertheless General Smith instructed me to go to 12 A.G. and see General Bradley personally and warn him. This would be about the first week in December. I saw General Bradley personally for about ¾ hour and he told me he was aware of the danger but 'that he had earmarked certain divisions to move into the Ardennes area should the enemy attack there . . .' ."

To General Bedell Smith Bradley said, "Let them come."

Right up to the eve of the attack Col. Dickson, U.S. 1st Army Chief of Intelligence, continued to report enemy troop movements of an ominous nature, particularly in the Bitburg–Wittlich area. This was one of the principal points from which the offensive was mounted, and Col. Dickson also reported the presence of engineers with bridging equipment. In addition, a German order was captured calling for speakers of the "American dialect" to report to Waffen SS Lt.-Colonel Otto Skorzeny's headquarters for special training. This pointed clearly to some kind of plan for sabotage behind the American lines.

Two days before the German offensive Col. Dickson's warnings grew more urgent, and on the 15th December the 1st Army estimate read (in part):

"Reinforcements for the West Wall between Dueren and Trier

[1]Letters addressed to Forrest Pogue, office of Chief of Military History, Washington, from Generals Strong and Bedell Smith, and dated: 31 Aug. and 1 Nov., 1951.

continue to arrive. The identification of at least three or four newly re-formed divisions along the Army front must be reckoned with during the next few days . . . . it is possible that a limited scale offensive will be launched for purpose of achieving a Christmas morale victory for civilian consumption. Many PW's now speak of the coming attack between 17th and 25th December . . . . "

None of this, the generals complain, was sufficiently definite to induce them to take action, and one wonders what they could have expected from their Intelligence advisers. It is the role of Intelligence to discover as many facts as possible, to keep track of enemy troop movements, and to appreciate the courses open to the enemy. This they did with remarkable accuracy.

In his book General Bradley wrote: "No one came to me with a warning on the danger of counterattack there (the Ardennes)",[1] which ignores or denies the categorical testimony of Generals Bedell Smith and Strong. In the same passage General Bradley remarks that he was commanding nearly three quarters of a million men spread out over a front of 230 miles. "It was impossible for me even to scan the intelligence estimates of subordinate units."

The fact is that not one of the generals was prepared to consider the possibility of enemy offensive action. They had made up their minds that the enemy was incapable of more than counter-attack, and that this would come in against the Roer front.

The Intelligence Chief of the 1st Airborne Army came nearer than anyone else in an accurate forecast, according to Lt.-General Brereton in "The Brereton Diaries", but these warnings were ignored because Airborne units were not in the line at that time.

The 21st Army Group headquarters had also followed with interest the German build-up, and had plotted the course of the 6th Panzer Army with the restlessness of an old lady searching for a pea in her bed. But their conclusions were coloured entirely by Field Marshal Montgomery's certainty that "von Rundstedt was running the show". Thinking on those lines they were accurate about what von Rundstedt would have done. It was believed also

[1] "A Soldier's Story."

that an enemy offensive was ruled out because it must lead to the more speedy defeat of the Germans, but Hitler was "running the show", and for him it was "All or nothing". He achieved complete tactical surprise.

III

The news of the German offensive reached General Bradley during the afternoon of the 16th December while he was in conference with the Supreme Commander and senior Staff Officers at SHAEF. "You've been asking for a counter-attack," General Strong remarked. "Now it looks as if you've got it."

"A counter-attack yes," said Bradley, "but I'll be damned if I wanted one this big."

Nevertheless it was three days before Bradley confided to Patton that it was a good deal bigger than he had thought, and nearly a week before the full extent of the offensive was realised. Characteristically, Patton had taken steps to commit one of his armoured divisions in order to avoid any interference with his own planned offensive. Equally characteristically he disengaged his whole army from the Saar on Bradley's orders three days later, and moved north with tremendous drive and speed. Patton's disengagement and subsequent move with six divisions was a masterpiece of ruthless generalship, for with very great skill he swung north at right angles to his original line of attack, and compelled the attention of the weak German 7th Army, and made Manteuffel nervous about his left flank.

At the same time Devers' 6th Army Group moved to fill the breach left by the 3rd Army, and in so doing dangerously uncovered Strasbourg and the Alsatian plain.

Immediately upon hearing the news of the attack at SHAEF Bradley had ordered the 7th Armoured Division to St. Vith, and the 10th Armoured to race up from Luxembourg to Bastogne. Generals Bedell Smith, Whiteley and Strong had at once appreciated the vital importance of holding the road centres of St. Vith and Bastogne, thereby squeezing the German armour into the defiles. The 18th Airborne Corps, refitting at Rheims after its long spell in the north since Arnhem, was ordered at once into the fight, and by the 18th the 101st and 82nd Airborne Divisions were racing overland to the rescue of the hard-pressed units holding out at the nodal points in the south and centre.

Already Hitler had been forced to cancel his plans for an attack by the 15th Army against Aachen, and had alerted Army Group H to prepare to assault across the Waal and the Maas. SHAEF, aware of these possibilities, urgently scraped the bottom of the Allied barrel for reserves, grateful that Antwerp was at last open. But the port was under heavy pressure from the torrent of V.2s, demanding immense efforts to keep the port functioning while fire fighting and attending to the needs of the population. In these weeks the Belgians were called upon to display all the fortitude they could muster. At the same time the problem of feeding the liberated people of Belgium and the Netherlands became acute, putting an added strain on Allied resources, not only in supplies, but in ships and aircraft. Without Antwerp it would have been impossible for the Allies to have met their obligations, or to have replaced and reinforced their own losses. And Antwerp was gravely threatened.[1]

Meanwhile Montgomery's swift action in halting the movement to the north of the 30th Corps, and almost at once ordering the Guards Armoured, three Armoured Brigades, and the 43rd, 51st and 53rd Divisions, to the area Louvain–St. Trond, had not only provided effective screening of the Meuse and the roads through to Brussels and Antwerp, but had also freed Hodges to put the whole weight of the U.S. 1st Army into the battle.

By the night of the 19th December, although it was becoming clear that enemy hopes of seizing crossings of the Meuse, and of exploiting bridgeheads for any further advances, had virtually disappeared, there were still many alternative courses the enemy might pursue with great profit to himself, and massive loss to the Allies. Already he had driven a wedge through the heart of the 12th Army Group, isolating Bradley from effective control of his armies in the North.

[1]Two-thirds of the houses of Antwerp were hit, and one-fifth destroyed. Liege suffered even more severely. In the 6 months, October-March, 8,000 Belgians were killed and 23,584 wounded by bombing, the worst of it coinciding with the German offensive. In January there was a dock strike in Antwerp.

On the evening of the 19th December, while the generals in the field were still thinking in terms of enemy counter-attack intended to divert Patton from his drive against the Saar, and Hodges from his offensive to seize the Roer dams, General Strong appreciated the true situation, and at once suggested to General Whiteley that Field Marshal Montgomery should be ordered to take command of the U.S. 1st and 9th Armies without delay. Whiteley agreed. Indeed such a move had become unavoidable, not only because Montgomery was the only possible man capable of the task, but also because he controlled the essential reserve of the 30th Corps. The two generals put their proposition to Lt.-General Bedell Smith. A quick check discovered that the 1st Army had been virtually out of contact with 12th Army Group headquarters for two days, and General Smith telephoned Bradley.

Bradley's reaction on the telephone was far less heated than his subsequent reaction to the definite decision of General Eisenhower to give the command to Montgomery.[1]

"Certainly, if Monty's were an American command, I would agree with you entirely," he said to Bedell Smith. "It would be the logical thing to do."

In that sentence all the difficulties between the Allies are expressed: they were of two races: they had to attempt to fight as one.

It was in fact the "logical thing to do". The north of the Ardennes had become "one battle front needing one Ground Force Commander". The enemy had prevailed when all Montgomery's arguments had been in vain. Awakened during the night of the 19th with the news of his appointment, the Field Marshal at once called a conference at 1st Army headquarters with Generals Hodges and Simpson, commanding the 9th Army, for the morning of the 20th.

The descriptions of the meeting on that morning in U.S. 1st Army headquarters emphasize a situation which, but for the integrity and simplicity of the two principals in the long command controversy, Eisenhower and Montgomery, might well have bedevilled and even disrupted the working of the Alliance. Chester Wilmot quotes a Staff Officer as saying: "The Field Marshal strode into Hodges' H.Q. like Christ come to cleanse the temple". Mont-

[1] Eisenhower's last words to Bradley were: "Well Brad, that's an order".

gomery's Chief of Staff confirms the Field Marshal's remarkable resilience and perkiness. It was, wrote de Guingand, just his "cup of tea".

Montgomery's whole mien and high spirits were in sharp contrast to the American generals. Hodges in particular showed signs of anxiety and strain. Both generals were weary men. They had been the rounds trying to gather precise information, and it must have been the more galling to find Montgomery with the situation, apparently, at his finger tips. His personal team of liaison officers, operating in scout cars, had brought him all possible news of the latest developments, and with masterly efficiency he unfolded his plan to the American commanders. The U.S. 9th Army would take over the commitment of the U.S. 1st Army on the Roer. The U.S. 7th Corps would disengage and begin to form a reserve under General Collins to await the precise moment of necessity. Few men were as well equipped militarily to deal with the situation as Field Marshal Montgomery; few men could have been less fitted to deal with Americans in their particular humour at that time, in that place.

Already for weeks the intense bitterness evident in 12th Army Group headquarters had been a source of worry to SHAEF, and nothing less than sheer necessity would have persuaded the General Staff and the Supreme Commander to appoint Montgomery to command American troops at such a time.

Montgomery's great problem from the outset was to restrain the Americans, and to build reserves. At a time when they wanted to throw everything they had into the battle the Field Marshal knew that it was vital to withdraw troops. He doubted the ability of the 3rd Army to halt Manteuffel's drive through to the Meuse on Givet and Dinant, and believed that he must face the probability that he would have to halt, and finally destroy, the 5th Panzer Army as well as the 6th. He was alarmed about the strained condition of General Hodges, uncertain for several days whether the general would be up to his job, and worried about what might happen if Hodges had to be replaced. Eisenhower quickly took that responsibility squarely upon his own shoulders, and Hodges settled the problem by recovering. In addition the Field Marshal found many American divisions below strength in infantry, some of them by as much as 7,000 men. In the rear areas the absolute confusion, the lack of any clearly defined lines of communication, the remarkable absence of security precautions in signals which were feeding information to Dietrich and Manteuffel as fast as to their own units and formations, must have offended his military sense. Yet he acted with great restraint, austere, uncritical, supremely confident, doing the job with an absolute certainty of touch, and unyielding in his resolution.

It was not easy. It required as much force of character as military skill. He had to force men to withdraw, to take up rear positions, to organize and prepare in patience, whose whole attitude to war was "amateur". His insistence that the 7th Corps must disengage filled the corps commander and Hodges with "dismay".

Decisions of extreme urgency were also called for at the heart of the battle, particularly in the fight raging for St. Vith. With great skill and courage Hasbrouck's 7th Armoured Division had checked and held the enemy, forcing the enemy armour into narrow channels to the north and south, but on the 22nd December Hasbrouck was outflanked holding a 25 miles crescent front round St. Vith, and under tremendous pressure. Knowing that he must be overwhelmed Hasbrouck sought permission to withdraw to strong positions west of the Salm. Permission was refused. Hasbrouck had no illusions but that this meant "the end of the 7th Armoured Division", but Montgomery, hearing of this astounding refusal, indefensible on any grounds, insisted upon withdrawal in the face of fierce and bitter opposition from Generals Ridgeway and Hodges. The brave defenders of St. Vith were saved.

Almost at once a similar decision had to be taken in regard to Major-General Gavin's 82nd Airborne Division. In this case the situation was complicated by Gavin's desire to be destroyed rather than withdraw. He realized fully that tactics, strategy, and even all reason, demanded his withdrawal, yet he supported his senior commanders. His cry: that his division had never withdrawn in "its combat history" held in it the whole tragic problem of the United States Army in war. It must be true that a division that has never withdrawn has no right to talk of "combat history", for the long story of war proves decisively that it is above all in withdrawal under pressure that men show their mettle and reveal the hard core of their morale.[1]

While Montgomery was fighting with Ridgeway and Hodges to save Gavin's division from itself, the enemy moved with speed to force Ridgeway's entire reserve into the battle, and gain a local tactical victory, forcing the loss of a vital defensive position that could have been easily gained and easily held. Only then was Montgomery able to insist on withdrawal, and to save something from the wreck.

No military man could have been in any doubt in either case that a tactical withdrawal was the only possible course of action, and a course of strength, yet to the Americans a withdrawal was tantamount to dishonour. In their terms of thinking the British Army had steeped itself in dishonour by its heroic withdrawal to Dunkirk, and from the beaches.[2]

The period of crisis reached the peak on the 23rd December when Manteuffel had an armoured spearhead within four miles of the Meuse. The spearhead had overrun its supplies, and was virtually impotent against the Allied attack. It was the first and last brief look the enemy had of the broad river, and the end of his hopes. On that day also the fog lifted from the Ardennes, and the Allied Air Forces swooped down upon the enemy supply lines, and the columns trapped in the narrow defiles. In four days more than 10,000 sorties were flown, and all that remained to the enemy was withdrawal. But Hitler was adamant, compelling his armies inexorably to their destruction, as he had done in Normandy. From that point forward it is probable that the Americans had a clearer idea of the German intentions than was possible for Montgomery. Hitler's strategy was in fact very like their own, while Montgomery's

[1]Chester Wilmot wrote: "The stubborn determination to stand their ground was a source of great defensive strength to the Americans." Yet he admits that it deprived them of "tactical flexibility and strategic balance". I hold the view that the American inability to withdraw deprives them of defensive strength. In many battles, not least in Korea, this view has been reinforced.

[2]In a letter to "The Times", 25.2.57, Sir Arthur Bryant commented on the magnificent feat of Gort and Alanbrooke in extricating the British Army in the retreat on Dunkirk. "Both made a vital contribution to saving the Army and enabling it to reach the coast. Had they not done so, and had it not been for the incomparable valour of that Army itself, the war might well have been lost."

military mind had to consider the probable moves of other military minds, such as von Rundstedt's and Manteuffel's.

Through these early days of anxiety Montgomery steadily held the northern jaws of the vice that must inevitably close upon the enemy, awaiting the precise moment to strike, holding back the Americans from premature counter-attack, while Bradley fumed in his headquarters, writing bitterly to Hodges, but unable to command him, or to divert Montgomery from his plan. The enemy, Montgomery knew, was defeating himself. In good time he would move to destroy the Germans, and ensure that few should escape to confront him in his final drive to the Rhine. Not for one instant did he lose sight of the course of Allied strategy.

IV

The Supreme Commander and Field Marshal Montgomery met in conference at Hasselt on the 28th December. Earlier on that morning snow had begun to fall heavily over the whole battlefield to mask the scars of war, and to slow the enemy armour as it sought to manoeuvre over the difficult ground.

On the 26th December Patton's armoured column had reached Bastogne at a moment when the enemy had begun to shift the weight of his attack to the south and south-west, and so to intensify the struggle for the key road centre. Already the American defenders of Bastogne had written an indelible page in the story of war. Now the long epilogue, which was to involve ten German divisions in a vain effort to its defeat, was about to begin.

All along the salient from Bastogne through St. Hubert and Marche to Malmedy and Elsenborn, the enemy offensive was firmly held. All roads to the Meuse were blocked. The tide of battle was on the turn.

None would deny that when Field Marshal Montgomery met General Eisenhower at Hasselt on the morning of the 28th December the British Commander had brought order out of chaos. He had taken over command of the U.S. 1st and 9th Armies to find the 1st Army off balance, under heavy attack, and in a state of confusion. In less than a week he had restored that army to equilibrium, while at the same time contriving a tactical reserve and holding the most powerful offensive the enemy was capable of mounting. He had used the British 30th Corps as a reserve with great skill, bringing the 29th Armoured Brigade and the 53rd Division east of the Meuse on the right flank of the U.S. 7th Corps. The 51st Division was moving through the 53rd Division to free the U.S. 7th Corps and the 1st Army for the counter-attack which must soon be mounted. Four divisions were on their way from England to Antwerp to help to restore the reserve position, and the despatch of new divisions from the United States was speeded up.

The task of regaining the lost ground and of destroying the enemy in the Ardennes now faced the Allies, and for this task the Americans considered the British Commander entirely unsuitable. Bradley had expressed himself strongly on this point to General Bedell Smith on the 26th December, and Patton endorsed his Chief's views. Bradley wrote: "Although I had hoped Montgomery would soon join our counter-attack with one from the north, I found him waiting expectantly for one last enemy blow on the flank. Not until he was certain that the enemy had exhausted himself, would Montgomery plunge in for the kill. Disappointed at the prospect of further delay, I headed back to St. Trond."[1]

Already Bradley was urging upon SHAEF and the Supreme Commander that the time had come for the return of his armies and the complete restoration of his 12th Army Group Command.

Montgomery, for his part, was uneasy lest Bradley and Patton should seek to drive through from the south prematurely, and force the commitment of reserves 'piecemeal'.

Meanwhile, far from the battle front, dangerous rumblings had begun to stir the fires of discontent. Criticism of the Supreme Commander had been given some prominence in the British Press, and, with that, support had grown for "one ground force commander". To the commanders in the field this was an old and bitter story, but to the Press it seemed brand new, and arising out of the Ardennes situation. All moments would have been bad for such criticisms, but there could not have been a worse moment than this, with passions rising high in the American camp. Reaction in the United States was swift, definite and uncompromising.

[1] "A Soldier's Story."

It was with this unfortunate situation nearing a climax that Field Marshal Montgomery, logically, as he saw it, pressed his old arguments for a single Ground Force Commander north of the Ardennes, and for confirmation of the British view of strategy that the full force of the Allied offensive must be in the north. Nothing seemed more reasonable to Montgomery than to press his claims at a time when his views seemed to have been vindicated by events, nor had the time seemed more ripe than at this meeting with General Eisenhower at Hasselt.

Pogue describes how Montgomery pressed the point that:

> "The key to future success lay in the assignment of all available offensive power to the northern line of the advance to the Ruhr and the establishment of one-man control of the whole tactical battle in the north."[1]

It was ironical that at this moment when Montgomery held the command he had argued for for so long, it had become impossible for him to retain it. General Marshall had cabled Eisenhower at once in reaction to British Press reports:

> "My feeling is this: under no circumstances make any concessions of any kind whatsoever. You not only have our complete confidence but there would be terrific resentment in this country following such action. I am not assuming that you had in mind such a concession. I just wish you to be certain of our attitude on this side. You are doing a fine job and go on and give them hell."[2]

Writing of the meeting at Hasselt Forrest Pogue states:

> "In reality nothing was said at this time that had not been stated on various other occasions by the 21st Army Group Commander and his advisers."

General Eisenhower, aware of the powerful undercurrents, remained, as always, restrained, patient and eminently fair. Montgomery, as a mark of the Supreme Commander's confidence, would retain the U.S. 9th Army for his attack in the north, and this would give the Field Marshal as many divisions as he could hope to deploy

[1] "The Supreme Command."
[2] Eisenhower personal file.

on that front. The U.S. 1st Army would return to Bradley. The old pattern of command, and of strategy, would be maintained. It had paid magnificent dividends.

But Montgomery, undismayed, and with the British Chiefs of Staff behind him, continued to press his point, and on the 31st December Eisenhower wrote thanking the Field Marshal for his "frank and friendly counsels" and uttering a warning. He would deplore "the development of such an unbridgeable gulf of convictions between us that we would have to present our differences to the CC/S. The confusion and debate that would follow would certainly damage the goodwill and devotion to a common cause that have made this Allied Force unique in history."[1]

The situation had reached the boil, and de Guingand, Montgomery's Chief of Staff, fearing the worst after a talk with General Bedell Smith, warned his Chief that if it came to a showdown "someone would have to go and it would not be the Supreme Commander."[2]

Montgomery was astonished. The storm of controversy raging round him had passed him by. Without wasting a moment he wrote at once to assure Eisenhower of his devoted loyalty. Between the two men it could not have been in doubt. The long command crisis in the field was almost at an end. At the conference table between the Chiefs of Staff it was only at its beginning.

V

The main purpose of the Hasselt meeting had been to reach agreement on the timing of the counter-attack in the Ardennes. Montgomery stated that he would be ready to begin to move over to the offensive about the 2nd or 3rd January. Eisenhower appears to have understood him to say the 1st January. In the event New Year's day itself belonged to the Germans, reminding the Allies that it was unwise to take chances with their terrible enemy even

[1]Eisenhower personal file, dated 31 Dec., 1944.

[2]The Supreme Commander's advisers at SHAEF urged him to force a showdown, see, "The Supreme Command", p. 386.
"Operation Victory", p. 434. By Major-General Sir Francis de Guingand.

in the air. On that day the Luftwaffe, mustering all its strength, struck in low level attacks against Allied airfields throughout Belgium and the Netherlands. It was the heaviest enemy use of air power in the campaign, and something of a shock. The losses of aircraft on the ground were severe, but far from crippling, and it was small consolation that the enemy had also paid a heavy price. For the enemy it had been a desperate throw.

Nevertheless it gave warning that it was time to press home the counter-attack, and on the 3rd January the U.S. 7th Corps went into the attack against the northern shoulder of the enemy salient. The snow was thick upon the ground. Guns and men moved with difficulty over a white wilderness, hiding mines without trace, and against an enemy resolved upon a controlled fighting withdrawal, an enemy moreover still capable of offensive action. The cold was intense.

Slowly from that day forward the jaws of the vice closed, and on the 7th January, knowing the battle won, and the final result beyond doubt, Field Marshal Montgomery gave a Press conference, which was doomed to set the seal upon the crisis of command.

Members of Montgomery's staff, fearing that their Chief would almost certainly say the wrong things, or the right thing in the wrong way, strove to prevent the conference. The Field Marshal was adamant. He owed it, he believed, to the Supreme Commander and to the Americans to put the record straight, and to correct some of the misunderstandings which had arisen from British Press criticisms of General Eisenhower. Few doubted that he would achieve the reverse.

Yet Field Marshal Montgomery's statement earned him the warm praise of *The New York Times* in an editorial: "No handsomer tribute was ever paid to the American soldier than that of Field Marshal Montgomery in the midst of the combat."[1]

His analysis of the battle was, as always, masterly. His tributes to U.S. commanders and men unequivocal. His sentiments unexceptionable. Nevertheless General Bradley and the U.S. commanders were "outraged" and utterly "exasperated". From that moment it became hopeless for the British Chiefs of Staff to press their views on strategy, or to pursue their suggestion for a new

[1] New York Times. 9.1.45.

Deputy Supreme Commander to replace Air Marshal Tedder, and to act as a "Ground Force Commander".[1]

When General Eisenhower tentatively broached the subject of a Ground Force Commander to General Bradley, the 12th Army Group Commander stated flatly that he would ask to be relieved of his command rather than serve under Montgomery. Moreover, the next offensive must be under American command. The American public would not stand for a secondary role.

It seemed then that Montgomery's battle of the Rhineland was in jeopardy, for it was becoming difficult for the Supreme Commander to hold to his intention that the main drive should be in the north. It had become politically essential that a secondary drive should take place, and that if possible it should steal the thunder. With Bradley and Patton out for blood it was not unlikely that, secondary or not, it would do just that.

Dr. Goebbels was quick to turn the controversy to German advantage. A broadcast in English, giving a skilfully distorted view purporting to be British, was readily believed, notably by General Bradley, despite the denials of Mr. Brendan Bracken. Churchill weighed in with handsome tributes to the Americans, emphasizing the Ardennes as an almost total American battle, and followed a statement in the House of Commons with a grave warning: "Let no one," he said, "lend himself to the chatter of mischief-makers when issues of this momentous consequence are being successfully decided by the sword."[2] It was, at least, a reminder that the price was being paid in flesh and blood.

The reaction continued to plague General Eisenhower for many weeks. It had bitten deeply into the minds of many American senior officers, and was not soon forgotten. In a letter to General Marshall,

[1]At the Malta conference of the Combined Chiefs of Staff 30th January-2nd February, the British pressed their strategic viewpoint, and also pursued the subject of a "Ground Force Commander". Alexander was designed for the role. The Americans would not consider it, nor would they budge from Eisenhower's "two-attack" strategy. See: Grand Strategy, vol. vi. "It (the discussion) was indeed vehement as well as prolonged." It provoked "the most acrimonious dispute between the CC of S during the war." See also: "The White House Papers of Harry Hopkins", vol. ii. "One can read the official minutes of these meetings without suspecting that a single harsh word had been exchanged. But they were very angry men."

[2]Hansard 1944-45, 407 H.C. Deb.

Eisenhower wrote that it was the most difficult incident with which he had ever had to deal.

It must be clear that Field Marshal Montgomery's statement to the Press of the 7th January, harmless though it was in content, and intended to clear the air, served to spark a situation that was already primed and ready for explosion. The passage singled out by General Bradley, and which roused his bitter and lasting anger, reads as follows:

> "When Rundstedt attacked on 16 December, he obtained a tactical surprise. He drove a deep wedge into the centre of the United States 1st Army and the split might have become awkward; the Germans had broken through a weak spot, and were heading for the Meuse.
>
> As soon as I saw what was happening I took certain steps myself to ensure that if the Germans got to the Meuse they would certainly not get over that river. And I carried out certain movements so as to provide balanced dispositions to meet the threatened danger; these were, at the time, merely precautions, i.e., I was thinking ahead.
>
> Then the situation began to deteriorate. But the whole Allied team rallied to meet the danger; national considerations were thrown overboard; General Eisenhower placed me in command of the whole northern front.
>
> I employed the whole available power of the British Group of Armies; this power was brought into play very gradually and in such a way that it would not interfere with the American lines of communications. Finally it was put into the battle with a bang and today British divisions are fighting hard on the right flank of the United States 1st Army.
>
> You have thus the picture of British troops fighting on both sides of American forces who have suffered a hard blow. This is a fine Allied picture.
>
> The battle has some similarity to the battle that began on 31 August, 1942, when Rommel made his last bid to capture Egypt and was 'seen off' by the Eighth Army."[1]

[1] See: "The Supreme Command", and for comment.

Taken out of their context these words and this mode of expression might be irritating to highly susceptible men, but it was not so much Montgomery's words as his manner, his "what a good boy am I" attitude, that so infuriated the Americans in the field. But it was Bradley's "calculated risk" that had brought these results, and was costing an average of more than 2,000 American casualties each day of the battle. He was the man responsible for dragging the whole weight to the south in constant support of Patton at the expense of the 1st Army. Perhaps, indeed, his anger sprang out as a result of some such inner awareness.

"There was a danger that Bradley's high prestige *vis-à-vis* his troops might become undermined," wrote de Guingand,[1] referring to the Field Marshal's statement, but Bradley's high prestige with his troops could not be undermined by any words of Montgomery's.

Throughout this storm the two men most concerned, Eisenhower and Montgomery, maintained their dignity and their balance. Montgomery, for his part, seemed almost unaware even that General Bradley bore him anything but goodwill and the warmest regard.

[1]"Operation Victory", by Major-General Sir Francis de Guingand.

9

THE MOMENT OF TRUTH

I

AT no time in the whole war was the enormous extent of the Nazi military power more apparent—and, in a way, more awe inspiring—than in this January of 1945, when, assaulted from east, south and west, the vast military machine moved into its dance of death, and strategy into its last phase. It is possible to fix the moment of truth with some precision.

In the north, while the Battle of the Ardennes was at its height, it had been a time of vigilance, of incessant patrolling, of many severe, but limited encounters, and constant menace. All along the line of the Maas and the Roer rivers the enemy had a resurgence of hope and energy, even borrowing from the Chinese some of the violent noises of battle. Amplifiers dinned the rumble of armoured columns into the ears of the men manning their brens in the forward positions. Men of 47 Royal Marine Commando fought a tremendous battle with a German parachute division on the island of Kapelsche Veer in the middle of the Maas north-east of Breda. A small but powerful force of enemy crossed the Maas at Wessem. All along the right flank of the 2nd Army from Sittard to Geilenkirchen the activity was intense, and it was clear that a major battle would have to be fought to clear the Heinsberg triangle and open up the last stretch of the Roer from Linnich to Roermond. That battle, postponed under the name "Operation Shears", because of the assault in the Ardennes, was ready to go in in mid-January under the code name "Operation Blackcock". The 12th Corps had earmarked the 7th Armoured Division, the 30th Armoured Brigade, the 43rd Wessex Infantry Division, and the 52nd (Mountain) Infantry Division, for the job. The men lay there in the snow, keyed up and ready, their outposts in Germany, and their waggon lines in Holland, their ears assaulted by the new Nazi "music of battle".

At the southern end of the Roer the great dams remained securely in enemy hands, and would demand a major effort from the U.S. 1st Army if they were to be taken and Schmidt revenged. Fierce enemy attacks came in against Dueren, and the threat to Aachen was at times severe.

But it was in the south that Hitler chose to strike a major blow at the very climax of the Ardennes battle. Taking advantage of Patton's move to the north the enemy had mounted an offensive driving south and west of Bitche, while at the same time a strong force crossed the Rhine north of Strasbourg to link up east of the Vosges with an attack planned to strike north and west out of the Colmar pocket. The plan was bold and extremely dangerous, threatening Strasbourg and precipitating a crisis with the French. For an agonizing twenty-four hours it seemed that Strasbourg might fall again into German hands, and with appalling results. The whole Alsatian plain was threatened at a moment when the U.S. 6th Army Group, manoeuvring to shorten its lines, had left Strasbourg uncovered, and would have been prepared to yield the city to the enemy had such a course proved as politically possible as it seemed militarily expedient.

General Schwartz, the French Commander of the Strasbourg Garrison, strongly supported by Generals Juin and de Gaulle, reacted with horror. The thought of the reprisals the Nazis might wreak upon the people would have been alone sufficient reason to deny Strasbourg to the enemy at all costs. Three hundred thousand people in Alsace were in fear of their lives. Churchill flew anxiously from London in response to a plea from de Gaulle to sit in at a conference with Eisenhower and the SHAEF Chiefs of Staff while the French generals disabused the Americans of any notions of expediency. There was no need for the Prime Minister to do more than sit there with his head thrust forward, his jaws hard set, saying nothing at all. President Roosevelt had refused to interfere.

The enemy offensive, under the code name NORDWIND, had opened on the last night of the old year to reach its maximum intensity in the bridgeheads north and south of Strasbourg between the 5th and 7th January. At that point the French took over responsibility for the defence of the city.

In the Colmar pocket the enemy continued to hold, and on the 23rd January, with an enemy threat to the Saverne Gap still potent, a very outspoken meeting took place between the Supreme Commander and General Juin. The French had been starved of reinforcements, waging a bitter war in the Vosges for months, and now in January, with their front doubled in extent, they could make little headway. When Eisenhower expressed the hope that the French would be inspired "to excel their own former records",[1] General Juin reacted with a sharp note on the following day, pointing out the extent of the French effort and criticizing "the goings-on in the neighbouring Army further to the North".[2]

"The important thing to-day," General Juin's letter ended, "is that you win the battle of Alsace as you have won the battle of the Ardennes. That, in my opinion, as I told you yesterday, should be your sole preoccupation of the moment."[3]

It was, however, a moment of many grave preoccupations for the Supreme Commander, a moment when great prospects were opening ahead.

But by the 25th January the Germans had fought themselves virtually to a standstill in their bid for Alsace. They had fought themselves to a standstill everywhere. Now in the west they stood with their backs to the Rhine as, in the east, they had their backs to the Oder.

II

The worst of the Allied troubles in the Ardennes were over at the time of the enemy offensive in the south. On the 10th January, while the enemy threat to Alsace was still being furiously maintained, although in fact past its climax, Field Marshal Montgomery and General Bradley issued their joint orders for a combined counter-attack by the U.S. 1st and 3rd Armies. This would strike the enemy a knock-out blow, and regain all the lost territory.

Feeling that his work in the Ardennes was virtually at an end

[1] "The Supreme Command."
[2] U.S. 7th Army.
[3] Letter, Juin to Eisenhower, 24 Jan., 1945.

Montgomery wrote generously to Bradley on the 12th, the eve of the combined attack:

"My dear Brad,

It does seem as if the battle of the 'salient' will shortly be drawing to a close, and when it is all clean and tidy I imagine that your armies will be returning to your operational command.

I would like to say two things:

First: What a great honour it has been for me to command such fine troops.

Second: How well they have all done.

It has been a great pleasure to work with Hodges and Simpson: both have done very well.

And the Corps Commanders in the First Army (Gerow, Collins, Ridgeway) have been quite magnificent; it must be most exceptional to find such a good lot of Corps Commanders gathered together in one army.

All of us in the northern side of the salient would like to say how much we have admired the operations that have been conducted on the southern side; if you had not held on firmly to Bastogne the whole situation might have become very awkward.

My kind regards to you and to George Patton.

Yours very sincerely,

B. L. Montgomery."

A copy of this letter was sent also to General Eisenhower with a covering note saying: "It has been a very great honour for me to command two American armies."

While there is every reason to believe that these notes express Montgomery's genuine sentiments, there is equally every reason to believe that anything Montgomery could say added only gall to General Bradley's load.

In the dawn of the 13th January the 1st and 3rd Armies moved from north and south to crush the enemy out of the salient. Already the 6th Panzer Army had been ordered out of the line by Hitler, and was about to rush east to add its remaining strength to the troops fighting desperately to halt the Russian avalanche.

On the 16th January, units of the 1st and 3rd Armies joined hands across the stream of the Ourthe where it runs deep in the gorge through the little township of Houffalize.[1] The heavy snow lying in deep drifts in the narrow defiles blanketed the offal and debris of war, but seemed to enhance the desolation of the little towns and villages, reduced to blackened skeletons in the ebb tide of war, in the wake of "Les sales Boches", 1914-1918, 1940-1944. In the villages women buried their dead, and old men searched in the ruins of homes for some treasure. Rochefort, Champlon, Bure, and Houffalize itself were in complete ruin, but Houffalize on the morning of the 17th January was the symbol of the American victory. Powdered snow drove fiercely in the bitter wind, so that the ground had a virgin look, unmarked by wheel or footprint, as infantry patrols moved forward soon after dawn. Within an hour the snow had erased all signs of their passing. A man approaching from the south saw no signs of life, and knew only a loneliness as of the grave, a strange calm within the distant noises of battle. Shattered tree stumps stood up in grotesque shapes on the slopes of the steep gorge, and icicles veiled the outcropping rocks. Houffalize was no longer a place of human habitation. A cat ran startled out of a heap of rubble, wavered, uncertain which way to turn, and crouched in terror under what had been a road block. Presently a very old man leaning on a tall stick came slowly up the hill. There were no other signs of life.

At the foot of the hill a handful of American troops straddled the timbers of the blown bridge, clambering across to shake hands with a patrol from the north. Engineers moved about like housewives with heavy floor polishers looking for mines.

"Bea't, ain it!" said a soldier.

The battle of the Ardennes was to rage on into the fourth week of the month as the enemy fought to extricate something from the wreck of his last hopes, but Houffalize on that morning meant the end. The enemy had inflicted a tactical reverse upon the Allies, compelling the postponement of their planned offensive, but the cost had been far greater than he could afford to pay. The wreckage of at least 600 tanks, and of countless trucks, lay over the roads, and in the rear beyond the Rhine immense quantities of rolling stock had been smashed to ruin by Allied air attack. Above all the

[1]A recce force of tanks entered from the south on the 16th.

drain on the last remaining German manhood had been severe. At the lowest estimate the enemy had suffered 80,000 casualties in the battle. It was probably nearer 100,000. It had cost the Americans very little less. It had been their battle. They had lost 75,482 men against the British total of 1,408. That is the measure of it.

Again, as in Normandy, Hitler had imposed catastrophe upon his armies, refusing to permit withdrawal while withdrawal was possible, refusing to agree alternative objectives until it was too late. Yet, although Hitler may be said to have lost the Battle of the Ardennes, Field Marshal Montgomery deserves very great credit for his part in it. Beset by Bradley, and to a lesser extent by Hodges and Ridgeway, his whole plan and tactics loathed and condemned, and even at times compromised by impulsive action, Montgomery kept the battle firmly under control from beginning to end. I would say that he saved the American 1st Army 20,000 casualties, including the U.S. 7th Armoured Division. The blood was American; the brains and moral courage were his.

Moreover his handling of the British 30th Corps was consistently masterly. Unless he had concentrated his mind upon the "maintenance of the Objective" in the north, the battle of the Ardennes might well have cost him the battle of the Rhineland, taking the campaign out of British hands, and condemning the 21st Army Group to a minor role.

Nothing would have been easier—or brought him higher praise from the Americans—than to commit the 30th Corps to the battle. Instead, he most carefully avoided entanglement with the U.S. lines of communications while using his troops to the best advantage. Their role was to guarantee the line of the Meuse through the time of crisis, to provide security and a vital reserve, and at the last by strengthening the right flank of the U.S. 1st Army to lend it manoeuvreability.

On the day of Houffalize the 30th Corps divisions were pinched out of the battle, having served their purpose admirably. On that evening of the 17th January the U.S. 1st Army returned to the operational command of the U.S. 12th Army Group. It behoved Field Marshal Montgomery to withdraw his troops, to re-group with all speed and to move north.

III

The 12th January 1945 is perhaps the most easily recognizable of the decisive dates in the history of war, for on that day vast forces were set in motion which were to change the face of Europe, and to mark a decisive turning point in the story of European civilization. Of those few who were aware of these things at the time it is unlikely that any, apart from Stalin and Churchill, saw the portent. For Stalin it was enough to observe with satisfaction. For Churchill no action was possible.

Yet the promise of these things had stirred Churchill and Eisenhower to something like exaltation. From early December Eisenhower had been anxious to have some news of Russian offensive plans for the winter. No news had been forthcoming. Early in January Air Marshal Tedder had set out by air for Moscow to see Marshal Stalin, but on the night of the 5th January his aircraft was grounded in Cairo. Impatient at the delay Churchill sent a personal cable to Stalin on the 6th, and had a reply the next day promising "large-scale offensive operations against the Germans along the whole Central Front not later than the second half of January". Churchill at once cabled his grateful thanks for the "thrilling message".[1]

At dawn on the 12th January Marshal Koniev advanced from his bridgeheads on the Vistula, and two days later the armies of Marshal Zhukov, crossing on his right flank, swung north over the Pilica, while on his left General Petrov's army threatened Jaslo. On the extreme right of this violent assault, which swiftly enveloped Warsaw and Cracow, Marshals Rokossovsky and Chernyakhosky advanced upon Tilsit, obliterated East Prussia, and gained bridgeheads over the Vistula in the north to join with the right wing of Zhukov's armies. In the south, stiffening the pressure which they had never relaxed throughout the winter, Malinovsky and Tolbukhin enveloped Budapest, and the roads to Vienna and Berlin opened ahead.

In three weeks, moving at an average rate of 14 miles a day as the crow flies, the Russians were on the river Oder 280 miles from

[1] "Churchill Memoirs", Vol. vi. Triumph and Tragedy.

their start point. From north to south 300 Russian divisions backed by 25 tank armies and hordes of Cossacks, rolled back the Germans with an irresistible force. East Prussia and Poland were engulfed; Bulgaria plucked like a rotten fruit, Hungary doomed in violent struggle, Roumania shattered, while the fate of Czechoslovakia could not be long in doubt.

That, I believe, gives a glimpse of the overwhelming significance of the 12th January, 1945, in human affairs, and it is impossible not to state the fact here, even though it may be by now a mere platitude.

By the time Field Marshal Montgomery was ready to mount his offensive in the Rhineland, the Russians were within 40 miles of Berlin with their centre, and their right flank on the Baltic, and their left ready to sweep on Vienna.

It may be unfair to say that the Western Allies "fiddled while Rome burned", but at this moment, as the great tragedy—which was world tragedy—unfolded, moving into its final phase, the U.S. 1st Army was still trying to take the Roer dams, and undo the battle of Schmidt. The U.S. 9th Army, under Montgomery's command, was not only immobilized behind the Roer river awaiting the taking of the dams, but was also awaiting the return of its divisions involved with the 12th Army Group.

Thus, at the end of January, Allied strategy was in chains, and German strategy had ceased to exist. For the Germans there was no to-morrow. The war had moved beyond the point when all previous wars have ended, and this, I believe, was inevitable. The Allied policy of "Unconditional Surrender" has often been blamed as perhaps the principal reason why the war did not end at that point. But this cannot be true. Unconditional surrender is, in any case, a meaningless form of words, for there are always terms or conditions, and millions of Germans did surrender on those "terms".

Hitler, and Hitler alone, bears the whole weight of responsibility for the beginning and for the end. His were the terms, and the terms were these: he would bring down the Reich in chaos, and divide Europe with his last strength, demented and steeped in evil, eyeless in the bunker.

Eighty-five divisions faced eighty-five divisions west of the Rhine, on the last battlefield, and in its death throes the German Army in the west was still a most terrible and potent force.

PART THREE

BATTLE OF THE RHINELAND

10

MAINTENANCE OF THE OBJECTIVE

THROUGH all December, while the attention of the world was focused almost exclusively upon the Ardennes, and the subsequent developments round Strasbourg, the Canadian 1st Army and the British 2nd Army had achieved considerable feats of organisation and of arms in the maintenance of the offensive projects in the north, and in preparations to mount them with the smallest possible delay. These tasks had been complicated by the absence of the 30th Corps, which had been actively involved not only in the early planning of "Operation Veritable", but also of "Operation Blackcock", an essential preliminary to the Rhineland battle.

While the build-up for these offensive actions progressed steadily, aided by the growing traffic out of Antwerp, it had been necessary to hold a long front against an enemy inspired with new hopes, and capable of launching severe attacks at a number of key points. It was a period of great strain and unceasing vigilance. The Canadian 2nd Corps deployed its troops in the Nijmegen bridgehead, seeking constantly to improve its positions, and the British 1st Corps held a 125 miles front on the Maas, alert to meet an expected enemy drive with four divisions aimed through Breda against Antwerp. This had been a part of the Ardennes plan Hitler had been forced to abandon, but it had remained a very real and potent menace at the height of the Ardennes offensive.

The British 2nd Army had also been busy, its headquarters involved in the complex planning for the Rhine crossing, an amphibious operation envisaged as second only to the Normandy landings, and posing difficult problems of engineering. 2nd Army troops also held the line of the Maas from Roermond to Cuijk, uneasily aware of the thinly held right flank south to Aachen. Indeed the position on the flanks, both north and south, amply demonstrated the power of the German offensive in the centre which had sucked the bulk of four armies instantly into the battle.

But above all in December urgent consideration had to be given to "Operation Blackcock", the clearance of the Heinsberg triangle to close the line of the River Roer from Linnich to Roermond, and to remove this awkward salient from the joint of the British and American armies. It was impossible to wait for the release of the British 30th Corps, and the task was handed over to the British 12th Corps. On the 31st December planning instructions were issued to all troops available for the battle. These consisted of one armoured division, two armoured brigades, elements of the 79th Armoured Division, and two infantry divisions. Corps and divisional artillery would be greatly strengthened by the 3rd and 9th Army Groups Royal Artillery. In addition the British 8th Corps would give artillery support on the left while the U.S. 13th Corps performed a similar function on the right.

These were formidable forces, amply justified by the nature and urgency of the task confronting them, a task moreover which was unlikely to bring praise in its execution, to capture the attention of the audience, or to be noted outside military circles. Nevertheless, Allied success in this battle was as vital to the opening of "Operation Veritable" as the seizure of the Roer dams would be to the opening of "Operation Grenade" by the U.S. 9th Army.

On the 10th January, Field Marshal Montgomery issued his final orders for "Blackcock". He had also agreed a target date with the Supreme Commander for "Veritable" to open on the 8th February, and with "Grenade", it was hoped, to go into action two days later. The time table was rigid, allowing of no more delays, and no more arguments. There were still plenty of worries. The U.S. 9th Army was down to a strength of five divisions as a result of Bradley's demands upon it. These demands might increase rather than diminish, and Montgomery had pressed Eisenhower to make up the 9th Army to sixteen divisions. Finally he had been promised twelve divisions. The Field Marshal also felt some doubts as to the urgency with which the U.S. 1st Army approached the difficult task of seizing the Roer dams before it was too late. Nevertheless, convinced that he had achieved all that was possible he at once became wholly absorbed with his tasks in the north.

On the 14th January the 30th Corps headquarters moved north to join the Canadian 1st Army in the final planning stages of "Operation Veritable" and on the 21st January the 21st Army Group issued final orders for the battle. The intention was to destroy all enemy forces between the Rhine and the Maas from Nijmegen to the general line Julich–Dusseldorf.

The back areas of the Canadian 1st and British 2nd Armies had become an appalling turmoil of traffic over utterly inadequate roads, and only the freight trains rumbling out of Antwerp made offensive actions possible. At times, as the V.2s rocked the city with their diabolical explosions, it seemed a miracle that the docks and railways kept the supplies flowing. Roads crumbled constantly under the immense weight of traffic, and tens of thousands of tons of rubble were brought forward to enable the engineers and pioneers to reconstruct four hundred miles of roads, and to build one hundred miles of new.

In addition to these difficulties the heavy rains of December had flooded the Maas up to one thousand yards on either bank, and had swollen the River Niers to the east.

On the 15th January, with the 30th Corps troops moving laterally across the supply lines, the 12th Corps embarked upon "Operation Blackcock", one of the worst and most difficult battles to be fought in the campaign. The weather was appalling, a sudden thaw turning the roads to "glue pots" of mud to hold up the main assault of the armour.

One of the main provisos of the plan was that the ground should be suitable for the use of flails and armour, but the time for provisos had passed. The battle must be fought and won. It was, therefore, on the morning of the 15th January that the 1st/5th Battalion of the Queens Regiment moved to secure the start line.

11

THE "BLACKCOCK" REHEARSAL

I

THE weather for "Operation Blackcock" provided all the possible variations on a theme of winter except sunshine, bright and cold. It thawed, froze, fogged, snowed and rained, sometimes all five in a mushy mixture within twenty-four hours. It was always bitterly cold. The white snow suits provided for most of the forward troops, the careful white camouflage of armour, including flails, crocodiles, troop-carrying kangaroos, and almost all vehicles, was not in vain. It was more often "whitish" with snow or dank and dim with fog than anything else, and the nights were long and dismal, lit in the hours of night attacks by searchlights reflecting down from the clouds in "artificial moonlight". It was a battle for infantry.

But the pattern of warfare was new. It was fought out on a small confined stage inside Germany, from river to river and brook to brook, from copse to copse, hamlet to hamlet and house to house. Yet, in common with every major process of "mopping up" since the Normandy victory, it lacked the essential of a battle: the enemy could not win. At best the enemy could hope to slow down the momentum of losing while awaiting a political miracle. Only the Ardennes had borne the characteristics of a major battle, and even there the possibility of enemy victory had seemed unreal, even in the worst moments.

"Operation Blackcock" was a very unpleasant and important example of the long mopping-up process ahead. In that narrow triangle of difficult, deceptively undulating country, with Roermond at the apex, with the sides held in the west by the line of the Maas and the Juliana canal, and in the east by the intricacies of the rivers Wurm and Roer, the enemy had constructed three defensive trench systems protected by trip wires and minefields. The first of these was anchored on Linne and the powerful defences covering Roermond, thence following the eastern bank of the Maas and the Juliana canal to a point just south of Roosteren. The line then followed the stream of the Saeffeler beek along the southern base of the triangle from the Juliana to the Siegfried Line pill box system on the Roer above Linnich. The second defensive line was anchored on the Juliana canal at Echt and ran diagonally to link into the Siegfried defences sited to prevent an advance down the Roer valley. The third line was a short trench system covering Heinsberg.

Every enemy village was a strong point, every stream a heavily defended obstacle, the crossing points covered by mortars and artillery. The numerous small copses of the centre woodlands of the Echterbosch were ideal points from which to inflict heavy casualties upon the attacker. Civilians were very few. The whole area was a battlefield, and the heart of it was inside Germany. It had become a fortress held by two infantry divisions, and a first class regiment, Regiment Hubner, garrisoning Roermond. Some ninety field guns, including self-propelled guns of 7.5 cms. calibre, were available to the enemy within the triangle, and some support might be expected from the heavy guns of the Roer. There would not be reserves. These men would fight, die, or be captured or retreat beyond the river barrier. Their counter-attacks would be strictly local, and by their courage or cowardice nothing could be gained or lost, except time. Their army had suffered a ferocious purge of its officers, and behind them their country was disintegrating rapidly in physical, spiritual and moral ruin.

Henceforth this in essence is the nature of the campaign in north-west Europe, and in this it is unique in the history of war. It is endowed with a rare and terrible quality of tragedy, of wastage of life and courage, a vain, empty, suicidal, self-inflicted total defeat growing worse with every hour, availing nothing, and nurturing the seeds of chaos.

The Allies had allotted ten days for the elimination of the Heinsberg triangle. A careful plan had been prepared, detailed yet flexible in the hands of good commanders. A skilful regrouping had been carried out calculated to deceive the enemy. Two brigades of the 43rd Division had relieved the 52nd Division on the extreme right. The 52nd Division had moved to the centre to relieve the right flank of the 7th Armoured Division, and it was hoped that these moves would encourage the enemy to expect a stalemate to continue, or that an attack would be aimed direct on Heinsberg from the Geilenkirchen sector.

Instead the 12th Corps plan was to strike on the extreme left, driving north to open the roads Sittard–Limbricht–Holtum–Dieteren–Echt–Maasbracht, and the main Sittard–Roermond road running with the railway some two thousand yards to the east.

It was intended to develop immediately two left hooks, using the 8th Armoured Brigade, a brigade of the 52nd Division, and the 22nd Armoured Brigade. These two forces would swing east to embrace the central woodland area bounded by Aardenburg, Waldfeucht and Koningsbosch. The 1st Commando Brigade would spearhead the attack on Maasbracht and Linne while the main force of the 7th Armoured Division advanced north-eastward on Montfort, Posterholt and the Roer river at St. Odillenberg.

At first light on D plus two the 52nd Division was timed to attack in the south centre, assaulting across the Saeffeler beek, seizing Hongen, clearing its left flank and swinging right handed on Bocket. It would then develop its attack eastward on Heinsberg.

On or about the 20th January the 43rd Division would come into action on the extreme right, moving east from Waldenrath to close the river Wurm south of Heinsberg to the junction with the U.S. 102nd Infantry Division thrusting north from Linnich.

Artillery support was on a massive scale, seeming designed to blast the enemy out of the ground. Typhoons, fighters and fighter bombers were ready to take advantage of all breaks in the weather. The enemy had already suffered a great weight of bombs, harassed constantly at all salient points.

The British troops were acutely aware that they would be fighting inside Germany for the first time, and that their initial assault would heave the Germans from one of their last holds on eastern Holland south of the Waal. Doubtless the enemy was also aware. "Operation Blackcock" had a special savour.

II

At first light on the morning of the 15th January a company of the 1st/5th Queens moved silently out of its forward positions escorted by three flail tanks. From its size it might have been little more than a powerful fighting patrol to probe the enemy defences. Its purpose was to take the village of Bakenhoven, one mile to the north-west of Susteren, seize a good crossing point of the Vloed Beek, and secure a good start line for an attack against Dieteren.

Preliminary work had already been done on the approaches to the beek. At nine o'clock on the night of the 15th the Royal Engineers, covered by the 9th Durham Light Infantry, a machine gun platoon, an anti-tank battery, and a squadron of flail tanks of the Lothians, would move to the crossing point and bridge the Vloed Beek ready for the armour to surge into the triangle.

It was a grim morning, greyish white, the snow beginning to mush with the sudden thaws. The thin coating of ice on the roads was turning to a film of grease. The Queens reached Bakenhoven almost without incident. The flails beat a way through the minefield to the south, finding the going difficult. Belts of woodland enclosed the village on the east and west. A copse came down to the water's edge of the Vloed Beek on its eastern bank and fringed the north side of the road which runs from Gebroecht to Susteren. Bakenhoven was strangely quiet. The weather worsened. The flails beat the mushy ground, and very soon the mortar bombs began to burst in confused fierce patterns, spattering the village and the approaches to the beek. Grey shapes, running swiftly from cover to cover in the fringes of the woods, drew the fire of the Queens. They had studied the ground with care, and the menace of the woods had not escaped them. All through that day of the 15th the company fought an isolated battle in the village, on the approaches to the Vloed Beek, and in the woods. The flail tanks revealed that they were not simply armour bearing revolving drums with chains to beat the ground, but fighting vehicles, not to be despised. The Queens held on, sections fighting hand to hand with bayonet and grenade. By afternoon they knew that they would have to hold on all night as well as all day.

By early afternoon the state of the ground and the uncertainty of the weather had decided the commander of the 7th Armoured Division to postpone the follow through until the morning. It was half past seven o'clock on the morning of the 16th before the Royal Engineers with their supporting troops moved up to the beek under mortar fire. The 9th Battalion of the Durhams went through the Queens and took the village of Dieteren. Enemy mortars concentrating on the crossing point of the Vloed Beek took a steady toll of the engineers. Armour attempting to move up smashed the prepared approaches, the tanks slithering on the grease. Medium artillery added weight to the enemy mortaring. Two bulldozers were knocked out. It was a dreary, deadly day without promise.

All through the night of the 16th-17th the engineers worked under heavy mortaring and shell fire. The infantry held on in the villages. An isolated flail tank fought a brave action and beat off a counter-attack coming in from the woods bordering the stream. By morning on the 17th the Vloed Beek was bridged, but it seemed as though the enemy merely waited for the light to bracket the position and blow up the bridge with a direct hit. Grimly the R.E.s dragged their equipment two hundred yards down stream and began again. A day and a half of valuable time had gone. The plan of the swift armoured thrusts to the north and east had faded. The pattern was becoming clear: it was, and would be, a battle for infantry all the way, of swift adaptation from hour to hour, from village to village, while the engineers fought to bridge the beeks and open the roads.

In the detailed plan of the battle, phase followed phase in sequence, and each phase was sub-divided in sequence. Thus the opening phase, code-named ANGEL, was sub-divided into ANGEL I—II—III. At the outset a stodgy, timid or unimaginative command would have bogged down the whole operation by sticking to the book of the words. Such a course would have been disastrous, threatening the delicate and elaborate time table of the Rhineland battle. Fortunately the two divisional commanders most closely concerned, Major-General L. O. Lyne of the 7th Armoured and Major-General E. Hakewill Smith of the 52nd Lowland Division, were men of action, initiative and moral courage. The commander of the 7th Armoured Division swiftly appreciated the situation, and by the evening of the 16th had switched his opening sequences to meet the case. At dawn on the 17th the 1st/5th Queens crossed the Vloed Beek on foot to move on Susteren in ANGEL III, while ANGEL II formed up in the rear. Armour, flails, flame throwing crocodiles and troop carrying kangaroos would be fed through as and when possible. Meanwhile the infantry would press on. It was clear that an immense burden would fall upon the Royal Engineers, for without bridges and roads the armour would not be able to move in strength and would be held to a crawl.

Awaiting his moment of attack in the centre Major-General Hakewill Smith, the commander of the 52nd Division, keeping in close touch with the opening developments, realized that the success of "Blackcock" might depend upon the speed and ability of his troops. The armoured thrusts designed to move eastward to embrace the central woodland area would undoubtedly move behind time, and a brigade of the 52nd was with the southern thrust. With his remaining brigades Hakewill Smith must move, therefore, with all speed on Waldfeucht, Koningsbosch and Echterbosch, possibly without support. The high ground at Bocket on the road to Waldfeucht must be taken without delay.

By the afternoon of the 17th the Queens had gained Susteren, and the 2nd Devons, leading the advance of ANGEL II, had struggled up to their start line at Dieteren. The going was appalling, the combination of trip wires and mines deadly in the mess of ice, snow and slush. Two troops of tanks had crossed the Vloed Beek at a bulldozed crossing to join the hard-pressed Queens in Susteren. A few tracked vehicles had got through to Dieteren with ANGEL II, only to bog down. It was half past three o'clock in the afternoon when the 2nd Devons struck off across country from Dieteren, a few tracked vehicles struggling along behind. The plan was for one column to move on the western route to the north through Ophoven on Echt, while the right hand column opened up the main road from Susteren to Schilberg.

The left column made good time, fighting a stiff sharp action in Ophoven, and getting its forward companies in the outskirts of Echt by nightfall. It was necessary to press on, night and day.

On the right the main column of the brigade—the 131st—struck trouble a mile and a half outside Susteren. At this point the railway crosses the road. The enemy had dug in on the embankment, and supported by S.P. guns held solid. Without armour the infantry could not storm the strongly entrenched position. It was then dusk. Snow had begun to fall.

By five o'clock that afternoon the engineers had the main bridge in commission across the Vloed Beek, and the armour began to move across, the roar of tank engines bringing cheer to the infantry ahead. It was impossible for the tanks to manoeuvre off the road, but all through the night infantry and tanks battered at the enemy road block.

It was clear at this early stage of the battle that hold-ups could not be permitted. As fast as the engineers could bridge the beeks, men, armour and 'Funnies' moved into the battles, the infantry humping all that they could carry on their backs. A relief column moved up swiftly on the western route to find Echt occupied by midnight. There, joined by crocodiles, the relief column prepared to attack eastward on Schilberg to outflank the enemy and break the road block on the main road position north of Susteren.

At half past six o'clock in the morning the attack went in, and at that hour the 4th/5th Royal Scots Fusiliers of the 156th Brigade of the 52nd Division launched their assault north-eastwards from the village of Tuddern across the Saeffelen Beek. Hakewill Smith had decided not to wait upon success on the left. The balance of power was moving his way, and he grasped it. Directly ahead of his troops lay the formidable obstacle of the Saeffelen Beek, twenty feet wide, with marshy approaches made worse by the mixture of thaw and freeze, and with a high bank shielding the north. In the opening phase the cluster of villages north of the beek had to be taken to gain a firm bridgehead, and the key town of Hongen must be won to establish the main route of advance.

Three hundred guns supporting the assault of the R.S.F. fired their programme on the villages of Stein and Lind before the leading infantry had reached the Saeffelen Beek under concentrated enemy mortaring, small arms and spandau fire. It was nearly nine o'clock before sappers had the first of two assault bridges in place, and the infantry, humping their mortars and everything they could carry, climbed up and over the northern bank. Nothing on wheels or tracks could follow, not even a weasel. The forward observation officers of the gunners crossed with the infantry, but wireless links with the guns broke down.

By this time the congestion growing on the battlefield was reflected in the congestion of the artillery. An immense fire plan had been arranged, but the air was so filled with a confused pattern of signals, and the going was so slow and unpredictable, that the gunners had to adapt to conditions as best they could.

Nevertheless the 156th Brigade pressed on, the 6th Cameronians moving up under heavy mortaring over one thousand yards of open ground to cross the beek on the second assault bridge. Three tanks had managed to cross by the first of the bridges in early afternoon, only to bog down. Three flails suffered direct hits at the approaches to the second bridge. The enemy in the villages of Stein and Lindt were fighting like demons, using communication tunnels from house to house, snap shooting from all angles, and at one point heaving grenades into a group of wounded. It was a grave mistake. It inspired the Royal Scots Fusiliers to a burst of fury which wiped out the enemy before dusk. It was a costly day. Seventy-five men of the leading companies lay dead or wounded in and around the village of Stein. More than forty such villages lay ahead on the divisional road to the key town of Heinsberg.

III

The 18th January was a day of desperate infantry fighting, and the key day in the battle of the Heinsberg triangle. By their determination to go forward regardless of support by armour or artillery, and without much hope of being served by anything larger than a jeep, the 4th/5th Royal Scots Fusiliers, the 5th Highland Light Infantry and the 6th Cameronians of the 156th Brigade, broke through the main enemy defensive line at a crucial point, and opened the way through to the whole area of the Echterbosch.

In the early stages the Canadian rocket battery had fired three of its salvoes in devastating support of the crossing of the beek and the gaining of footholds in the hamlets beyond. The battery, consisting of twelve rocket projectors each of thirty-two barrels, fired ripple salvoes at 5 to 7,000 yards, bringing down three hundred and eighty-four rockets, each the equivalent of a 5.5 in. shell, into an area two hundred yards square. From the villages of Breberen and Havert the enemy emerged dazed, shocked and speechless from the cellars to totter blindly into walls and into the hands of the attackers. Each salvo obliterated the area upon which it fell, but the battery swiftly shot its bolt.

The 6th Cameronians, following swiftly on the heels of the Royal Scots Fusiliers, went forward in the face of terrible mortaring, skirting Stein, where the fusiliers were fighting bitterly from house to house, and swooping on right-handed to Heilder. With Heilder taken, the key point of Hongen could be assaulted from the rear, and the main divisional route opened across the Saeffelen Beek. All day the mortar platoon of the 6th H.L.I. blanketed Hongen in the smoke from 11,000 smoke bombs to mask the direction of the drive, and add confusion to the enemy.

The continuing thaw immobilized all vehicles and forced the 52nd Division to organize eight hundred men as carriers while the 5th Highland Light Infantry crossed the beek and secured the left flank of the bridgehead, storming through Havert, assaulting Schalbruch, and securing the small lateral road network Nieuwsted–Schalbruch–Havert. Meanwhile in Stein the battle raged fiercely through the day and far into the night, its issue in the last resort depending on the personal valour and sacrifice of individuals. It was here on this day that Fusilier Donnini, charging in the face of machine gun fire, regardless of grievous wounds, and pressing home his attack to the point of death, earned the Victoria Cross. It was a fitting symbol of that day of struggle.

By the dawn of the 19th the German town of Hongen was cleared by the Cameronians attacking down from the north, and the 52nd Division became the first to establish their headquarters on German soil. Swiftly the Engineers put a Bailey bridge across the beek, and opened the road from Sittard. With that the wheels and tracks, the flails, the crocodiles, the kangaroos, the weasels, and the whole array of battalion and brigade vehicles began to move steadily forward into the bridgehead to supply and sustain the forward troops on the lateral road network to the outskirts of the Echterbosch.

It was as well that the 52nd had pressed home the attack with such energy, for it was clear by the evening of the 19th that the 8th Armoured Brigade with the 155th could not get through on the southernmost of the hooks to embrace the Echterbosch. There was no alternative but to withdraw the armour back through Sittard, and to put it through on the 52nd Divisional axis. But this also had become impossible, and had to be abandoned. To the north the column of the 22nd Armoured Brigade, striving to open up the way through to Montfort, and to swing right upon Aardenberg, fared little better. The enemy resistance in the north was proving of a more durable quality than that in the south. A tremendous fight had begun to gain the village of St. Joost on the direct line of advance. Backed by skilfully placed S.P. guns, prepared to deny every yard of ground and to fight independently for every house and barn and strong point, the enemy held firm against the repeated attacks of the 1st Battalion the Rifle Brigade. The tanks of the 8th Hussars, confined to the icy roads, could do little in support, and for thirty-six hours the weary men of the Rifle Brigade, having fought and endured for five days and nights of the severest weather of a severe winter, battered themselves against an enemy amply reinforced by elements of the crack Regiment Hubner covering Roermond, and the extreme apex of the triangle. It was becoming apparent that the enemy regarded the north as the hard core to which he must hold.

Without delay the 52nd Division brought its artillery across the Saeffelen Beek, and with its infantry closely supported pressed on with all possible speed, clearing the villages to the east and north, and preparing to assault Waldfeucht, the central core of the enemy defences. Artificial moonlight guided the troops by night under its strange, sometimes greenish pallor. The alternate thaw and freeze made the going treacherous for men and machines, but there was safety from schumines in the tracks of the flails, even though the flails themselves were hampered in their beating by the snow. The news from all sides was of a struggle against blizzard, snow, fog, ice and slush. One company of the 7th/9th Royal Scots, trying to get through to assault Heide from the west, rashly attempted to move on the ice through a tunnel under the railway embankment, only to find themselves neck deep in icy water. But the three brigades of the 52nd Division were all in the battle. Swarming over the bleak and broken countryside, assaulting villages, clearing coppices, and constantly crossing the narrow channels of the beeks, a score of platoon and company sections gradually formed a coherent picture of sustained assault. On the morning of the 19th the 4th K.O.S.B. had reached the woods to the west of Koningsbosch, and were ready to attack the straggling village. At the same time the 7th Cameronians attacked Saeffelen in the face of terrific enemy concentrations of mortars, spandaus and small arms.

The pressure was maintained relentlessly by day and night. On the 20th, Bocket fell to the H.L.I. with very little trouble, and opened the way for the attack on Waldfeucht and the Echterbosch. The recurrent blizzards seemed to confuse the enemy more than the mountain trained British infantry, and it became clear that the enemy was off balance. An enemy counter-attack in battalion strength and supported by Tiger tanks had been ready mounted against Bocket. It failed to come in. Because of this Waldfeucht was taken by the 5th K.O.S.B. in a night attack with three companies while the fourth company moved into Echterbosch. It was in these two villages throughout the 21st January that the 5th K.O.S.B. were to fight the stiffest action of "Operation Blackcock".

The night of the 20th/21st January was bitterly cold. The whole countryside lay under thick snow, and the village of Waldfeucht with its ancient gateways wore a peaceful look. Moving in almost soundlessly in the early hours of the morning the 5th K.O.S.B. swiftly moved into all-round defensive positions in a silence that was uncanny. Before the dawn enemy shelling heralded an attack, and at half past six o'clock two Tiger tanks loomed out of the grey light followed by infantry in two small groups. Four of our own tanks were swiftly knocked out by enemy shell fire, but the anti-tank gunners held on until the enemy Tigers were cruising in the village street and within one hundred yards. Only then did the men manning the 6-pounders open up to smash the two enemy tanks with direct hits. It was the beginning, not the end, a mere prelude to a major assault.

As the enemy shelling grew intense six Tiger tanks with at least four Panthers, and all draped with German infantry men came swiftly out of the north. Fifteen self-propelled guns in close support began to rip buildings to rubble, filling the narrow channels of the streets with flying fragments and insane din. Under this cover the enemy infantry infiltrated from the north-east cutting off one company. A solitary Tiger tank, penetrating to the heart of the village, roared like some berserk and invulnerable beast up and down the main street, rotating its gun turret, blasting houses point blank with its 88 mm. gun. German civilians emerged from their cellars to shout warnings and directions to the tank crew while infantry men stalked the invader with sticky grenades and P.I.A.T.s.

Two men manning a P.I.A.T. in a bedroom ducked under the long barrel of the Tiger's gun as it poked through the first storey window and blasted room and house to a chaos of rubble and plaster. The solid old brick gateways at each end of the street were too narrow for the Tiger tank to pass, and in the narrow confines within the gates the tank fought for three hours, seeming immune to the many grenades and bombs exploding against its armour. The Regimental Aid Post was shot up, and many of the wounded were again wounded or killed. Finally the enemy tank battered a way through to its own troops in the north-east corner of the village, and for eighteen hours the three companies of the 5th K.O.S.B. held on until relieved by their sister battalion, the 4th. Even then the enemy fire was so accurate, and the battle so closely waged in the streets, that a soldier received five bullets through his hand as he raised it from cover to signal to the relieving troops.

That day and night in Waldfeucht was an indication of the nature of the struggle ahead. Waldfeucht was one of the first of the larger German villages to fall to our troops, and the contrast to the fighting in the Dutch villages was striking. There would be no more safety, no more helpful civilians, no more welcomes in friendly and grateful homes, no more of that kind of relaxation. On that day, I think, on the northern front, a new sense of the grimness of the struggle was in many minds.

The German counter-attack on Waldfeucht had been pressed with strength and determination, but an operation order captured from the 341st Army assault brigade revealed that the attack had been originally mounted against Bocket, and had been hastily remounted against Waldfeucht. The speed of our advance had been well repaid. With the capture of Waldfeucht the way was open for the final assault against Heinsberg.

IV

By the 22nd January there was also good progress in the north. The 22nd Armoured Brigade, battling on dourly with small groups of armour supporting infantry as best they could, helped the Devons into Aardenberg. The 1st Commando Brigade, moving north out of Echt and screening the left flank, was ready to assault Maasbracht. But it was not until the morning of the 24th that the 1st/5th Queens, having taken over in Aardenberg from the Devons, attacked Montfort.

The 131st Brigade were by now making good progress on the right flank of the northern attack, and advancing north-eastward from Aardenberg upon Reutje. When on the night of the 23rd-24th January the 7/9th Royal Scots and the 4th K.O.S.B. moved out of Aphoven in two columns upon Heinsberg only the last splinters remained of the thorn which had festered for so long in the right flank of the 21st Army Group.

The village of Aphoven lies some three or four miles to the south-west of Heinsberg. The countryside is open, with trees lining many of the roadsides, and from the ridge of the valley the ground falls away in a gentle slope to the banks of the rivers Roer and Wurm and a skein of confusing waterways. The village of Aphoven was the start line for the final assault upon Heinsberg. Before midnight on the 23rd January the troops for the assault began a long march from the Bocket area. At Laffeld the 7/9th Royal Scots split into two columns, each column with one company of the 4th K.O.S.B. The moon was well up, and the night sky was lurid with the crimson flashes of shells, and the slow parabolas of tracer. Yet the march was tedious. The roar of the tanks of the 8th Armoured Brigade, and the rumble of the tracks of crocodiles and flails, made harsh patterns of sound, weaving in with the crunch of boots on the thin ice covering the road. At times the beams of the searchlights mixed a greenish tinge on the confused palette of the sky. There was little danger. The wild confusion of sound and colour seemed divorced from the long column of marching men, borne steadily forward as though impelled by the monotonous rhythm of their boots.

It was two o'clock on the morning of the 24th when the columns passed through Aphoven on the last lap of the journey, one column moving to the left, the other to the right, to encircle Heinsberg before the dawn. The remaining two companies of the 4th K.O.S.B. with battalion headquarters and support troops would follow through and clear Heinsberg on the centre line from south to north.

The flanks were well held. The 129th and 130th Brigades of the 43rd Division, coming into the battle on the 20th, had moved east to clear the road through Waldenrath to Dremmen. Opposition was slight. The U.S. 102nd Division moved north up the valley of the Wurm to close the last gap in the south.

Once over the eastern ridge of the valley the twin columns of encircling troops could see the roofs of Heinsberg luminous with frost, reflecting the macabre disorder in the sky. It had been a town of 5,000 people, an ancient town of tall thin buildings with dormer windows in steep roofs above narrow streets, and all huddled within the massive gate houses. It was no longer a place of habitation, but a warren of cellars and rubble after constant hammering from the air. Yet for a little while, in the night, it held the illusion of a sleeping town, the roof tops belying the reality.

All at once, it seemed, the shell fire, which through the night had seemed remote, became personal, and a body of some sixty enemy clothed in white, materialized out of the snow, to put in a fierce attack on the left flank. A Tiger tank roared its challenge in close support, but the column met the onslaught with controlled machine gun and anti-tank fire. The rhythm of the night was broken. Moving swiftly the encircling columns drew a noose round Heinsberg before the dawn, and dug themselves in, watchful and waiting.

It was almost exactly six o'clock in the grey half light when the remaining two companies of the 4th K.O.S.B. moved upon Heinsberg from the south under intense mortar fire, and grateful for the partial cover afforded by a sunken road. In the main the country was open. A mile short of the town a massive wooden cross held the crucified Christ under the shelter of a tree stricken by shell fire, and the tall thin spire of a church gave form to the misty shape of Heinsberg, rising from the snow like the hummock of an island. A sense of aching desolation seemed graven upon that place.

There was no great battle for Heinsberg, no great determination in the German rearguard of defenders. The scorching bursts of flame from the crocodiles brought many up from the cellars with little stomach for a fight. Grenades crashed in the dark enclosed caverns of the houses, and here and there pockets of men fought with terrible fury, each man knowing his enemy, while the mortar bombs and the scream of bullets held attackers and defenders alike in invisible cages of death.

The two flanking companies of the K.O.S.B. swiftly joined their fellows in Heinsberg's last moments of truth, but an enemy strong point came suddenly to life on the southern outskirts of the town to trap B Company on open ground as it attempted to follow through. In the first burst of mortar and machine gun fire the company commander and the company sergeant major were seriously wounded, and the second in command killed. There was no way forward or back, no conceivable cover beyond the low shelving of a ditch or hummock. Alone in all that remained of company headquarters Lance-Corporal Leitch of the Royal Corps of Signals lay with one leg almost severed, and the other gravely wounded, striving none the less to make contact with the guns. His voice, "with the Lowland lilt in it", the gunners say, came to them clearly through all the confusion and hubbub of signals traffic, and calmly, yet in unconventional terms, directed fire and smoke upon the enemy with such speed and accuracy that the company was saved.

Long before evening Heinsberg was secured, and the last of the villages had fallen to the 52nd Division on the banks of the Roer. In the north the 1st/5th Queens, still in the van, the Durham Light Infantry, the Devons, the 5th Dragoons, the 11th Hussars and the 5th Royal Tanks, combed the last pockets of woodland, secured Posterholt and took St. Odilienberg. From those points they could look down upon the last remaining enemy bridgehead of Vlodrop, secure for the time being under his own guns. It was less than a grain of sand between the toes of the advance, and could avail nothing. In the south, for thirty hours the enemy heavy batteries east of the Roer poured shells into the rubble of Heinsberg, and by the end of the month the last bridge capable of bearing vehicles across the Roer had been blown. Such was the nature of the battle of the Heinsberg triangle, a battle of a hundred villages, a battle made up of scores of fragments, and with the attacker eating swiftly into the soft spots, surrounding and reducing the hard cores. It revealed the need for the swift regrouping of brigades, for rapid changes of plan, for the constant leap-frogging of small groups of infantry, tanks, flails and crocodiles. On a much larger scale this would be the pattern of the last great battle.

12

"VERITABLE"—THE PREPARATION

I

THE opening of the port of Antwerp had enabled General Crerar, commanding the 1st Canadian Army, to assemble a vast weight of materials in the Nijmegen bridgehead in preparation for "Operation Veritable", the Battle of the Rhineland.

The final period of the build-up began on 25th January, and by the end of the month the whole region behind the northern front bore the unmistakable imprint of Field Marshal Montgomery. Seldom, if ever, has so much activity, so immense an expenditure of energy, taken place in so confined a space. It resembled the incessant toiling of ants. Seven divisions, two Armoured brigades, and an immense weight of artillery under command of General Horrocks' 30th Corps, moved steadily into the assembly area behind the battlefield. Two more divisions of the British 2nd Army were ready to move in as soon as there was room, finally to swell the ranks of the Canadian 1st Army to a total of thirteen divisions, three armoured brigades, the 30th Brigade of the 79th Armoured Division, five A.G.'s R.A., two A.A. brigades and the Canadian rocket battery. The ration strength of the Candian 1st Army, together with attached personnel, reached a peak of more than 470,000 men of which nearly 400,000 were fighting troops.

All these would funnel through the narrow space between Grave and Nijmegen to debouch into the Reichswald forest, and close the west bank of the Rhine from Emmerich to Wesel, from the Nijmegen–Cleves–Emmerich road on the left to the Geldern–Xanten road on the right.

It is essential for the layman, in considering such a battle, to lend his imagination to the meaning of such numbers of men and quantities of equipment, in terms of movement, food, ammunition, and the expenditure of the intricate paraphernalia of warfare as it was in the mid-twentieth century, for only by so doing is it possible to form judgements on matters of strategy. Thirty-five thousand vehicles and 1,300,000 gallons of petrol were needed to move these troops and their equipment to their assembly points. Many hundreds of trains and thousands of vehicles in constant transit were essential to their supply and their continued movement. 1,880 tons of bridging equipment were used to bridge the river Maas at four points prior to the battle. Seven bridges would be needed, and because of flooding four hundred feet of folding boat equipment was brought forward to meet the emergency.

A steady intake of 7,250 tons of supplies each day had enabled General Crerar to amass 250,000 tons in his stock piles. In the last stages before the battle the daily maintenance reached 10,000 tons, which included 2,800 tons of ammunition. The variety of goods was very wide, from drugs and medical supplies; toilet rolls, and boots to shells for the super-heavy guns. A great array of buoys to mark channels in the flooded areas seemed grotesque, adding a whiff of the sea to the saturated inland scene, and this impression was enhanced by large numbers of amphibious vehicles constantly to be observed in the forward areas.

In addition to the immense road making and repairing tasks of the engineers and pioneers it was necessary to build 95 bridges, each seventy-five feet long, to span huge flooded craters twelve feet deep and up to seventy feet in diameter, blown by the enemy with 500 lb. bombs in the few existing roads. Traffic control police in close collaboration with the engineers were forced to re-route traffic each day, and to add to these problems essential traffic moved mainly by night, especially to the gun sites. The dumping programme for ammunition began on the 25th January and was completed on the night of the 1st/2nd February. In that period five hundred thousand rounds of ammunition of three hundred and fifty different kinds, and weighing eleven thousand tons, were moved forward to the gun sites and camouflaged. At that time many of the batteries, comprising a total of 1034 guns of all calibres, including more than 300 mediums, heavies and super-heavies, had not reached their positions. Errors in distribution would eliminate batteries. There were no errors.

Anticipation of extensive flooding had caused the assembly of more than half a million gallons of fog oil for burning in a probable 100,000 smoke generators in case it should be necessary to mask the whole of the left flank. These were in addition to the normal smoke stores.

Signals also made heavy demands and supplies included more than 8,000 miles of four different kinds of cable, 151,000 yards of assault cable, and 14 pairs of double armoured submarine cable to be laid across the Maas.

It would be possible to compile a dozen lists equally impressive, and all these materials had to move constantly under cover through Nijmegen and over the Maas–Waal canal, through Grave to Mook, or over the few minor roads between these two points. On the 8th February, it was estimated, trains would run into Nijmegen itself, right behind the battlefield, and in the month of February alone 350,000 tons of supplies would feed the stock piles.

On the 31st January a thaw added suddenly to the burdens of the army of road maintenance personnel, and served further to compress the great weight of transport moving in continuous streams into the area held within the loop of the Maas between Nijmegen and Grave. In every village and town the troops were assembling fast. Tilburg and s'Hertogenbosch were crammed with men and vehicles. Conferences were in constant session, and commanders from generals to second lieutenants studied the 800,000 special maps and 500,000 air photographs together with massive sheaves of orders, which had been prepared for them.

II

Operation Instruction No. 47 issued on the 3rd February announced simply: '30 Corps will destroy the enemy between the R. Maas and R. Rhine and break through in a southerly direction between the two rivers."

The simplicity of such instructions contrasts oddly with the immense complications of the tasks involved. On the 4th February the troops detailed for the opening attack began to move forward into the six mile wide funnel between Nijmegen and Mook. They moved essentially on two roads, the one through Nijmegen itself to the left flanking positions, and through Grave to the right flank. In scores of towns and villages of south-west Holland the forward brigades of the 15th Scottish, the 53rd Wessex, and the 51st Highland Divisions, who, together with the 2nd and 3rd Canadian Divisions, would provide the spearhead, made ready for battle. The pipe band of the Camerons had marched through Breda to thrill even the jaded inhabitants and to excite their own hearts in celebration of the birthday of Princess Beatrix. In every town and hamlet there had been outbreaks of "spit and polish", and the "loads of bull" which often in the British Army presage rough times ahead.

Reacting with remarkable patience and kindness to the upheavals which seemed in five months to have become a part of life, the Dutch wished the men God speed, and even produced in some villages concertina bands to cheer the marching troops. Perhaps, at last, the end was in sight.

In scores of headquarters, commanders of battalions, brigades, divisons, corps, and armies, focused their whole attention upon the battlefield. To the west, along the line of the Maas and facing north, the Canadian 1st Army maintained responsibility, which included dummy positions and concentrations intended to mask the intention of the Rhineland battle and to suggest to the enemy an attack directed upon Utrecht. In the north centre the 30th Corps confronted the mass of the Reichswald forest and the flooded complexities of its flanks. To the south the greatly depleted forces of the 2nd Army maintained a watch on the Maas. It would not take part in the battle. Farther to the south the U.S. 9th Army assumed responsibility for the still strongly held enemy positions at Venlo and Roermond and prepared to cross the River Roer in "Operation Grenade". On the right flank the U.S. 1st Army at last moved against the Roer dams.

Thus on the morning of the 4th February four armies from the Nijmegen bridgehead to the Ardennes stirred to the opening phases of mounting the greatest battle of the campaign since Normandy. Here from the Ardennes to the extreme north was one front, one battlefield, plain for all to see, and beyond a shadow of doubt. Field Marshal Montgomery had seen it for many months, and now his long argument for one ground force commander north of the Ardennes was underlined by topography, strategy and military necessity. It was underlined above all by the Roer and Erft river dams.

But the argument was an argument no longer, thrown out by the Supreme Commander, and so bitterly opposed by General Bradley that its further pursuit would have had grave consequences. Yet the broken strategy inherent in the positions of the U.S. 12th Army Group was never more apparent.

There was no longer any attempt on the part of General Bradley to veil his dislike for Field Marshal Montgomery. Even at the end of January, with Montgomery committed to the battle of the Rhineland, Bradley continued to urge upon the Supreme Commander to permit his armies to drive through the Eifel to the Rhine, and to relegate the northern battle to a secondary role.

Eisenhower, however, was adamant. He had always intended that the major thrust should be in the north, and all Bradley's eloquence failed to move him. On the 1st February Bradley was ordered to halt his armies. It was time—past time—to move troops to strengthen the U.S. 9th Army. It was also past time for General Hodges' 1st Army to attack, and to gain control of the Roer and Erft dams. This was a task Bradley had wished to avoid, for the control of the dams by the enemy strengthened his argument for the main thrust in the south centre, and it is difficult (for this writer) to avoid the conclusion that the immense strategic importance of the dams in the northern battlefield coloured General Bradley's thinking. Eisenhower, however, ordered Bradley to employ a force of "two or three divisions" to do the job, and on the 4th February Hodges attacked. Once again the key target was Schmidt.

At the same time General Bradley told Patton and Hodges to press on with their advances until the 10th. Patton, in any case, had no intention of halting, although he realized the need to keep his intentions quiet. Patton continued to advance in the Eifel north of the Moselle under the impression that he and General Bradley were "putting something over on SHAEF", and above all upon Field Marshal Montgomery. "The matter was kept quiet so as not to draw objections from Field Marshal Montgomery."[1]

But the Field Marshal, with his vision ranging over the whole

[1]Pogue. "The Supreme Command."

northern battlefield, was well aware of these things, and he maintained a stream of protests that "the operations in the north were not being properly backed".

Only Field Marshal Montgomery can say how much or how little he relied upon the opening on time of "Operation Grenade" as the right arm of the embrace he had designed to crush the German armies in the northern Rhineland. It is certain that he viewed the slow progress of the attack upon the dams with grave misgiving, and was resolved to fight with his strong left arm, even if his right remained tied behind his back. He knew that his forces would face the most powerful troops and defensive positions remaining to the enemy on the western front. He knew that if Hodges failed in his attack on the dams and the enemy succeeded in flooding the Roer valley, thereby immobilizing the U.S. 9th Army, massive reinforcements would become available against the Canadian 1st Army. With memories of Caen and the great battle of the hinge in Normandy such an eventuality may have seemed fore-ordained, an eventuality even to be wished for. Indeed, it is possible that such considerations played a part in the massive build-up of men and weapons.

Such then is a glimpse of the position on the front north of the Ardennes on the eve of "Veritable". It was a vision which did not greatly concern Lieut.-Gen. Horrocks, commanding the British 30th Corps and the 2nd and 3rd Canadian Divisions in the opening phases of the coming battle. His immediate problem was one of construction, the launching of more than 200,000 men and their armour "through the eye of a needle".

III

The Reichswald forest, a dark coniferous mass some ten miles in depth from west to east and five miles wide, filled the centre of the immediate battlefield facing the British 30th Corps. The forest is flanked on the north by the town of Cleves, and to the south by the railway and road junction of Goch, the heart and main anchor of a powerful defensive system. In the north-west corner the gently undulating forest land rises to a height of 150 feet, and between the edge of the forest and the town of Cleves a narrow neck of high ground forms an escarpment to shelter the town from the south.

The Canadian 2nd and 3rd Divisions had maintained their forward defensive localities on the fringe of the forest proper in the area of Groesbeek immediately facing the forward defensive system of the Siegfried Line running from Wyler to anchor on the Maas south of Mook. Throughout all the long winter of preparation these troops alone had held the bridgehead, actively patrolling and denying information to the enemy. Up to the very eve of battle no enemy patrol could hope to gain the identification of any unit other than Canadian.

The Canadian positions round Groesbeek would be the start line for the attack which would open the battle of the Rhineland. It would be essential for the Canadians to secure the village of Den Heuvel, gain Wyler, and thus open the main road through from Nijmegen to Kranenberg.

The Reichswald was a State forest cut into rectangles by long tracks and rides, giving long fields of fire to the defenders. The forest was closely planted, and giving a visibility of no more than a dozen yards except in the clearings and along the rides. Old clearings had become thickly overgrown with low scrub, but the new clearings would give fields of vision up to two to three hundred yards. There were small groups of deciduous trees. Maps were unreliable, and air photographs had failed to add precise knowledge of the conditions on the ground. Many of the rides and tracks were overgrown, others were sandy. It was certain that the going would be hard or impossible for wheeled or tracked transport.

Two new roads of concrete ran through from north to south, from Cleves converging at Hekkens, the one curving through Kranenberg–Frasselt, the other through Bedberg. These roads enclosed roughly the central third of the forest area, including the neck of high ground known as "the Materborn feature", and covering the town of Cleves.

From the Hekkens crossroads the road runs west to Gennep and south-east through Asperden to Goch. The main Cleves–Goch road bounds the forest to the east. Beyond it lies the railway and the small forest of Cleves, a tight square mile of trees in the centre of the position.

The heavily fortified town of Goch, normally a considerable manufacturing centre of some 15,000 inhabitants, was surrounded by a maze of concrete pill boxes, and anchored to the two main defensive systems of the Siegfried Line, the westernmost covering the Kranenberg–Frasselt–Hekkens–Goch road, the other anchored on the defences of Cleves in the north, passing behind the forest of Cleves, sited east of the railway line to Goch. Beyond this lay a third main defensive system running from Rees forward of the Hochwald forest and continuing south to Geldern. This was known as the Hochwald lay-back, the last line of defence covering the Rhine and the Wesel road and rail bridges.

The immediate enemy defences of the whole area consisted of continuous trenches along the east bank of the Maas, and an anti-tank ditch covering the western edge of the Reichswald forest. These first defensive positions were organized for two thousand yards in depth. Road blocks and anti-tank guns covered all roads, rides and tracks. Trench systems had been dug to defend the Materborn feature linking in with the main defences of Cleves. Further trench systems and strong points had been developed at Nutterden and Donsbruggen on the road between Kranenberg and Cleves.

Isolated farms in the Reichswald, and small villages everywhere, were known to be strong points and self-contained "boxes of defence". Minefields and wire had been laid on an elaborate scale. The whole area of the battlefield comprised the flood plains of the Rhine, Maas and Niers rivers, low undulating forest alternating with marshes, backwaters and flood channels. Tall poplars revealed the lines of many ditches, and orchards often surrounded the smaller villages.

The river Maas was flooded up to 1,000 yards on both banks, and the river Niers had overflowed to turn its water meadows into swamps. In the north the Rhine floods had converted the land north of the Nijmegen–Cleves road to a series of inland lakes.

This whole formidable area, with Cleves and Goch as the hinges of its powerful and narrow jaws, had to be forced against the finest troops remaining to the German army in the west, the 1st Parachute Army under Army Group H. These troops, paratroops only in name, were none the less highly trained, young, and dedicated to the defence of their homeland. The 84th Division defended the Reichswald forest, and with the 180th, 190th and 606th Divisions in close reserve, supported by a probable 114 guns.

It was clear that if the U.S. 1st Army's assault on the Roer dams should fail, and the U.S. 9th Army should be immobilized, the enemy would be able to move heavy reinforcements to the northern battlefield. There also remained the possibility of further extensive flooding on the northern flank, and the whole battlefield wore an aspect of isolation, an island in the midst of its rivers and floods, and without possibility of expansion.

A sense of excitement, of decisive events in the making, was inescapable. It seemed to imbue all ranks as they struggled forward, manhandling trucks, guns, equipment, brewing up thick brown tea by the roadsides, extraordinarily patient. Even the least observant among them could not fail to be aware of the immense weight of guns and armour building up, and few doubted that the story which had begun on D-day on the Normandy beaches was at last nearing its end.

IV

The troops immediately available to Lieut.-General Sir Brian Horrocks, commanding the 30th Corps, were the 2nd and 3rd Canadian Infantry Divisions, the 15th (Scottish), the 43rd (Wessex), the 51st (Highland) and the 53rd (Welsh) Infantry Divisions, the Guards Armoured Division, the 6th Guards Armoured Brigade, the 8th and 34th Armoured Brigades, and the 30th Armoured Brigade of the 79th Armoured Division. These were supported by the guns of the Canadian 2nd A.G.R.A. and the British 3rd, 4th, 5th and 9th A.G.'s R.A., the 74th A.A. Brigade, the 106th A.A. Brigade and the Canadian rocket battery. In the air the 2nd Tactical Air Force would provide close support, while on D minus 1 one thousand bombers of the R.A.F., supported by heavy and medium bombers of the U.S. 8th and 9th Air Forces, would attempt to blast the key towns of Cleves, Goch and Emmerich from the face of the earth.

All this, together with the opening barrage of more than 1,000 guns, to which would be added the fire pattern of three machine gun battalions and the 8th Armoured Brigade's tanks revealed

Field Marshal Montgomery's intention to shoot his way in to the battlefield, and to force the jaws closing the way to the Rhine.

But the tactical plan and the tactical battle on the ground belonged in the early stages to General Horrocks. He had decided to attack with five divisions up, to force the narrow Materborn gap, to open the road through Cleves, and to burst out into the more open country. It was a plan which would have been optimistic over hard ground, for it entailed the swift passage of one armoured and two infantry divisions on a single main axis of doubtful capacity. Over the saturated and flooded ground ahead it loomed as a nightmare, a nightmare to be faced, none the less, with that wry humour and dogged courage which, although it may seem old fashioned, has been one of the distinguishing characteristics of British troops at least since the Crimea.

The line up, and the intention, was as follows:—

Right:

51st Highland Division, to capture, clear and hold the high ground north of the south-west corner of the Reichswald, to swing south and hold down enemy attempts to move troops to the north. To open route Mook–Gennep–Hekkens–Goch.
Take over Goch from 43rd Wessex Division.

Inside right:

53rd Welsh Division, to seize the high ground on the northern edge of the forest, and move east through the northern half of the Reichswald.

Centre:

15th Scottish Division, to capture Kranenberg; to breach the Siegfried Line north of the Reichswald, capture Nutterden and the Materborn feature. To attempt to capture Udem and Calcar with mobile columns, and clear Emmerich road to west bank of the Rhine. To clear and hold Cleves.

Inside left:

2nd Canadian Division, to capture Den Heuvel and Wyler, and open the main road to Berg-en-Dal.

Outside left:

3rd Canadian Division, to protect the left flank, to capture and clear the low ground between the main road Wyler–Kranenberg–

Cleves and the Rhine up to the line of the railway Cleves–Griethausen. The 43rd Wessex Division to follow up and pass through the 15th Scottish Division, to capture Goch. Prepare to hand over to the 51st Highland Division, and exploit south-east to Weeze, Kevelaer, Geldern.

Guards Armoured Division, to pass through Materborn behind the 43rd Division, and advance on axis Udem–Hammerbruch–Wesel. To capture and hold the high ground north of Sonsbeek. Push forward mobile columns to capture Wesel bridge (if intact). Capture Xanten.

In support:

22nd Dragoons
141st R.A.C.
6th Assault Regt. R.E.

At 5 o'clock on the morning of the 8th February the barrage would open. At half past seven o'clock a smoke screen would be laid by the guns for ten minutes, to be followed by ten minutes of silence to give the Survey Regiment a chance to locate any enemy batteries which might be active. At twenty minutes past nine o'clock a barrage of high explosive and smoke would open to be followed by a complete barrage at ten o'clock, heralding H hour at half past ten o'clock.

That was the bare bones of the programme which would launch five divisions into the battle. The detail was immense. It was studied in the days before the battle by all the commanders concerned, and especially by the brigadiers of the 15th Scottish Division, for they were the spearhead. On them, on their ability to thrust through with speed, must depend the whole timetable of events to follow. The heavy thaw had set in, and through the mud by night the brigades heaved themselves with great difficulty and determination into their forward positions.

V

Each night of the first week of February, as soon as it was dusk, the armoured brigades, the machine gun battalions, the Field Regiments of Royal Artillery, the Field Companies of Royal

Engineers, and all the strange and varied paraphernalia of warfare, moved forward on converging lines through Grave and Nijmegen to add their fire power to the opening barrage, and to drench the forward positions of the enemy with lead. The Field companies of the Royal Engineers would open the way.

Only two axial roads were available, the one from Eindhoven through Mook to Nijmegen, the other from Tilburg through s'Hertogenbosch and Grave to Nijmegen. All movement by day, except for reconnaissance groups, was forbidden forward of the Eindhoven–s'Hertogenbosch road.

On the night of the 4th February in pitch darkness and in relentless rain the leading brigades of the 15th Scottish, the 53rd Welsh and the 51st Highland Divisions, began to move. All divisional signs had been removed. Each truck, each kangaroo with its load of men preserved an anonymity, and it was as though eyeless creatures felt their ways through a nightmare. The road Eindhoven–Mook–Nijmegen swiftly collapsed and became a morass, ill defined, of liquid mud in which the Provost companies, the R.E.s and the Pioneers toiled with a desperate, yet inspired, fatalism, bulldozing, laying mattresses of logs, creating diversions where no diversions were reasonably possible, always saturated, yet always sustained by a relentless driving force, directing the tortured streams of men and vehicles through the hours of darkness. Only by efforts beyond all normal expectation were the roads cleared by daylight. There was no comfort, no possibility or expectation of comfort, no hope of reward, and no wish for anything other than to do whatever task there was to do. Such was the spirit animating this great body of men, and which seemed like a miracle, and which, making war possible, could, if it could be produced in peace, make peace possible also. It existed in all those who must fight, and in most of those who, directly in contact, aided them to fight.

The rain beat down in that incessant steady rhythm of permanence, and neither by day or night did the sky show a loophole of hope. An all pervading blanket submerged men and vehicles in morasses of mud. Yet there were very few signs of depression in those long columns, which were still as often as they moved. The suck and squelch of many boots, the roar of engines, muffled curses and a multitude of metallic noises filled the nights. In the trucks many sat, lay, sprawled, according to their luck, invariably in silence, some few sheltering the glow of cigarettes in the cups of hands grown red and calloused.

No rewards of peace could have induced men to this patience, to this readiness for incessant effort, to labour until they dropped, to live in mud, and often to sleep in it, to feed upon biscuit and bully beef and mugs of "char" of a more horrible milk-and-sugared kind than they had ever known. Above all to die, to crawl over wire and mines to drag back some person previously unknown, to share a last cigarette.

It was—it is—a miracle impossible for me to define, a platitude of war which must be stated, a phenomenon, perhaps of human perversity, perhaps a pointer to the possibility of human greatness. All men who have known this experience must hunger for it, a vision as unattainable as the Holy Grail, proving what might be.

But something had happened in that first week of February to renew drooping spirits. For months men had been lost, directionless in scores of bleak wildernesses, all different, all with a dreadful drab sameness, the dereliction and emptiness of war which must be filled with the human spirit to render it tolerable. Week after week men had filled recurring vacuums of mud, in barns, billets, dykes and dug-outs, unaware of where they were, or why—except in the larger sense that this was the madness of war, and its demands were infinite. As men arrived wet and weary at a journey's end it might prove, as often as not, merely a beginning. They might be urged irritably to double back on their tracks. They would enter the first dry billet they had known for weeks only to about turn before their blankets were down. Always death might be in the midst of it. Few men of the 15th Scottish, the 53rd Welsh, the 51st Highland, were unaware of that, old Baldy, young Toby, Jenks—the lists were lengthening—had "bought it". These were their milestones.

In the course of a few weeks those who followed and tried to keep track would encounter the same battalions in a dozen different places, whether in Belgium or Holland very few knew or cared, one week in south-western Holland watching the grey Maas, another in the snows of the Ardennes. Then back again. Some were often under fire, knowing an enemy, others almost never, alerted, taking cover, digging in, waiting, mortared and shelled. Off again. It seemed purposeless, undoubtedly mad. It was war. Yet in all the frustration a response was evoked from every kind of man which no other human activity on a large scale has been able to approach. Men were at the same time individuals and a part of a great whole. All the petty irritations and stresses of life had been removed, and replaced by fundamentals. There was always humour.

And then, suddenly, on the 4th February there was the sense of direction for which thousands had been waiting, knowing that it must come. It came down from the top, from the Field Marshal visiting his old division, through the Corps Commander inspiring the battalions of the 15th Scottish, and setting off such a glow with his words, his controlled yet infectious enthusiasm, that it spread down through all ranks. In many diaries are the words—"This might be the end."

Everyone knew where he was going. It was eastward at last, east and always east, into Germany, to engage and defeat the enemy in his homeland.

Thus on the nights of the 4th, 5th and 6th February the three leading divisions forced their ways through morasses of mud over two roads, one of which was not a road, and through drenching rain in complete darkness. For a week the infantry had worked with the armour, the tank crews, the men of the flails and kangaroos, petards, crocodiles, and a host of strange devices. As they came into the bridgehead the reconnaissance parties went forward into the Canadian F.D.L.s, into Nederijksche wood and Groesbeek, looking out over the flat land between them and the first line of enemy defences, and to the dark barrier of the Reichswald towering on the rising ground, formidable and forbidding. To the left there was nothing but flood water beyond the Nijmegen–Cleves road, the main axis, flood water of uncertain depths hiding the wire and mines of the ground defences.

The enemy was aroused to mortar the road to Groesbeek as the Field Companies of Royal Engineers laboured to make it possible for men and armour to reach their start lines. The mines were very deep and difficult to locate. Bulldozers pushed trees off the road, and exploded mines. Many dykes were bridged and ditches filled while mattresses of logs were laid over the worst stretches. It was routine work, work which had been done again and again, work which was never done, but this time the R.E.s felt a new rhythm in it. They too knew where they were going.

Farther back on the western edge of the forward area the crews of tanks, flails and kangaroos were "marrying" up with the infantry they would support and carry. On D minus one the guns were still coming up, finding their camouflaged sites and stocks of ammunition, digging in with not a minute to lose. By dusk the 46th Infantry Brigade was on its mark to the left, the 71st Infantry Brigade was in the centre, the only Welsh voices in all the lilt of Scots, and on the right the 154th Infantry Brigade, the assault brigades of the 15th, the 53rd and 51st Divisions. From Groesbeek back through Nijmegen and Grave to Tilburg every square inch of sodden ground, road and ditch was packed with men and vehicles and guns. It was the end of silence.

13

"VERITABLE"—THE OPENING PHASE

I

THE downpour abated in early afternoon, and towards evening on the 7th the rain ceased. The sky, which had been like mud for some days, had cleared to the pale colour of oysters. In the waiting silence it seemed that some giant metronome measured off the minutes, soundless yet insistent. The spires of the churches of Cuick and Gennep rose above the sable belt of the Maas like steel grey spears, austerely beautiful, borrowing pale light from the pale sky. Yet the impression in that serenity of the swollen river, the flooded meadows, the dark forest, the villages, the spires piercing the sky, was one of menace.

It was impossible to believe that the enemy was ignorant of the huge force ready to burst upon him, of the stillness of fifty thousand men wedged into the narrow bridgehead. Between six o'clock and nine o'clock there was scarcely a sound in all the region of the Maas from Nijmegen to below the village of Cuick. Men lay or squatted or stood about in barns, schools, vehicles, heads propped on hands, waiting, seeming thoughtful, some sleeping. The darkness came like a benison, and shortly before nine o'clock a muffled roar grew out of the western sky, rose to a crescendo overhead, and within seconds exploded in the opening deluge of the air bombardment. Nearly two thousand tons of high explosive thundered down upon the ancient town of Cleves to heave it out by the roots in eruptions of dreadful violence. Most men knew the meaning of that shuddering impact of sound:

D minus one. Heavy bombers will obliterate Emmerich, Cleves, Goch . . . .

Not only Emmerich, Cleves and Goch but also the smaller townships of Weeze, Udem and Calcar, key links in the main enemy defensive line. Each one of these was uprooted to subside in a shapeless chaos, admirable for defence and impassable for the armour and vehicles of attacking troops. Over all the area of the coming battlefield the sky flickered with gun fire, with a colour wash reflected from the surging flames. The river mirrored the crimson trails of tracer, and on its banks scores of simple men, of the Gordons, the Black Watch, the Royal Welsh Fusiliers, the Oxford and Bucks, the East Lancashires, reflected some of the meaning in their eyes, and their reddened faces, intensely alive. Forward from Groesbeek and Nederijksche wood there were the valiant echoes of a valiant past, in the names of the regiments, all England, Scotland and Wales, the Glasgow Highlanders in the van, the Cameronians, the Argyll and Sutherland Highlanders, the Scots Guards and the Coldstreams, the Derbyshire Yeomanry, the Lothians, the Fife and Forfar, the names like the music of tradition sounding down the years.

Soon after midnight it was apparent that the narrow muddied axes of the 46th and 227th Brigades forward of the river would be of doubtful service even to sustain the initial assault. Even the flails and tanks in support of the leading battalions might fail to get through, and to think beyond that was unprofitable. The difficulties would be immense: it would be necessary to surmount them.

These considerations were very clear to battalion commanders and engineers, less clear to divisional commanders, and might have escaped the attention of those higher up. It was certain that the road Nijmegen–Wyler–Kranenberg–Cleves must be opened without any delay, and that the road Mook–Gennep and thence to Goch must swiftly become available. Without these two roads it would be impossible to fight the battle of the Rhineland.

The Regimental Aid posts had been established as far forward as possible on the start lines. Engineers and pioneers worked tirelessly to keep the muddied tracks open.

On the northern flank of the Reichswald the Regiment de Maisonneuve and the Calgary Highlanders of the 5th Canadian Brigade of the Canadian 2nd Division, prepared to seize Den Heuvel and Wyler, and to open up the main axis. Until that was done the 44th Brigade of the 15th Scottish Division and the 43rd Division behind them would be immovable in Nijmegen. Already in the hours of darkness the waters were rising to threaten the road, and to force the Canadian 3rd Division into the water over the whole northern flank.

All through the night the men of the infantry battalions were moving to their assembly areas over the deeply rutted tracks through the gun lines. Many spent the entire night in kangaroos, jogging, jolting, slithering and slewing yard by yard. A few, mainly of the leading brigades of the 51st and 53rd Divisions, enjoyed some sleep, and the first entry in the war diary of the 1st Battalion the Oxford and Bucks light infantry for the 8th February is a laconic comment on the opening of the heaviest barrage fired by British guns in the Second World War:

0500 hours. Reveille!

At that hour all those troops still passing through the gun lines felt the tremendous impact of one thousand guns bursting suddenly into action. Reveille may have been at an earlier hour for many that morning: it is certain that for none was it later. The effect on those who lay or moved under the guns was awe inspiring, constraining a new awareness, a tentative appraisement of what might lie ahead. Impossible to imagine the effect upon the enemy as the air vibrated with incessant thunder to deaden the senses, and the earth shuddered.

It was some time before eyes and ears adjusted to the din and the gigantic panorama of the sky, and at no point, I think, was the spectacle at once more splendid and awe-inspiring than on the banks of the Maas in that stretch of the river between the steeples of Cuick and Gennep. All the wild pattern of the sky kindled the grey water to the semblance of a boiling cauldron of fire and flame. Soon it was possible to distinguish the instruments in the vast uproar, the heavies and mediums in layers above the threshing and burping of the smaller weapons. Underneath the great weight of the barrage the bofors were firing flat while the tanks of the armoured brigades and the machine gunners of three battalions drenched the forward positions of the enemy.

Slowly the sky lightened, and at half past seven o'clock the barrage lifted for ten minutes of an eerie silence in which all normal movement seemed deadened and unreal. Tanks, kangaroos and a host of vehicles lumbered forward all lurid with cerise fluorescent panels, giving them a look of fury as though they had come up dripping with blood and fire from hell, or the depths of the Maas.

When the barrage lifted from its opening phases at half past ten o'clock, and the forward troops advanced on its heels through the minefields, it seemed that no man could have lived in the enemy positions, that no tree could still be left standing in all the Reichswald forest. The Glasgow Highlanders, leading the attack in the centre, were within five hundred yards of the enemy. All but one of their flail tanks had bogged down on the start line, and the infantry went on alone. Behind them the one remaining flail cleared a path through the minefield for the tanks, and the tanks of the Coldstreams surged through to engage anti-tank guns and 88's before they, too, bogged down. But the Glasgow Highlanders had brushed aside the slight opposition from the dazed enemy in the forward trenches, and were on the German frontier with their right flank on Lubertsche Straat, and their centre overwhelming the villages of Haus Kreuzfuhrt and Hettsteeg. The enemy had been called upon to endure a sustained weight of fire calculated to dull the senses, and it is astounding that he was able to react so well. On that small stretch of front the Glasgow Highlanders had the best of it, but on their left it was more difficult. The Canadians had swooped upon Den Heuvel with scarcely a shot fired, but the Calgary Highlanders, fighting to clear the vital road point at the small town of Wyler, met a resolute enemy behind a maze of mines, and as the day grew towards dusk heavy artillery and bombers were called to their aid. It was night before Wyler was cleared, and the road was not yet open. The rain had begun again soon after dawn, and all through the day the 44th Brigade of the 15th Scottish had waited to go forward from Nijmegen to join the 46th and the 227th. But the 46th and the 227th looked to their fronts. The Argyll and Sutherland Highlanders, leading the attack on Kranenberg, rode the tanks of the Scots Guards through an old minefield left by the U.S. Airborne troops, and were at once under heavy enemy fire. The flails and all the carriers had bogged down in the sea of mud churned up by the Churchill tanks. A sergeant, striving to blaze a trail through the minefield, lost a foot. Heavy mortaring began to take a steady toll, killing off all the officers of the company on the left at a single blow. Rallied by the company sergeant-major the company went on, and within the hour the Argylls were on the German frontier while the H.L.I. struggled through to join in the assault on Kranenberg.

The light outer crust of the enemy defences had crumbled without much difficulty. The Cameronians, going in behind the Glasgow Highlanders, soon after middle day had time to curse their own artillery for falling short, while some said that the gunners seemed to have forgotten about hill clearance after so much time in the flat lands of Holland. Patrols of the Cameronians probing into the outskirts of Frasselt in the valley found the village strongly held, and the battalion called for armour and crocodiles to aid in the main attack. On the fearsome shambles of the brigade axis pioneers and engineers worked like demons to help the armour into the battle.

Before dusk the H.L.I. had got across the main enemy anti-tank ditch to join with the Argylls in the assault on Kranenberg. One tank of the Scots Guards had somehow churned its way through with the Argylls only to bog down within sight of Kranenberg railway station. It had done fine service.

In the late afternoon these troops on the high ground round Kranenberg had been cheered by the sight of the Cameronians searing their way into Frasselt behind flame-throwing crocodiles, and fighting with grenades from house to house. By nightfall the forward battalions, in awful discomfort on the sodden earth, knew themselves inside Germany, never to look back. For some of them there was that night the miracle of a hot meal, for battalion and company cooks had caught the inspiration of the drive into Germany proper, and men toiled forward on foot, in and out of ditches, caked in mud, bearing the precious containers to put warmth into the troops.

The two leading brigades of the 15th Scottish had done well, but they were not alone. On their right the Cameronians could see the Royal Welsh Fusiliers going into the forest with the flails of the Westminster Dragoons and the tanks of 147 R.A.C. It was heartening, but on the mind of every battalion commander was the acute awareness of the shambles of the axis, and the knowledge that his men might be isolated and without armour, to stick it out without much cover and less comfort, very thin on the ground. Each battalion was without its transport, and behind them A.V.s R.E. of every kind, some bearing fascines and bridges for the anti-tank ditches, were fouling the trees at the sides of the narrow tracks. It seemed impossible that men and armour would be able to get through. It was a fight against nature, against the rising floods already ominous, more than against the enemy.

On the right the way to the forest for the 53rd and the 51st Divisions, and the way to the Mook–Gennep road was easier in the early stages. The 1st Battalion the Black Watch with ten Churchills, crocodiles and flails, had found the going comparatively easy at first, and were more than three hundred yards inside the Reichswald itself by 12.45, and on high ground inside Germany. On their left the 7th Battalion of the Black Watch was also making progress with one troop of tanks supporting each company, and with its A.V.s R.E. and fascines churning along somehow.

On the extreme right the 2nd Derbyshire Yeomanry was performing miracles with the 5th/7th Gordons, and by midnight they too were established on the high ground to the south-east, having reached their objective in the midst of an enemy take-over. For more than an hour the Gordons, heavily outnumbered, had fought fiercely hand to hand in the forest in the pitch darkness before they beat off an enemy even more confused than themselves.

In the centre the 71st Brigade of the 53rd had achieved its miracles. The H.L.I. had forced their way forward on the right of the Royal Welsh Fusiliers, while on their left the Oxford and Bucks crossed the anti-tank ditch and were inside Germany by early afternoon.

Thus by midnight at the end of the first day four brigades of three divisions had reached their objectives with their assault battalions and odd fragments of their armour. The Gordons of the 227th Brigade had been forced to wait back in Nederijksche wood to come under command of the 44th Brigade when the 44th could get through.

By all reasonable measures the way in on the axes of the 46th and 227th Brigades was non-existent, and the main road was not open through Wyler, and thus on to Kranenberg, before nine o'clock at night. The Canadians had had a tremendous struggle to make good their opening role, and the mines were deadly. All through the day and far into the night of the 8th February the troops of the 44th waited in their kangaroos on the outskirts of Nijmegen, exposed to the cold incessant drizzle which had begun soon after dawn, and to the minor but unpleasant attentions of the Luftwaffe. The struggle of the armoured force supporting the 44th to force its way forward to join battle is itself an epic of the determination and endurance of men. All along that hopeless shambles of the brigade axis men laboured to get the armour moving, many with tears of rage seaming faces thick with grime, others drawn and haggard beyond all normal measurements of exhaustion. The scene was nightmarish, wild with the stark monstrous patterns of massive vehicles, the huge shapes of the bridging tanks, cranes, fascines, bulldozers, standing out against the outlines of splintered trees. All these in a lurching, towering, roaring, heaving chaos of sound and movement. Deep ditches lined the narrow track on the 46th Brigade axis. There was no room to manoeuvre, and when at last the armoured force had ploughed through over that diabolical route, its men worn out with the struggle, there was then forthcoming the leadership and the strength to press on. By that great effort the anti-tank ditch was reached and bridged, and the way cleared for the assault on the main defences of the Siegfried Line.

In such conditions as these Brigadier Cumming Bruce commanding the 44th Brigade passed his brigade through to mount attacks on the vital twin hills of the Materborn protecting Cleves. That great effort to get through had finished the axes available to the 15th Scottish Division.

Meanwhile the Canadian 3rd Division had embarked on its watery task of clearing and covering the whole northern flank to the Rhine banks at Emmerich. Embarked is the literal word. Already the rising floods had washed out the bridge on the Canadian 7th Brigade axis, and because of this, and the flood probabilities still to be considered, the division had exchanged its tanks for buffaloes. In these lightly armed and lightly armoured amphibious vehicles the Canadians sailed in the late afternoon of the 8th February from Wainwright Beach, named after the Canadian buffalo reserve, and set forth into the night over the mines and wire at the northern limits of the Seigfried Line. The 7th Brigade took Zyfflich while the 8th Brigade "landed" at Zandpol and Leuth. The water was by that time at least three feet deep over most of the flood plain beyond the Rhine bunds, and rising to lap the main Nijmegen–Cleves road. Those troops which had assaulted their objectives on foot in the early stages were swiftly marooned, sharing the first floors of houses and the roofs of barns with surviving livestock and the enemy.

II

The 9th and 10th February were critical days at the extremities of the entire northern front. On the 9th the U.S. 1st Army was once more in Schmidt with its troops bearing down irresistibly upon the Roer and Urft river dams. It was too late. Holding their positions to the last moment, but not beyond it, the Germans opened the sluices to release a cataract of water to surge through Duren in a great wave to join the flooded Maas at Roermond. On the morning of the 10th February the British forces committed to the Rhineland battle knew that "Operation Grenade" would not take place; that the U.S. 9th Army was immobilized for an unpredictable period, and that they would fight alone.

At once the enemy began to move reinforcements from the Cologne plain to confront the 30th Corps in its attempts to burst through and out of the Reichswald forest area. For the Germans the time for strategy had passed; all that they could do was to fight from day to day, and without thought for the future. Troops were committed piecemeal to the battle as they arrived, for the situation was desperate. Five hundred thousand refugees were reported to be pouring into and through Berlin as the victorious Russian armies drove on through Silesia, and this news was as alarming to the enemy as it was heartening to the British. Yet the morale of the enemy was high, and there was no inclination at this stage to underestimate the fighting capacity of men making a last stand before the Rhine.

For at least two weeks it seemed certain that the battle of the Rhineland would be isolated with the British and Germans locked in a death struggle in forest, bog and flood, and almost surrounded by water. The tremendous barrage fired to launch "Operation

Veritable" had successfully eased the assault battalions onto their first objectives, but beyond those points it was clear by the end of the second day that the enemy was resolved to fight bitterly for every yard of German soil back to the Rhine.

In the extreme north the Germans had also called their last water resources to their aid. The main Rhine dykes had been breached at the outset, and the weight of flood water swiftly collapsed the Quer Dam and threatened the essential British axis of advance, especially on the stretch of road from Wyler to Kranenberg. To reinforce this flood the enemy blew the northern gates of the Spoy Canal, and with that the whole area north of the Cleves–Calcar road became a lake, lethal with submerged obstacles at unpredictable and varying depths.

The troops of the 15th Scottish were at once forced onto the railway line through Kranenberg, but even that was under water by the 12th February, and the main axis was under three feet of water with the troops and vehicles of elements of three divisions piled up in appalling confusion as the 43rd Division strove to get through.

Probably, partly as a result of this immense flooding of the Rhine and Roer, the Maas and Niers continued to rise steadily to hamper the bridging operations, and the forward movement of supporting troops, armour and artillery.

In attempts to counter the floods Royal Engineers blew the dykes north-east of Nijmegen on the advice of the Dutch, and sent two million gallons of water an hour in a counter barrage to roll back water with water. The enemy at once breached the dykes of the Alter Rhine, and it seemed to the troops struggling over the Nijmegen–Cleves road that they fought along the shores of an inland sea with the tide steadily rising. The spires of churches, the crowns and tattered sails of windmills, roof tops and telegraph poles, with here and there the branches of trees, stood out ominously from a wild waterscape as broad as the estuary of the River Plate. Over this waste of water, whipped to white horses by a fitful wind, and under an incessant drizzle of rain, the Canadian 3rd Division developed a form of "naval" warfare piloted by British crews in ungainly buffaloes, weasels and amphibious jeeps. Navigating with land maps, taking bearings on steeples, and constantly attempting to avoid the elaborate wire and minefields of the hidden defences, the buffaloes, buffeted by the waves, taking water aboard across their blunt bows, moved steadily upon their objectives, answering bursts of spandau fire from windmills and roof tops with bursts from their brownings and brens.

The work of maintenance of the fleet of amphibious vehicles in addition to the immense labours to build ramps and bridges and roads, put a massive burden upon the engineers. In the midst of the waters men worked with wire cutters, their hands and arms blue with cold as they strove to release the tracks of the buffaloes from the wire. Weasels were often at the mercy of the curious cross currents, and almost as many vehicles lumbered awkwardly "hove to", stranded on wire or submerged obstacles, as moved to the attack. Now and then a vehicle heaved up out of the flood with its human cargo floundering, maimed in the water, after squatting upon a mine.

To protect the whole northern flank from enemy artillery three thousand five hundred tons of smoke supplies were brought forward, and 85,000 smoke canisters burned 500,000 gallons of fog oil to pour dense clouds of smoke across the water. Wainwright Beach was a scene of immense activity, an improvised shipyard resounding to the clang of iron on iron and steel on steel as mechanics laboured without rest, and sodden to their bones, to keep enough craft in service. For there was a danger that many of the assault troops would be as hopelessly marooned as were many of the enemy. It must be doubtful if ever before in warfare have men at the back worked so hard and tirelessly, and with such ingenuity, to supply and serve fighting troops. And they too worked often under fire.

The work of detecting and blowing up mines under water and of marking "safe" channels with improvised buoys, was in itself remarkable and highly dangerous, not alone on the main floods, but on the "dry" routes to the Materborn, Kranenberg and Cleves. All along the line pioneers and signals men matched the efforts of the engineers, laying corduroy tracks over the slush of scores of dangerous trails, laying and maintaining cables and wire, and somehow keeping supplies of ammunition and food on the move.

By nightfall on the first day the gunners had fired 500,000 shells, and as they manhandled and bulldozed the guns forward to new advanced positions new supplies followed them, as it seemed, by countless minor miracles.

All forward tracks were given names, and all laterals were numbered, in the forest regions. Coded traces were issued to aid battalions moving forward on compass bearings by day and night, "navigating" the forest by following white tapes knotted at every one hundred yards, while flank parties struggled through the undergrowth to protect the main bodies. It was warfare of a remarkably blind nature, groping for, and often encountering groups of enemy hand to hand in the darkness.

In the wake of the infantry the gunners were having a tremendous struggle, even themselves surprising pockets of enemy, especially on the 51st Division axis. There on the road to Gennep a loop of the Maas held enemy positions to harass the advancing Scots on both flanks, and on the western fringes of the forest Canadian Scottish had guided the Highland Scots to their F.D.L.s with the music of the pipes. It was in this area that gunners of the 63rd A/tank Regiment flushed the enemy out of a magnificent dug-out equipped with a piano, a grandfather clock still ticking and showing the right time in spite of the bombardment, and with pots on the boil on the stove.

By the end of the second day "Operation Veritable" had become a tactical tangle, impossible to unravel, and the story of the battle can only be built up from a mass of fragments if anything in the nature of a narrative is to be attempted. Brigade orders were changed several times a day. Battalions seldom knew what they were meant to do for more than two or three consecutive hours. Orders from the top had become meaningless, and in this situation the waging of the struggle devolved upon the shoulders of brigade and battalion commanders. Out in the front they knew what must be done, and what could be done, and they did it. The elaborate movements and timings, the steady leap-frogging planned for infantry and armour, were so much waste paper. Reliefs were impossible. Brigades, let alone divisions, could not hope to pass through those in front, and those in front stayed in front, while behind them a wedge of men, armour, guns, carriers, cranes, bridging tanks, fascines, bulldozers and a whole host of vehicles bogged down.

Yet no one faltered, and slowly order began to grow out of chaos, and the patterns desired were attained. Indeed, in the records of corps, even of divisions, very little can be learned of the Rhineland battle.

Strangely, in these early stages, simplicity lay on the flooded northern flank. The fleets of buffaloes sailed on, marooned friends and foes were steadily rescued. Gulls soared and swooped over the ragged "flotillas", and wheeled hopefully above the numerous craft trapped by the underwater wire, and escorted the lonely men struggling to reach land in collapsible boats. Magpies and crows regarded the buffaloes and their crews from the roof tops and telegraph poles. Signposts sticking out their arms above the waters indicated the invisible roads to submerged villages. A small herd of Friesian cattle huddled on a mud bank in the yard of a half submerged and shell holed farmstead, and on a strip of land a foot deep under water a solitary black horse trotted up and down, up and down, pausing only to whinny sadly. Canaries still sang in their cages framed in glassless windows. A spotted dog rushed barking furiously through the loft of a barn to stand framed in a shell hole torn in the wall. Geese, ducks, poultry, pigs, grunted and cackled, and above all was the crash and mutter of heavy guns, the harsh threat of spandaus, and the answering bursts of the brens.

Over this battlefield the Stormont, Dundas and Glengarry Highlanders, piloted by British crews, reached the Spoy canal on the 10th February, and assaulted Duffelward and Rindern, closing in to the north of Cleves, and observing the wreckage of the town. On that evening men lay out upon the Rhine bunds on the banks of the last barrier between them and the heartland of Germany.

Five miles of the main road to Cleves were then under three feet of water, and DUKWS moved forward over the flooded tracks through Kranenberg.

From the high turret of a mansion on a piece of high ground in the midst of the floods to the north-east of Cleves it was possible, even before Cleves had fallen, to look far out over all this wilderness of war, and to discern the beginnings of order on the left. Elements of an enemy parachute regiment were marooned some two thousand yards away on a small island, helpless but still dangerous. Buffaloes and weasels were busy taking blankets and food to troops isolated in the floods and to First Aid Posts. Those unfortunates marooned for the night in their buffaloes stretched tarpaulins athwart their "ships", posted look-outs, and prepared to make the best of it. The earphones of the radio telephones buzzed with messages. From somewhere out on the water a colonel asked insistently for "Control":

"Hello, Control! I say, there are six very wet and weary men out here. We're coming in soon. Hot food and a fire. How about it?"

"Can do," said the voice of Control.

Nevertheless, in this strange manner the northern flank was swiftly covered, and patrols were out on the Rhine bunds, all at a very small cost in lives. Without the 79th Armoured Division, without the vision and dogged persistence over many years of Major-General Sir Percy Hobart—for he had "conceived" and made possible all this collection of "Funnies"—it is hard to imagine how this battle, and many others in north-west Europe, could have been fought at all.

14

THE BATTLE OF THE REICHSWALD

I

BY four o'clock on the morning of the 9th February the 44th Brigade had contrived, with a dogged determination beyond all praise, to heave itself into the forefront of the battle. The 2nd Battalion the Gordons, coming under command, moved out of Nederijksche wood two hours after midnight to enter Nutterden seven hours later after battling with mines, felled trees, wire and the hazards of the trail, rather than with the enemy. Kranenberg was clear and the way was open for an assault upon the twin hills of the Materborn feature, the essential preliminary to the attack on Cleves.

Under artificial moonlight the brigade had crossed the anti-tank ditch guarding the Siegfried defences, and soon after first light the 6th Battalion K.O.S.B. had reached the narrow belt of the Reichswald immediately to the south of Nutterden. Brigadier Cumming Bruce, commanding the 44th, realizing that having got his brigade into the lead he would almost certainly stay there, reacted to the demands of the hour with energy and skill. In mid afternoon he launched the 8th Battalion R.S.F. supported by Grenadiers against one side of the Materborn while the 6th Battalion K.O.S.B. in kangaroos went in against the other.

The speed and power of these twin assaults surprised the enemy. Footholds were swiftly gained and secured, but a desperate and bitter struggle developed for control of this citadel defending Cleves, and for the escarpment and woodland belt dominating the last section of the main road. Both sides knew that every hour counted. Enemy reinforcements of quality and supported by self-propelled guns were rushing to strengthen the Cleves garrison and block the Calcar road, and the chances of "bouncing" the town, and exploiting with fast armoured cars to Calcar were rapidly diminishing.

By last light on the 9th the K.O.S.B. and the R.S.F. were secure on the feature, but a hard core of enemy remained. At the same time a squadron of the 15th Scottish Recce Regiment attempted to exploit to the south of Nutterden on the road to Hekkens through the forest. It was no easy matter to keep troops on the move in the darkness even with the help of artificial moonlight, but one battalion was established firmly on the road. A group of enemy trying to find the way forward to reinforce positions already lost fell into the hands of patrols of the Recce squadron, and two officers and fifty men added new identifications to the growing tally. Seven battalions from three reserve divisions had already been encountered, and it was clear that the enemy was moving troops with all speed through Geldern and Xanten to the north. It was also clear that the furious artillery bombardment and the constant air strikes had disrupted enemy communications and spread confusion throughout their forward defensive positions.

Meanwhile throughout the 9th the 46th and 227th Brigades had been steadily consolidating their gains, and rescuing their armour and vehicles from the mud. The padre of the 2nd Battalion the Seaforths had taken advantage of the near impossibility of further forward movement to bury the battalion dead. The Glasgow Highlanders were readying to aid in the fight for the Materborn as soon as they could get there. The 7th Battalion the Seaforths were totally involved in a battle against mud, mines and flood. Towards evening it began to sleet, and then—mildly—to snow.

Soon after dusk the enemy shelling and mortaring became severe and accurate. A direct hit on the Command Post of the 2nd Battalion the Gordons killed eleven men and wounded five, including two officers killed and one wounded, a savage end to a successful day, and a foretaste of the fire power still available to the enemy, and of the bitter struggle ahead.

It was at this hour, in these conditions of rising floods, with the axis of the 15th Scottish beyond use, and with every way forward blocked with men, vehicles, mud and water, that the 30th Corps ordered the 43rd Wessex Division to advance out of Nijmegen, to pass through the 15th Scottish, by-pass Cleves, and strike south towards Goch. It is unlikely that a more optimistic order has ever been given. It was based partly on the belief that Cleves had fallen, but it also reveals a strange failure to appreciate the true conditions forward.

In a spirit, therefore, of "theirs not to reason why"—or how—the 4th Wiltshires led the 129th Brigade of the 43rd out of Nijmegen on the night of the 9th February with the intention of advancing through the Materborn gap and the slender neck of the Reichswald east of Nutterden. It was a night of bitter cold with the rain driving in sudden fierce squalls over the water from the north-east, "a ghoulish night", according to the keeper of the record and to memory, a night with searchlights, flares, bursting shells and burning buildings revealing the desolation of water and bog in nightmarish fashion.

When the head of the brigade reached Nutterden on the fringe of the shambles of transport and armour in the wake of the 44th, and was confronted with the rising floods, it was clear that a new way forward must be found. Undaunted by the confusion, reconnaissance parties at once explored the possible secondary routes. Air photographs had given the impression of a secondary with a concrete surface. In fact the surface was of sand. The way was blocked by felled trees, skilfully mined and covered by spandau fire, but the 4th Wiltshires pressed on with the 5th Wiltshires and the 4th Somerset Light Infantry close behind.

The record of that night lives only in the minds of those who travelled that road, fighting in the pitch darkness with an invisible enemy, firing at gun flashes, and steeling nerves against the murderous bursts of mortar bombs. The remarkable truth is that at first light the 4th Wiltshires reached the outskirts of Cleves near the junction of the Goch–Bedburg road. Southward lay the planned line of their main attack, for the divisional task was to roll up the Siegfried Line from north to south while the 15th Scottish pressed on beyond Cleves to Calcar, the 53rd cleared the forest, and the 51st, having secured Gennep and thus opened the 30th Corps axis, pressed on to attack Goch.

But all this was no more than the rough outline of intentions in that drab dawn of the 10th February when the 129th Brigade, having produced itself through the "eye of a needle" in the wake of the 15th Scottish Recce Regiment, suddenly attacked the enemy in Cleves. Fierce fighting had again erupted with the dawn on the

Materborn when the brigadier of the 129th ordered the 5th Wiltshires and the 4th Somersets into the attack.

In the ensuing battle fought by the 15th Scottish and the 129th Brigade in and over and through the shocking rubble of Cleves the confusion of the enemy proved even greater than the confusion of the attackers. So unexpected was the attack that the German garrison commander had no chance to deploy his reinforcements of men and guns. Fighting was intense, incoherent, unpredictable and deadly, for the enemy paratroops, although very few of them had ever worn parachutes, or ever would, had been chosen for such a role, and were of the highest quality youth still available.

All through the 10th and the night of the 10th/11th fierce fighting raged as isolated enemy groups fought for the shapeless rubble of Cleves, and clung to the heart of the Materborn. Sporadic bursts of fire still came from the mounds of rubble until afternoon of the 11th. It was a Sunday. From dawn until noon the bark of spandaus answered bursts from stens as troops of the 15th Scottish advanced over the flooded main road running in the shelter of their armour. On the western approaches the neat "suburban" homes were burning fiercely like torches in the water. It was still dangerous to move unwarily, and it was not until early afternoon that the last burst of machine gun fire from the armour silenced the last men in the last rubble heap, and Cleves was ours.

"What always will rankle in the minds of those who fought at Cleves is the oafish stupidity of the attack by Bomber Command," wrote Major-General Essame.[1] It is a harsh but just comment, for if Cleves had not been bombed at all it is probable that the 43rd would have gone through with comparative ease.

The ruin of the old Swan Tower, which it was said, had once been the meeting place of smugglers, stood above the hideous confusion like the hub of some shattered wheel, one of the very few recognizable objects on which the eye could focus. The normally peaceful waters of a canal rushed in spate in a narrow channel through the rubble, and a white goat led a section of infantry across the tangled wreckage of a bridge.

From a high point the Canadians could be seen landing at the village of Rindern, a mile or two over the floods to the north-east,

[1]The 43rd Wessex Division at War 1944-45.

busily consolidating their hold over all the outcrops sprouting from that desolation of water, littered with all the garbage of war, and with the buffaloes moving against the trailing backcloth of the smoke screens.

The situation over the main axis was worsening steadily. The head of the 214th Brigade had reached Nutterden with the divisional commander refusing, in spite of a high fever, to hand over any of his responsibility at such a time. It was impossible to bring up the third brigade of the division. The news of all these difficulties had reached the 21st Army Group Commander, and he had at once resolved to see for himself. No fire engines rushing through the entrails of Covent Garden at the peak of business, or brushing aside the massed traffic of Oxford Street at noon, have ever made demands comparable with the demands made by the Field Marshal and his transport on that day. The water was more than two feet deep in places, and still rising. DUKWS were moving troops forward through Kranenberg, and the platforms of the railway station were as crammed with men as any suburban line station on a weekday morning. Hundreds of men were wrestling with transport, and using all their energies and ingenuity to keep traffic moving. Perhaps it is one of the tragedies of the exalted that, with the best will in the world, they can never discover life again as it really is, that they can never again share, or know, the common lot. To those struggling on those blocked ways, and attempting to repair the additional burden of the Field Marshal's progress, it was a matter for relief that the Monarch and the Prime Minister had not chosen this day to see for themselves. It was a memorable Sunday.

But while there was darkness in the rear there was a glimmer of light forward. A special force of armour with the 7th Seaforths strove to exploit through towards Calcar against enemy astride the road in strength. The 129th Brigade moved to secure the high ground east of Bedburg, and thus to be in a position to pinch out the Staatforst Cleves, opening the way to the Goch escarpment from the north.

In Cleves, the 15th Scottish, having played a prominent part in the forefront of the battle for the town, handed over to the Canadian 3rd Division, and began to shake themselves loose. The original hopes of the Recce regiment "to flood the country with armoured cars" from this point on had become idle dreams, nevertheless there were hopes that men and armour might soon gain a grip on solid earth ahead.

Opposition was hardening fast when on the 12th the Scottish right flank linked up with the Welsh left some three thousand yards east of the Cleves–Hekkens road. Conditions forward were still frightful. The 9th Cameronians, attempting to dig in, struck water at 9 inches, and were very wet. Magnificent efforts were being made all along the line by the master cooks, and in the most unlikely places troops were heartened by the sight, smell and flavour of hot food. The good humour seldom faltered. A rifleman of the Cameronians, moving up from a reserve position, remarked: "It must be dangerous here, the Colour Sergeant's wearing a steel helmet."

The period of alarums was at its height, with orders reversed within an hour or two of being given. In the woods south of the road to Moyland and Calcar fighting was intense.

II

The progress of the 53rd Division through the dank and dark Reichswald forest had in it something of the macabre, evoking flashes of vivid memory implanted in childhood by the German myth and legend of the brothers Grimm. By the 10th February the divisional axis had ceased to exist. Everywhere the sandy or muddied tracks had become impassable morasses until fortified with poles lashed together into corduroy bases by the pioneers. These in turn soon sank. All vehicles were banned in the forest, except jeeps, and even these often had to be abandoned. Battalion commanders habitually moved with their forward companies, and brigades strove to keep close up behind the battalions, maintaining communications by means of liaison officers and runners—though "runners" is a peculiarly inept word to describe the dangerous activities of the men struggling through quagmires and dark undergrowth, everlastingly alert for enemy.

Danger lurked in scores of hide-outs, impossible to mop up in the early stages, and sudden death was imminent at every intersection of the long "rides" and trails. Enemy self-propelled guns and well-sited machine guns were able to criss-cross the forest area with barriers of fire which might well have proved impassable to troops less resolved to gain ground and to struggle through to the light of day.

Immense efforts were made to bring up anti-tank guns using Loyd carriers with some success. In darkness, in confusion, in a sombre wilderness lit by a kind of greenish twilight by day and submerged in the dark blackness of the tomb by night, companies, battalions and brigades struggled on, their progress punctuated by sudden brief and deadly encounters. Small groups of men, usually in platoon strength, came face to face, and at such times the battle was to the bayonet.

The whole forest had the feel of some stagnant pool, and was almost as wet. The preliminary bombardment, while killing very few of the enemy, had toppled the crowns of scores of trees and shattered hundreds to matchwood. In such conditions the 53rd steadily progressed to cross the Cleves–Hekkens road, one of the two concrete roads running through the forest from north and south, and to press on towards the Cleves–Goch road, and daylight. P.I.A.T mortar teams fought in pairs, stalking and attacking the enemy self-propelled guns with success, but only twelve bombs per company could be carried by troops already festooned with the chattels of war. Artillery support was of little value, but the searchlights helped movement by night.

In the moments of rest men had some comfort from the tins of self-heating soup they carried, but there was not much time or opportunity for rest. The companies moved in tight formations with two platoons up. It was dangerous to straggle, and the tails of battalions were always in danger from determined nests of enemy awating their chances to strike.

On the 11th and 12th enemy opposition hardened all along the line, but on the 12th the leading battalions of the 53rd Division were in sight of the Cleves–Goch road, and with solid contact on the left. By the 13th the whole central mass of the forest had been cleared, and the weight of the 30th Corps attack had begun to turn, to bear down in a slow right-wheeling movement on the central hub of the 53rd, to the south-east, massing inexorably against the fortress town of Goch and the ramifications of its surrounding defences.

There was no doubt in any mind that Goch would prove a very tough nut to crack.

III

The 51st (Highland) Division in the right flanking role had the easiest road to travel on their main axis, and the hardest battles to fight. Inevitably the two things went together. The road ran south-eastward from Mook to Gennep with a loop of the Maas flats on the right and the escarpment of the south-western ridge of the Reichswald on the left. A light railway line, battered to uselessness by shell fire, ran in places tight up under the escarpment and the fringe of the forest. It was a dangerous road to travel, deeply cratered and mined, covered by mortar fire, and enfiladed by spandaus on either side.

The township of Gennep, protected by the formidable barrier of the Niers river in spate, was a vital part of the powerful defensive system of which Goch was the core. The opening of the road to and through Gennep was essential to the development of the battle, for while Gennep commanded the rail and road crossing of the Maas it was impossible for the British 2nd Army to bridge the river and to open up a main axis for reinforcements and supplies. A major assault across the flooded Niers and the capture of Gennep was, therefore, a priority task of great urgency for the 51st Division. The secondary task was the clearance of the southern part of the Reichswald, the taking of Hekkens and Kessel, and the opening up of the good roads through the forest. On the whole right flank of the battle the enemy defensive line faced north in its natural defensive features rather than east.

On the morning of the 8th February the 153rd Brigade advanced in the wake of the barrage down the road to the south from Mook, while the 154th moved south from Groesbeek to clear the southern fringes of the Reichswald and thrust with all speed upon Hekkens. Supported by the Derbyshire Yeomanry, and by the 107th Armoured Regiment, R.A.C., with the Fife and Forfars under command, both brigades struck determined enemy opposition. Swiftly on their first objectives on the high ground in the forest the 154th with the 152nd Brigade pressing in behind them fought fiercely astride the

Frasselt–Hekkens road all through the 9th and 10th. It was war with the bayonet and grenade, with P.I.A.T.s and anti-tank guns attacking enemy self-propelled 88's and strong points. Mines were deadly and skilfully concealed. Every barn and building housed resolute groups of enemy armed with automatic weapons and holding their fire. Strong points silenced by heavy mortaring erupted suddenly into fierce action, the occupants directing deadly fire upon the tails of advancing companies. In such conditions the kind of leadership, commonplace thirty years before in the days of those tens of thousands of never-to-be-fathers, at 1st, 2nd and 3rd Ypres, was demanded and given. Company and platoon commanders, leading their men in furious assaults against enemy strong points, were the first to die. On the 9th the 7th Battalion of the Black Watch paused to bury its dead while armoured bulldozers heaved the rubble of victory out of the path of troops going through, and armour attempted to tow the jeeps out of quagmires.

The half-tracks were blowing up on the Frasselt–Hekkens road as the 5th Seaforths strove to go through on Hekkens. Miraculously battalion cooks brought up hot food at night, and the men were fortified with rum rations. By the 11th the 5th Seaforths were down to two and a half companies, and with two companies organized as platoons. The battalion commander was wounded in the neck, and the toll of officers had been heavy.

The slogans painted in large white letters upon the walls of barns and houses revealed something of the desperation of the enemy. Phrases such as "Der feigling ist ein lump", "leben tot as slav", together with the familiar, "Ein volk, ein Reich, ein Fuhrer", dissolved into dust at the impact of the mortars, and were heaved out of existence by the armoured bulldozers. Whole villages disappeared without trace as the Seaforths, Black Watch and Camerons bore down upon Hekkens and Kessel, and the 53rd Division wheeled down through the forest and on the twin converging roads behind them. On the 13th the battered Seaforths were astride the Cleves-Hekkens road making way for the 53rd Division to put in a fresh assault on the fiercely held road centre of Hekkens. By that time the Black Watch and the Gordon Highlanders were fighting from house to house in Gennep, harassed by spandau fire from all sides, and meeting heavy counter-attacks.

IV

It was not an easy passage down the river road to Gennep; nor was the going simple through the deceptively close country on the fringes of the Reichswald flanking the road to the north-east. Here, where the forest peters out, giving way to scrub and thin groups of trees, scores of tracks, and as many hamlets and farmsteads, interlace the scrub and tree clumps, giving good fields of fire to the defenders, and a confused vision to the attackers.

Here was no vague invisible enemy. At the outset the 5th Black Watch and 1st and 5/7th Gordon Highlanders were in the midst of enemy groups, harassed by spandau fire and swiftly moving snipers, as they struck south out of the Reichswald to cut the road and comb the fringes of the forest on the left flank. On the road itself the Derbyshire Yeomanry led off with great dash, perhaps inspired by the fact of hard ground under the tracks of their armour. At once the road was covered with cross fire as every house and hamlet and strong point manned by resolute men threw down gauntlets of fire in the face of the attackers.

All through the 9th and 10th scores of fierce platoon and patrol actions blazed from end to end of the road and over the network of villages on the flanks. Ambushed at half a dozen points the men of the Derbyshire Yeomanry dismounted from their armour to go in furiously with grenades against an enemy immovable by other means. By the morning of the 10th they had jumped the road crossing to the north of Gennep to assault the large village of Ottersum.

All three battalions of the 153rd Brigade had fought their ways through ambushes and road blocks, the 5/7th Gordons blooded in a terrific fight at the first road crossing, swept on devoid of cover, giving tongue at sight of the enemy, and literally in full cry. They reached Ottersum close up behind their supporting tanks, and the spearhead of the Recce squadron.

The enemy defence of Ottersum was a foretaste of the battle ahead, and it was clear that the whole line of the Niers river was held in great strength. The first to make the crossing was a lieutenant of the Black Watch, leading his platoon with great skill and courage in assault boats, and infiltrating under cover of darkness to the outskirts of Gennep without disturbing the enemy deep in his dug-outs. In his wake the whole company got across to hold on grimly against spandau, machine gun and mortar fire, while behind them in Ottersum the battle raged with grenades and automatic weapons from house to house, from cellar to roof top. Artillery support, serving to alert the enemy, was more of a menace than an aid in an operation that had become fluid and confused, blazing spasmodically at hidden strong points all along the line of the attack. Prisoners were few. The 5/7th Gordons advancing down the main road in an attempt to seize the main bridge into Gennep saw it blown before their eyes. That night under heavy shelling the battalion crossed the river in buffaloes. Accurate artillery fire now proved vital in breaking up counter-attacks coming in furiously against the Black Watch and Gordons in attempts to hurl them back into the river.

All through the night of the 12th, Guards sappers worked under murderous shelling and mortar fire directed by an enemy knowing the range of the target to inches, and by morning they had thrown 110 feet of Bailey bridge across the Niers, and opened the way for the armour. By that time the main axis of the 51st Division had collapsed, demanding eight hours of dangerous labour before it could be restored.

Nowhere was the Royal Engineer contribution to the battle more evident than over all the axis of the 51st. Perhaps only because it was more easily to be seen and more striking in its scope than in the grim and muddied entrails of the forest, and in the morasses of flood and swamp. All through the days and nights the bridge builders and the road builders worked incessantly on building and maintenance. By night searchlights illumined the crossing points of the Maas to sparkle like necklaces over the water, and threw huge shadowed caverns of darkness under the escarpment of the forest above the Mook–Gennep road. The din of battle was incessant, and in an uproar which seemed at times to embrace all nature huge vehicles bore their vast and varied loads forward to the brink of the battle. Under the escarpment above the Mook–Gennep road the men manning the armoured bulldozers and the platelayers toiled incessantly, and the light railway grew literally before one's eyes.

All along the north bank of the Niers the 51st and 53rd Divisions were closing up, and a bitter fight raged over all the region of the Hekkens crossroads. In Hekkens village not one stone or brick stood upon another, and armoured bulldozers heaving the rubble from the way heaved all sign of Hekkens from the face of the earth.

To the left the anti-tank guns supporting the Cameron Highlanders blazed away at enemy artillery O.P.s and smashed the church steeple of Kessel, while the 3 in. mortars of the Argyll and Sutherland Highlanders hurled their bombs into the midst of enemy groups across the Niers. Armoured bulldozers moved into action with their guns blazing to fill an anti-tank ditch barring the way to the 5th Seaforths, and it was clear that the pressure building up on the north bank of the river was irresistible. Grimly the Argylls moved down the road to Kessel to assault across the Niers in buffaloes. Behind them came the Seaforths. On either flank were the Black Watch, and the enemy shell fire was deadly and accurate at all possible crossing points.

But the heart of the battle was in Gennep and to the south on the line of the railway, and in the flanking woods. Here the enemy built up counter-attack after counter-attack, his assaults bringing him at times within yards of battalion headquarters to make of every man jack a fighting soldier. It was essential for the British to anchor their right flank tight on the Maas, and this they did at a point where the river loops eastward at the village of Heyen. Yet it was in the narrow ways of the shattered township that the fighting was the most furious and deadly. Spandau fire blazed from cellar, attic and rooftop; snipers sniped with ruthless efficiency, and the mortar bombs splintered the rubble-dusted air with hidden death.

No form of warfare makes greater demands upon the physical and nervous resources of men; no form of warfare demands higher qualities of courage, of morale, and resource. The 5/7th Gordon Highlanders and the Black Watch were equal to the task, of which this was a mere foretaste. Led always with steadfastness, often with great skill, and at times with heroism beyond the normal demands of brave conduct, moving from house to house, from cover to cover, knowing always the deadly high-pitched whine, and sickening thud of bullets in flesh, coming from all angles, Gennep was slowly but inexorably cleared of enemy, while infantry and armour eased the pressure on the flanks.

The same lieutenant who had first led his platoon of the Black Watch across the Niers in assault boats led also the Black Watch in the fight for Gennep when his commander and second in command were killed. That was leadership at its most resourceful and heroic best.

V

When on the 13th February the 51st Highland Division had anchored the right flank on the Maas at Heyen, and cleared Gennep of the enemy, the first phase of the battle of the Rhineland was at an end, and the battle of the Reichswald was won. In the centre the 53rd Division had cleared the whole of the main forest region, and the good laterals were open from north to south. But even the good roads had sustained the worst ravages of war, and there was a stretch out of Hekkens, a main axis, bearing the sign—"The Liver Mile". Every yard of this corduroy was a jolting torment for men and vehicles, but it was passable. Roads and tracks everywhere presented a shambles of bogged tanks, bulldozers, A.V.s R.E. and vehicles of all kinds. Movement of vehicles remained an intolerable labour, but was no longer impossible.

On the left of the 53rd Division the 129th Brigade of the 43rd Division had secured the high ground north-east of the Staatforst Cleves and gained Bedburg. With this the 43rd was poised for its southern thrust, outflanking the still powerful enemy defences east of the Cleves–Goch section of the main railway line.

Meanwhile the 15th Scottish was heavily engaged on the Calcar road, in the woods flanking the road to the south, and still unable to make much impression on an enemy as unyielding as a wall of steel in front of Moyland, and resolved to bar the way to Calcar. Enemy reinforcements were pouring in, and supported by first class artillery. The worst was yet to come. Across the floods north of the Cleves–Calcar road the Canadians had anchored their left securely on Emmerich. The floods showed no signs of abating, and the levels of the Maas and Niers rivers continued to rise.

That was the position on the 13th February. The jaws of the enemy had been forced open, but the hinges of the jaws still held, and the constriction of the front remained acute. From Cleves to Goch is a distance of eight miles, and in that area bounded by the Nijmegen–Cleves road on the left, by the Gennep–Goch railway line on the right, and backed by the Maas, four divisions plus two armoured brigades, a brigade of the 79th Armoured Division, a great mass of artillery and supporting troops, were crushed together like a phalanx in a shambles of mud, flood, and shattered timber, bathed in a dismal drizzle, and upon which, it seemed, the sun would never shine. There was no chance to dry out.

Through four days and nights from the 13th to the 17th the battle raged all along the line with a growing intensity, and especially along the line of the Niers river and on the approaches to Goch. South of Gennep the enemy held on to the last man in trenches twelve feet deep in sand, and could only be moved by assault with grenades. Counter-attacks supported by self-propelled guns came in again and again, the first savage counter-attacks experienced by the 51st Division since Normandy. Enemy strong points continued to fight until overwhelmed.

By the 15th the attack was closing in with irresistible force on the road to Asperden, astride the railway line, and astride the Cleves–Goch road. The 43rd Division was rolling up the enemy line from the north, and from three sides the attack on the Goch hinge was building up to its last moments of truth.

15

THE SECOND PHASE—GOCH–CALCAR

I

THE 15th February was a key day. The waters of the Maas and Niers had reached their peaks, and no further flood possibility remained to the enemy. Even the weather showed signs of improvement, and with that there was a glimmer of hope for the U.S. 9th Army waiting impatiently at the turbulent barrier of the Roer. If no more rain should fall even that broad torrent must soon abate.

On the right flank of the Canadian 1st Army, sappers of the British 8th Corps greeted the signs of improvement with relief. They had worked like beavers to construct and to open a bridge to span the Maas at Gennep. Hundreds of feet of Bailey pontoon had been rising and falling with the erratic floods over the approaches; now the pontoons began to subside to sit upon the squelching earth. A small sign bore the legend—"Gennep bridge—4008 feet". When it was finally opened to heavy transport at dawn on the 20th it represented a major achievement of engineering under atrocious conditions, and often under fire. Seven bridges then spanned the Maas on the Canadian front to feed shells and supplies to the men ahead.

In the pale sunshine of the dawn of the 15th February hopes began to rise all along the line. Troops, whose horizons of life were bounded by the hour, by a few yards of grey landscape, the ominous shells of farmsteads, the rubble of villages, began to scour themselves of the grime of battle, and to get their second wind. North of Gennep men stood under the showers of mobile baths knowing a luxury greater than anything they could remember in all their lives, something to be described in diaries as "magnificent". Battalions, temporarily out of the line, cleaned up and cursed as they strove to get the muck out of their rifles. But it was not given to any visitor to know how they felt; how they felt was known only to themselves, and perhaps not even to themselves. Life had taken on new meanings, and only the abnormal was real, the sudden explosion which took away a man's arm in the act of eating—or his life, the incessant murmurous whisper of death, the strange orchestra of a hundred weapons each of which, unknowing, men came to know. The men in the forward positions had lived in an uncharted wilderness for more than a week. It had become timeless. They were the P.B.I., and bemoaning their lot it is doubtful if many would have exchanged places with others in less danger, less mud, less everlasting misery in which there was a kind of happiness, perhaps unattainable elsewhere.

At noon of the 15th February the Canadian 2nd Corps began to come into the battle behind the 15th Scottish on the left, to drive on to Calcar while the British 30th Corps wheeled south-eastward upon Goch. On the right flank the British 52nd (Lowland) Division came in on the right of the 51st to strike south along the line of the Maas through Afferden, and east towards Weeze. The going was very hard. Nine enemy divisions were now identified in the battle, one Panzer division, one Panzer grenadier, three infantry, and four paratroop divisions, and supported by good artillery, self-propelled guns and mortars. Outgunned by a margin of perhaps ten weapons to one, and almost helpless against air attack, the enemy gunners yet managed to meet the attackers with the heaviest fire most of them had ever experienced. This was the enemy version of "We shall fight on the beaches . . . . ". It had the feel of a fight to the death: there was no give anywhere.

The 15th Scottish, striving to make good their positions in the woods flanking the Cleves–Calcar road opposite Moyland had fought themselves almost to a standstill. The 10th H.L.I. under command of the 46th Brigade had advanced to within a mile of Moyland village, and captured the high ground to the south-west, but again and again the counter-attacks came in supported by self-propelled guns. Enfiladed by heavy machine guns from the uncleared woods on their flanks and with one of their companies overrun, they held on grimly for three days and nights while the 4th Canadian Infantry Brigade forced a way through on their left.

Since the day of the fall of Cleves the 15th Scottish had fought by day and night on that stretch of road and in the flanking woods.

Under artificial moonlight by night, and with creeping barrages lifting three hundred yards every twelve minutes, and helped by directional tracer, they battered away. Fighting or not fighting there was no rest by night anyway.

The 9th Cameronians attacking all through the night of the 15th with the 10th H.L.I. in support, met a terrible counter-attack against their right flank in the mists of dawn, and were overrun. Only steadfast courage on the part of every man saved companies from disaster.

The 7th Seaforths, putting in a night attack on the 16th south of the Moyland road, surprised the enemy, and "dug themselves into shallow holes and prayed" one hundred and fifty yards short of Schloss Moyland. They had suffered heavy casualties for three days and nights. They had sand in their rifles, and sand in their guts. On the 16th they lost eleven men to our own artillery.

On the right of the Seaforths that morning the 9th Cameronians were moving on a square of woodland known as "Ian". It must be cleared at all costs, said the brigadier. The shelling, mortaring and spandau fire was deadly, but at first light on the 16th tanks were coming up in support, and the Calgary Highlanders were going through. The pincers were closing in on Moyland from three sides, and the Typhoons were driving down out of a clear sky on the Schloss, once the summer palace of Frederick the Great.

Such was the position when the Canadians took over on the left flank to open the way through to the Hochwald, and the 15th Scottish Division leaving a brigade under Canadian command, turned south to pass through the 43rd Wessex Division for the attack on Goch. It would not be any better at Goch, but it would be different.

In all this warfare in which armour had found it costly and often impossible to attempt to spearhead infantry, the armoured personnel carriers called "kangaroos" had proved themselves, and their crews had been worthy of the vehicles. They had carried infantry into battle all along the line, often producing men behind the enemy forward defences, and gaining initial advantages that would have been impossible otherwise. The kangaroo crews, overworked and vulnerable, had suffered heavy casualties. In the early stages this had been hard to avoid, for harassed commanders did the best they could. It was said of the kangaroos that "nothing since the substitution of the musket for the crossbow has been comparable (with them) in modern warfare." It may not be an exact tribute, but it is a just one.

II

To the men of the infantry battalions in the line the 15th February was little different from any other day, and no less dangerous. It was a day of intense fighting from north to south. The differences were that letters were arriving, that wounded were getting back more swiftly, that hot breakfast was not a thing dimly remembered, that orders began to take effect. There was a chance of minor comfort out of the line of battle, to shave, to bath, even to sleep. Above all there was a sense of form, of order out of chaos, not perhaps discernible to the troops advancing upon some target known as "Shrimp" or "Toad", or squatting in the mud and scrub of "Clapham Common", but to the brigadiers and major-generals. At last they had begun to see daylight. Battalions passed through battalions, brigades through brigades, and even divisions through divisions. There was more room to manoeuvre. The axes were drying out. The confusion looked worse to the eye, but this was because there was movement. The weary dedication of hundreds of men working for days on the lines of communication almost in states of coma, gave way to the expression of feeling, to curses and bad temper.

All this began to have an effect forward. The 43rd Division, launched virtually in error on the road to Cleves, had broken loose, and having outflanked the main Siegfried defences east of Bedburg, was rolling up the enemy from north to south. But "rolling up", the division's own phrase, is not a good description. East of the Staatforst Cleves the 130th Infantry Brigade had a tremendous fight all through the 15th, and the 214th Brigade, passing through, fought its way yard by yard to the south. The enemy had to be scraped up, dug up, rooted out almost man by man. When on the 17th February the 43rd Division overlooked the battlefield of Goch from the escarpment to the north they had advanced ten miles from north to south, and had performed a major role in the development of the battle.

Thanks to that the 15th Scottish came down on their left without much difficulty, and ready to spearhead the attack on Goch from the north.

Through all this time the 53rd Welsh Division had suffered the appalling discomforts of the Reichswald forest, fighting its way through a tangled wilderness of dripping misery without landmarks. After a week it seemed to many battalions that they inhabited the entrails of some evil noisome beast, heaped with the rotting half-devoured carcases of its prey, and from which there was no escape. But on the 15th the 1st Battalion of the East Lancashires on the extreme right made contact with the 51st Highland Division, and the 53rd covered the left flank of the Highland Scots in their assault upon Asperden.

A deadly and ferocious battle plain for all to see was building up on all the western approaches to the inner fortress of Goch in an arc from Kassel running south through about 90 degrees to the 52nd Division fighting on the Afferden–Rempeld–Groote Horst road. Neither dusk, nor night, nor dawn was free from savage counter-attack. No village on all that tight perimeter was secure. Every gain had to be held grimly against constant attack and under heavy mortaring, shelling and incessant sniping.

Everywhere the noose was tightening round a tract of town and country that resembled an inferno, shuddering incessantly to the impact of explosions, shot through with great spouts of smoke and flame, and thunderous with appalling uproar.

The 32nd Guards Brigade, under command of the 51st Division, smashed its way through between the 51st and 52nd to capture Hommersum and Mull on the 15th, reaching Hassum on the 16th, and threatening Siebengerwald. It was the worst fighting the brigade had ever known, and severe losses on the line of the Kendal forced them to withdraw.

On the extreme right the Recce regiment of the 52nd Division probed out from Afferden to Rempeld, while the infantry cleared the thick woods flanking the road. On the night of the 16th the Royal Scots and the H.L.I. with the K.O.S.B. in support assaulted the last of the enemy in the south-eastern fringes, and with the dawn faced a prospect as dismal as any they had ever known. On their right two hundred yards of flood water augmented an immense anti-tank ditch running due east from the Maas. Seven hundred yards ahead across open fields stood the ancient moated Kasteel Blijenbeek. That seven hundred yards of open ground was to be a graveyard for the Churchill tanks of the 24th Armoured Brigade, and for the men of the 4th Battalion K.O.S.B. From behind the anti-tank ditch enemy self-propelled guns picked off the tanks, while mortars and heavy machine guns aided by medium artillery, ably directed from the O.P.s in the Kasteel, made the open ground impassable for men.

From the ground the enemy position was impregnable. The shells of our twenty-five pounders and 5.5's bounced off the reinforced walls. Again and again desperate attacks were easily beaten off, bringing only demands from the enemy that the attackers should surrender. Such was the spirit of the garrison of Kasteel Blijenbeek, a spirit which survived until Spitfires destroyed the castle and its garrison with 1,000 pound bombs. But it was impossible to extend the 30th Corps front another yard to the southward, and it was not until the 1st March, with the position hopelessly outflanked by the American advances, that elements of the 52nd Division Recce Regiment finally got across the anti-tank ditch. Between that line and the line of the Niers the enemy defences were almost solid.

It would be an exaggeration to say that Kasteel Blijenbeek was typical of the powerful enemy defences surrounding the fortress of Goch, but it would not be a great exaggeration. Five British infantry Divisions and two armoured brigades, supported by massive artillery and overwhelming strength in the air, in an arc from north through west to south bore down in relentless pressure upon a tight perimeter of concrete pill boxes with walls two feet thick reinforced with 4-inch steel plates all linked in with anti-tank ditches and fortified villages in a chain of strength that would only be broken by being blasted off the face of the earth, and by the bold and ingenious use of the varied engines of war provided by the 79th Armoured Division.

Not for the first time, or the last, men brooding upon that prospect on the night of the 17th February, on the eve of the battle for Goch, thanked God, not only as always for the infantry, but also for the "Funnies" of the 79th Armoured Division. Perhaps, even, it was here at this time and place that some men realized clearly the changed nature of this war, that there could be no end other than the destruction of the enemy, and that it seemed beyond the wit of man to make it otherwise.

For the enemy defending Goch there could not be hope, and the only possible line of withdrawal lay along the railway line to the east, for the road south through Weeze to Geldern was closely threatened. The words the destruction of the German army west of the Rhine meant exactly what they said, and the Germans had accepted that. There was not much point, as Hitler had said to von Rundstedt, "in transferring catastrophe from one place to another". And the smell of it was upon Goch.

III

It was estimated that three enemy divisions reinforced the garrison troops in the fight for Goch. Against them it was the task of the 51st Highland Division to clear the town south of the river Niers. The 53rd Division would maintain the positions on the escarpment between the river and the line of the Goch–Cleves railway. The 43rd Division would maintain the position left of the 53rd, and would secure eight crossings of the formidable anti-tank ditch immediately south of the escarpment. The 15th Scottish would then pass through to take Goch north of the river Niers.

All the approaches to the town were covered by dykes, anti-tank ditches, trench systems and pill boxes, and the whole area as the final attack opened was like the crater of a volcano in eruption. It seemed impossible that a single square foot of air could be free from screaming metal, and in the face of that on the night of the 17th/18th the 43rd Division gained and held crossing points over the anti-tank ditch. No man knows how. It was achieved by a kind of dogged madness by men who had passed through the barrier of ordinary fear to survive or to die in a limbo, known only to those who have experienced such things, and to each man differently.

Mattresses of rockets had reduced the township of Asperden to a heap of smoking rubble, and left an aftermath of fiendish din. Incongruously in that place a private soldier played quietly upon a piano while his colonel sat on a box under a wavering wall having his hair cut. Mortar bombs burst at short intervals spaced by the incessant whine and rattle of spandaus and rifles. Some men shaved. Some urinated. The battle was not yet personal, but it was unpleasant to wait. From that point down the road and across the railway line the Black Watch and the Gordon Highlanders led the direct assault of the 51st Division from the north-west, the subalterns leading their thin columns of men, humped with the tools of war, silent and with tight lines under the nostrils. Column after column disappeared into the smoke to probe into the lethal acrid rubble heap of the town of Goch.

It was half past seven o'clock on the night of the 18th when the 5th Black Watch approached the outskirts of the town, moving forward stealthily in the darkness to establish themselves by midnight like a Trojan horse. It was for the 1st Gordons coming in behind them to touch off the inferno of a defence that blazed from every house, crater and rubble heap. It seemed then that Goch erupted into a conflagration of war without shape or coherence, blazing out far beyond the outskirts, and which raged for three days and nights of incessant dust, din and death.

At three o'clock on the afternoon of the 18th the 8th Royal Scots had led the 6th K.O.S.B. and the 6th Royal Scots Fusiliers on the road from the north, and by midnight they, too, were inside the town confronted by a factory with enclosed overhead footways spanning the road. Through that night the 6th K.O.S.B. had fought for their bridgehead over the main anti-tank ditch, won it and held it under terrific machine gun fire and shelling, and enabled the kangaroos to shuttle the infantry forward. On the 51st Division axis a bridge was also secure across the anti-tank ditch, and in the dawn of the 19th the "Funnies" were lumbering forward blindly to the shambles, the crocodiles searing the eyeless sockets in the rubble heaps of homes. But the immense weight of air bombardment had effectively closed the way for armour beyond the fringes, and inside the infantry fought alone.

Early on the 19th a company of the Black Watch led by Major Brodie assaulted the hospital building and captured the garrison commander and his staff. With that Goch had officially surrendered, but it made no difference. Probably no one knew, nor cared. There were no communications and not much need for them within the vortex of the Goch inner perimeter, and not much need of them over all the wilderness of trench, concrete and dykes beyond. Even a week after the last German had fired a shot in the dust heap of Goch no man moved or walked by day with impunity in that desolation, acrid with the stench of cordite, and sour with vomit and the putrefying offal of men.

Day after day the slow processes of death and destruction gnawed away at the outer defences. The petard tanks, with the spouts of their huge mortars as wide as the funnels of tug boats, lumbered up through the swirling smoke of battle to within one hundred yards of the concrete forts and pill boxes, belched their bombs upon them, tearing out great jagged holes for the crocodiles to sear out the enemy with bursts of flame. That was the drill, the blasting and burning of a hundred strong points. But there were times when infantry, unable to call these great weapons to their aid, rushed up under cover of smoke to hurl grenades through weapon slits, and even to clamber upon the roofs seeking the apertures of chimneys and ventilators.

The trail of war was increasingly marked by the roasted bodies of men in armour, men in aircraft, men in pill boxes, men in cellars, their charred torsos swollen, rigid and terrible to see. And it seemed that the stench of burning flesh was as clinging in the nostrils as that of burning rubber.

But inside the town of Goch it was a more personal matter. Brave men vomited, and purged like lobsters plunged into that hideous cauldron of explosions, and fought with their entrails ready cleansed for death. By the night of the 19th two brigades, the 153rd and the 44th, were fighting inside the town, stumbling through fire and smoke in choking misery, half blind with smarting eyes and unaware of minor wounds, with every crater and rubble heap and cellar a death trap, blown up by mines and booby traps, and under incessant fire without coherence. No armour could penetrate that shocking rubble heap. Yet inside it men kept their heads, sorting out the strands of that maze of shattering sound and echo, planning their struggle, section, platoon, company. Whole companies cut off and leaderless found new leaders, and many survived.

On the 19th, Dutch-piloted Mitchells of the R.A.F. added to the death and dust, inexplicably mistaking Goch for Weeze, and adding to the infantryman's loathing of saturation bombing of towns. The bombing, said the infantry, frightened no one, killed very few, and presented the enemy with almost impregnable defensive positions in an impassable and formless shambles.

Slowly the battle for Goch, which was a score or more of battles, expanded on the flanks, drawing the noose astride the Goch–Weeze road, the Goch–Calcar road, and on the 21st the last of the enemy withdrew along the railway line to Udem, leaving Goch to the pitiless revenge of their artillery and heavy mortars.

As to facts, there are only simple facts. On the 20th, A Company of the 1st Battalion the Gordons was wiped out but for one N.C.O. and four men. The ambulances were struggling forward under cover of smoke to seek out and carry out the wounded. The R.A.M.C. men worked with a sublime indifference to danger that brought tears to the smarting eyes of those who saw. The War Diaries read soberly enough, for what can they say of it: "Black Watch fighting fiercely all through 20th and 21st at times completely surrounded . . . . Houses lousy with enemy . . . . 22nd, three more officers killed . . . . "

The men manning the kangaroos carrying the Gordons into the town south of the river and carrying the K.O.S.B. from the north, ran a gauntlet of fire from bazookas, heavy machine guns, spandaus, self-propelled guns, mortars and grenades. Visibility was seldom as much as fifty yards. The miracle is that so many survived.

In a cellar of Goch in the midst of appalling din and with all the earth shuddering and heaving to violent impacts, a major, his face tattooed with blood specks and yellow with iodine, read out a message—"Have you sent back your leave personnel?" It stretched men's faces in grimaces of laughter, and while they laughed the building above them disappeared, heaving every man in the cellar into a heap, still laughing, still alive.

A huge man in a white overall and with a red cross on his chest like a crusader strode through the rubble and lifted wounded men to shelter. A priest crawled about in the crypt of a shattered church muttering something about Communion wine.

On the 21st the battle had abated, and the sun shone upon the hideous carcase of the place. The railway tracks of the marshalling yards reared up in a chaos of tangled metal like snakes out of a pit.

Everywhere the sappers prowled about their dangerous business detecting unexploded mines and bombs. The arch of the great red brick gate house still stood on the lip of a giant crater at the heart of the town, and the sun glinted on the metal lettering of the words "Hitler Jugend". Two slender twisted pipes of steel, all that remained of the bridge, spanned the torrent of the river Niers, and deep in the cellars of the houses hampers of food were ready packed for flight, and bottles of fruit stood in rows.

With the fall of Goch the last great bastion of the main defences of the Siegfried Line in the north had been overwhelmed. On the roads out of the town to the south-east and to the north-east the battle was raging, down towards Weeze, east towards Udem, and in the north towards Calcar. Another and another "Goch", until the end. There were no illusions now. There would be no bursting through into the open. Eleven enemy divisions were wedged into the last bridgehead in the north, in the tract of country bounded by the Calcar–Udem–Kervenheim, Winnekendonk–Kevelaer–Geldern road, and held within the narrowing triangle of the roads converging upon Wesel. It was the last fight of the remnants of the German army in the north. It would go on like this day after day, a pitiless "killing match". It was astounding, when men had time to reflect upon it, how the enemy contrived to move troops and maintain men and guns in the fight under incessant bombardment from the air, Typhooned and machine gunned at every road junction and assembly point, and under constant artillery fire. Even the Wesel bridge, the last escape route, defied all the efforts of British and American bombers to destroy it.

IV

In the north the enemy, reinforced by a newly arrived Panzer Lehr division and an infantry division had maintained a tremendous resistance in the battle the Canadians had inherited from the 15th Scottish on the Calcar road. The great red brick pile of the Schloss of Moyland still standing pockmarked by shot and shell and shattered by the rockets of Typhoons had become the symbol of it. Six days after the Seaforths had come within one hundred and fifty yards of it to dig themselves in and pray the castle still held out. But on the 22nd February a dirty white flag was hoisted above the main turret, and half a dozen white cloths fluttered from the window sockets and embrasures to the south.

The capture of the Schloss of Moyland not only, with Goch, marked the end of the second phase of the Rhineland battle; it seemed to mark, also, the end of an era, an anachronism in its setting. The bright sunshine shone upon the dusky red bricks of its mellowed walls, and revealed the desolation of the surrounding lawns and parklands, laid waste by the violence of the fighting. Two antlered deer cast in bronze and mounted on stone plinths flanked the bridge over the outer moat. The swollen body of a dead horse lay in the drive. At the main entrance to the house stood two small sixteenth century cannon, and inside was a vast confusion of wreckage. In the great principal bed-chamber, the curving walls embellished with paintings of flamboyant nudes, the cooking stoves of a French Canadian company roared under pans of frying fat. Here Frederick the Great, at ease in the canopied bed on the raised dais, had once held the morning levee. In the magnificently appointed bathrooms of the state apartments groups of soldiers washed and shaved for the first time in a week. A record of "The Barber of Seville" was on the turntable of the radio-gramophone in one of the drawing rooms, but it was difficult to imagine that anyone had listened to music since the dawn of the 8th February.

The place had been a treasure house, and in scores of rooms all the bric-a-brac of an exquisite home of princely wealth lay jumbled in confusion. In the cellars of the castle Ilse Marie, Baronin Steengracht von Moyland, Geborn Baronesse Hahn, sat upright in the midst of her white-faced servants, seeming the lone survivor of a world long since dead. It seemed impossible to believe that a way of life such as hers had persisted until a week ago; impossible to imagine that such a life would ever again be possible.

Forward of Moyland the Canadians had come within one thousand yards of Calcar, but the town held firm. It was vital now to break through across the Calcar–Goch road at a point between Goch and Udem, some five miles to the east of Goch, and to capture a spur of the scimitar-curved ridge covering the Hochwald and Balberger forests. This was the central core of the last great defensive barrier running from the west bank of the Rhine near Rees, forward of the forests, and south to Geldern.

The front was still greatly restricted, but in the south the fall of Goch had enabled the 30th Corps to turn down towards Geldern. On the 23rd and 24th February the 53rd Division with a brigade of the 15th Scottish covering its left flank, and the 52nd Division on the right, was meeting tremendous resistance in front of Weeze in conditions that showed few signs of improvement. In the centre the 43rd with elements of the 15th Scottish and the armour of the Coldstream Guards battled doggedly to within two thousand five hundred yards of Udem. All complained bitterly of water problems. The 53rd found water at a depth of eighteen inches to make it impossible to dig in, the 15th Scottish found it difficult to wash and shave, the 9th Cameronians, half bogged in a stagnant marsh under heavy shelling by day and night, recorded thankfully the issue of a double ration of rum on the night of the 23rd.

In Goch itself on that day the 7th Battalion The Black Watch buried their dead while their 1st Battalion waded across a river three feet deep on the road to the south.

For the 51st and 15th Divisions "Operation Veritable" was nearing its end. It was the beginning of a period when it seemed to all but those taking part that all was quiet on the Canadian 1st Army front. As the Canadian Army regrouped for the final phase on the Rhineland battlefield the focus had moved sharply to the U.S. 9th and 1st Armies, at last across the swollen Roer, and soon racing for the Rhine.

16

"GRENADE"

I

PRECISELY at a quarter to three o'clock on the morning of the 23rd February the guns of the U.S. 1st and 9th Armies roared out their challenge behind the swollen Roer, and while the staccato pattern of the gun flashes danced in macabre confusion over the bivouacs and paraphernalia of a quarter of a million armed men, the bursting shells piled chaos upon chaos in the rubble of scores of towns and villages. Already in all the littoral of the river from Julich to Duren it would have been difficult to find two stones the one upon another, and the sight of a standing wall was a phenomenon.

Forty-five minutes later the assault troops of the 1st and 9th Armies launched their assault craft upon the still turbulent waters of the Roer, and the barrage lifted. It had been little more than a token, the harsh cry of havoc that unleashed the dogs of war. Ten divisions of the 9th Army, organized in three army corps faced the Roer between Julich and Duren, and to the south fourteen divisions of the 1st Army had awaited eagerly the signal to obliterate the last of the enemy between them and the Rhine.

The final plans for the launching of "Operation Grenade" had been reviewed at a conference on the 17th. It had been decided that unless one inch or more of rain should fall, or there should be an unlooked for increase in flooding, the attack would go in on the 23rd February. The U.S. 9th Army, crossing the Roer between Roermond and Duren, would drive north through Munchen Gladbach to the Venlo–Wesel road to link up with the British. It would clear the area on the left bank of the Erft to Dusseldorf. At the same time the U.S. 1st Army would cross the Roer south of Duren to protect the right flank of the 9th Army with its left while the centre moved on Cologne.

One felt then, and one feels in retrospect with all the inner records of those days available, that no one in those impatient American armies bothered to measure rainfall in that last week. Whatever the conditions, somehow on that morning of the 23rd the assault troops would have crossed the Roer. The conditions were grim. The river a full eighty yards wide flowed at five knots. A few enemy guns contrived to add to the difficulties of the men on the water, the inevitable mortars took a toll, but it was clear that the strength of the enemy defences had been sapped, and that little more than token resistance faced the U.S. armies. By noon on the first day under cover of the U.S. 29th Tactical Air Force, putting on its greatest effort of the campaign, the assault force was secure on the eastern bank, and a heavy pontoon bridge was in place behind them. In twelve hours sixteen battalions were enlarging the bridgehead, and six class 40 bridges, four class 5 infantry support bridges, and a number of footbridges and ferries were operating in support. It was a tremendous example of drive, energy, engineering skill and ingenuity, and only the rubble of the ancient city of Julich and the valley of the Roer impeded the progress of the troops. No more than four enemy divisions and scattered garrison troops remained to face two armies and to block the way to the Rhine. The entire enemy reserve of seven infantry and three armoured divisions had already rushed north to reinforce the parachute army in its suicide struggle against the Canadians and British in the Rhineland battle.

While the bulldozers shovelled paths through the rubble of the Roer towns the 9th Army built up its strength in the bridgehead, ready to burst out. On its right flank the 7th Corps of the U.S. 1st Army was racing for the Erft. By the 26th February the 9th Army had three corps on the general line Oberemdt–Opherten–Holzweiler–Venrath–Erkelenz. The 16th Corps on the left seized Kleine Gladbach against a beaten enemy, and with that the old British sores of Roermond and Venlo were at last eliminated without a battle. There was barely time or space for the remaining enemy to pull out from these, his last bridgeheads on the Maas.

A week after the assault crossing of the Roer the 13th Corps in the centre had entered Munchen Gladbach, the largest German city to fall into Allied hands, while the 19th Corps on the right was racing for the Rhine at Neuss opposite Dusseldorf, and the flank protecting role of the 1st Army's seventh corps was no longer necessary.

On the 1st March the Supreme Commander joined his 9th Army commander, General Simpson, in Munchen Gladbach, and had to put on his tin hat against the shell splinters of anti-aircraft guns attacking an enemy jet aircraft overhead. The Americans were jubilant. The assault of the 23rd February had sparked off the race for the Rhine from Wesel to the Swiss border. While the 7th Corps turned south on Cologne the 3rd Corps in the centre drove for Bonn, reaching Euskirchen on the 4th March. The 5th Corps on the right was almost upon the Rhine at Remagen.

The news of these things had destroyed the last of General Patton's slender store of patience, and with Bradley's blessing his 3rd Army accelerated its advance astride the Moselle upon Trier, and the path through to the Rhine was almost open. Patton had been swift to recognize that this was a chance for the repetition of the pattern of August 1944. Again the Canadians and British were fighting the German armies yard by yard on the left flank in a battle of "the hinge". It was for him again to break through with his armour, and as early as the 20th February he had pressed General Bradley to let him go. "All of us in high position," he wrote to Bradley, "will surely be held accountable for failure to take offensive action when offensive action is possible."

With some difficulty Bradley restrained him, pointing out that the major thrust in the north had been agreed, but of Bradley's sympathy there is no doubt. "Regardless of what you and I think of this decision," he wrote to Patton, "we are good enough soldiers to carry out these orders."

By the end of February Patton was beyond restraint, and the will to restrain him did not exist. It was rumoured that he towed his Rhine bridge behind him wherever he went, and that Hodges' 1st Army beating him to the Rhine filled him with envy, but that Montgomery's army might beat him to a bridgehead was more than he could bear. He need not have worried on that account. Montgomery had carefully planned every detail of his set-piece crossing, and fixed the dates. Nothing would move him an hour forward or an hour back.

In the first week of March Patton had his armour on the move through the Eifel on his left flank, and by the time the 1st Army's 7th Corps had swooped upon Cologne to clear the whole city within forty-eight hours, the 3rd Army was gathering momentum to clear the country west of the Rhine from Mainz to Koblenz.

Even General Simpson, commanding the 9th Army and under 21st Army Group command, showed signs of restlessness in early March. On the 2nd his spearheads had reached Neuss, and by the 5th March his army had cleared the Rhine bank from Dusseldorf to Mors. He had advanced some fifty miles with 7,300 casualties, and complained to the Supreme Commander that he had seven divisions he couldn't use. Why couldn't he make a surprise crossing of the Rhine?

But Montgomery was adamant. "He preferred the planned assault of the Rhine on a broad front between Rheinberg and Emmerich."[1] It seemed even that the Field Marshal had an *idée fixe* about crossing the Rhine; that to "jump a bridgehead", in the unlikely circumstances that such a possibility existed, was in some way undignified, and not in the book of rules.

The possibility did seem unlikely in the extreme. On the 3rd March, following the fall of Krefeld to the 9th Army, the commander of the German 1st Parachute Army, General Alfred Schlemm, received the first of a series of orders from the Fuhrer. In no circumstances was any bridge over the Rhine to fall into Allied hands, and yet the bridges must be kept open to the last moment to ensure supplies to the troops on the west bank. Failure meant death. When, soon afterwards, the Americans came dangerously close to the Homberg bridge, Schlemm wirelessed orders to blow it. The colonel in charge of the bridge hesitated, whereupon Schlemm replied that if the bridge was not blown immediately he would personally shoot the colonel and "anyone else he found near it".

Meanwhile on the 7th March the U.S. 9th Armoured Division of the 3rd Corps approached Remagen. Their orders were to move southward, but when the great Ludendorf bridge was seen to be still intact Brigadier-General William Hoge, commanding the 9th Armoured, ordered his men to seize it without hesitation. The story

[1]Pogue—"The Supreme Command".

of how the 9th Armoured grasped this unlooked-for opportunity of war has been amply told. It was a magnificent effort, and it sent Bradley into transports of delight. At that time General Bull of SHAEF was with Bradley, and he suggested that the Supreme Commander should be consulted before further forces were committed to the bridgehead. General Eisenhower himself has left a record of the ensuing telephone conversation.

> "I was at dinner in my Rheims headquarters with the corps and division commanders of the American airborne forces when Bradley's call came through. When he reported that we had a permanent bridge across the Rhine I could scarcely believe my ears. He and I had frequently discussed such a development as a remote possibility but never as a well-founded hope.
>
> I fairly shouted into the telephone: 'How much have you got in that vicinity that you can throw across the river?'
>
> He said: 'I have more than four divisions but I called you up to make sure that pushing them over would not interfere with your plans.'
>
> I replied: 'Well, Brad, we expected to have that many divisions tied up around Cologne and now those are free. Go ahead and shove over at least five divisions instantly, and anything else that is necessary to make certain of our hold.'"[1]

I have brought the story up to this point on the right of the 21st Army Group's harsh and sustained battle in the north, not only because it illustrates how inexorably the emphasis was moving away from the north, and the plans to which the Supreme Commander had adhered were steadily being fulfilled, but also because it points the great discrepancy at this stage between British and American strength. While the Americans had more divisions than they knew what to do with, the British were scraping the bottom of the barrel. Two divisions were moving up from Italy to reinforce the Canadians and the 2nd Army. In the north on the day that the 9th and 1st Armies had burst out across the Roer, the Canadian 1st Army began to re-group for the third phase of its struggle to

[1]Eisenhower—"Crusade in Europe".

destroy the enemy in the north. "Operation Grenade" had exploded to such purpose that it had stolen all the thunder. The eyes of the world had moved elsewhere, and it seemed often to the Canadians and the British, as it had done often before, that they fought alone in a kind of isolation.

It seems to me that General Eisenhower paid a great tribute to Field Marshal Montgomery when he wrote: "Progress was slow and costly (for the British and Canadians) and opposition became stiffer as the Germans began moving their forces from the Roer into the path of the Canadian advance. Montgomery was not too displeased by this transfer of German weight because of the promise it held that, once the American attack began, it would advance with great speed."

Would Generals Bradley and Patton have been "not too displeased" in a similar situation (and it must be remembered that this was fought before a world audience)? From 23rd February the Canadians and British fought out their long and bitter battle against the finest troops remaining to the enemy in the diminishing bridgehead narrowing upon the apex of Wesel. As the ground grew less the battle increased in fury, and the last day was worse than the first. The audience had long since left their seats.

II

The re-grouping of the Canadian 1st Army in the three days the 23rd February to 26th February took place against the background of a struggle in which the antagonists were locked solid. There was not a yard of give over all that narrow front, and the operation by which General Crerar planned to smash his way through was aptly named "Blockbuster". It was for this that the army regrouped its forces.

It would be tedious to attempt to unravel the day by day battle in all its horrible monotony of death and discomfort. It might tend to confuse rather than to illuminate. Nevertheless it is vital to my purpose that the realities of these days shall never be forgotten, or hidden behind such phrases as: The Canadian 1st Army re-grouped. There is always a feeling, however illogical, that this implies some pause. The truth is far otherwise. While a large-scale reorganization and movement of men and armour, of artillery and the many specialized implements of war, all involving great tonnages of transport and supplies, began to move over utterly inadequate roads, the battle raged with a fury demanding all the energies of those involved. It was not enough to hold: it was necessary to go forward, to insert wedges into the enemy's hardening barriers of defence.

At six o'clock on the morning of the 24th February (for example) the 53rd Division, supported by 13 field regiments, Royal Artillery, 6 medium regiments, 1 heavy regiment, 2 heavy anti-aircraft regiments, and by the 8th Armoured Brigade, and flails, crocodiles, kangaroos and A.V.s R.E. of the 79th Armoured Division, attacked southward from Goch against the town of Weeze. By noon of that day two battalions of infantry were astride the Goch–Weeze road some 4,000 yards short of the town, and its anti-tank ditch. The flame throwing crocodiles, moving in support of infantry and armour, had done their deadly work in the villages of Hohenhof and Host, villages that had long since ceased to function as villages, and had become outposts of great strength. The 71st Brigade got a company into a village called Rottum, and it seemed well named.

At a quarter past five o'clock on the morning of the 25th, twenty-four hours after the attack had been launched, it was brought to a standstill one mile short of Weeze. Enemy counter-attacks had inflicted heavy casualties and severe losses in tanks of the 8th Armoured Brigade. The way back, and the way forward, was littered with dead and the debris of war. Every way forward or back over the whole front of the 1st Canadian Army was a shambles of destruction, thick with smoke and stench, and shot through with flashes of the guns, and the reeking blasts of incessant explosions.

While the 53rd was fighting itself to a standstill on the road to Weeze from the north, the 52nd Division was blocked on the road from the west, and with one of its units engaged in a hand to hand struggle with the last defenders of the keep of Kasteel Blijenbeek. It was no better on the road to Udem.

On the 26th February the regrouping of the Canadian 1st Army for "Operation Blockbuster" had been achieved, and a slight but general improvement of the forward positions had been won. On the left the Canadian 2nd Corps comprised:

Canadian 4th Armoured Division
British 11th Armoured Division
Canadian 2nd Armoured Brigade
Canadian 2nd Infantry Division
Canadian 3rd Infantry Division
British 43rd Infantry Division

On the right the British 30th Corps:

Guards Armoured Division
6th Guards Armoured Brigade
8th Armoured Brigade
34th Armoured Brigade
British 3rd Infantry Division
15th (Scottish) Infantry Division
(to be relieved by 3rd British)
51st (Highland) Infantry Division
52nd (Lowland) Infantry Division
53rd (Welsh) Infantry Division

In addition there had been a redistribution of units of the 79th Armoured Division.

The inter-corps boundary would run right of the Canadian 2nd Corps through a point near Kervenheim to Sonsbeek.

That was the line-up for the last battle. The plans had been worked out in detail, and the outline of the intentions gives an idea of what remained to be done, and how, roughly, it would be done.

The intention was to break through between Udem and Calcar, produce two armoured brigades on the Hochwald ridge, and exploit through to Xanten.

Phase one was timed to begin at half past four o'clock on the morning of the 26th. Two brigades of the Canadian 2nd Infantry Division would secure high ground immediately to the south of Calcar, while a brigade of the 3rd Infantry Division, and two armoured regiments of the 4th Canadian Armoured Division secured hill spurs and features to points south of Udem. The 3rd Canadian

Infantry Division would then capture Udem while an armoured group closed in from the north-east.

These things having been done, almost, it was hoped, in three stages within the compass of a single day, the 11th Armoured Division would advance south-east, capture Sonsbeek and position its leading brigade on the high ground to the north of the town.

The way would then be opened for the Canadian 4th Armoured Division to advance east astride the road and railway running between the Hochwald and Balberger forests. The Canadian 2nd and 3rd Infantry Divisions would follow up to protect the flanks of both armoured divisions. Xanten and Wesel would then be within striking distance.

Such was the nature of "Blockbuster", and its opening was supported by 19 field regiments of artillery, 8 medium regiments, three heavy regiments, 1 Canadian rocket unit, and all the air support available.

17

ALL QUIET ON THE NORTHERN FRONT

I

INEVITABLY the focus of interest had moved to the right at the end of February. Names like Dusseldorf and Cologne, even Munchen Gladbach and Krefeld, were recognizable in the ears of the world, carrying with them the certainty of victory. Udem, Weeze, Sonsbeck, meant nothing, and but for a wife of Henry VIII it would have been difficult to arouse interest in Cleves. Goch was no more than an ugly word.

Not unnaturally a sense of excitement gripped onlookers, not only far from the battlefields, but on them, and it was difficult even to persuade any information about the left flank out of the headquarters of the 21st Army Group. Nothing, or next to nothing, was happening on the left. The re-grouping had been successful; all was going according to plan.

The British 2nd Army was deeply involved in the planning of the Rhine crossing, and with the 12th Corps was far more interested in mysterious exercises on a section of the Maas, than in the battles on the right or the left. Canadian 1st Army headquarters seemed depressed, and not without reason. Their great fight on the left flank in Normandy had passed almost unnoticed. Their unimaginative investment of the Channel ports had been dreary. Even their long sustained struggle for the Scheldt estuary had been overshadowed by the final assaults on Walcheren. And now, after months of plodding up the left flank, living in polder lands in dreadful conditions, they approached the climax of their greatest battle at a moment when all the world looked the other way. However unfortunate it may be, or appear to be, the audience had become an important factor in the Second World War; the more important because in the nature of things its eyes could never penetrate beyond the spotlight to the dim figures writhing in the smoke.

The first phase of "Blockbuster" had gone well. The high ground south of Calcar had been seized without difficulty, and forward troops had reached the outskirts of Udem. But the enemy defences swiftly hardened and the going was very heavy under wheels and tracks. Before noon on the first day the armour had begun to bog down. Before dusk the Canadian 8th Infantry Brigade suffered 25% casualties, and seventeen tanks had been lost to enemy anti-tank guns, panzerfaust and Panther tanks. Before the dawn of the 27th February no one had any illusions about "Blockbuster". It was going to be a grim and bitter fight to the finish. No one doubted that. The enemy did not give the impression of a brittle crust which might crack wide open. It was hard right through.

Udem was cleared on the 27th and eight civilians crawled up out of the rubble putting on an act of dubious welcome for which the troops had no time, and no response. They were no longer liberators, or if they were, they didn't feel like that. The streets of Udem were the accustomed shambles. Out of a window aperture overlooking a road deep in tangles of wire, wood, dust and stone, a succession of large plates crashed into the rubbish.

"The washing up, Sir," a young soldier said.

"You just chuck it out of the window?"

If he had said "Why not?" it would have been difficult to find a good answer.

Late on the 27th the Canadian 4th Armoured Division began to penetrate the Hochwald lay-back positions, and had elements on the threshold of the dangerous gap between the Hochwald and Balberger forests. It looked like a death trap.

Counter-attacks came in again and again, and were maintained with an almost demoniac violence, not only of men, but of heavy mortars, self-propelled and medium guns. Nothing like this had been encountered before anywhere on the western front. By the end of the second day one hundred tanks had been put out of action, more armour than any enemy panzer division could have mustered.

The Canadians pressed on, yard by yard, clinging to a grip on the spine of railway running through the gap. It made one think of Thermopylae, fixing one's thoughts on the failure of Antiochus of Syria, rather than of Leonidas and the Spartans.

It was, however, certain that the Canadians would get through. It was no more than a microcosm of an immense struggle, already resolved in military terms, and of which the new terms were not defined. Meanwhile the Canadian 2nd Infantry Division, moving down into the Hochwald to protect the left flank of the Canadian armour, ran into the garrison withdrawing from Calcar, and prepared to fight its way through to Marienbaum at all costs. Calcar itself was yielded in the end almost without a shot, but the price was paid in blood on the road.

On the right flank the 11th Armoured Division had been fighting its way to the south round the flank of the Balberger wood to capture the high ground north of Sonsbeck, well ahead of the Canadian 3rd Infantry Division whose role was to capture the Sonsbeck plateau. It was becoming clear that the enemy paratroops were resolved to hold a hinge position on which they might swing their troops away from the inevitable advance of the British 30th Corps. Their doom was being spelled out on their left flank.

Nowhere was the fight more desperate than in the narrow gap between the Hochwald and Balberger woods. There an assault battalion of paratroops, supported by self-propelled guns and heavy mortars, sold the pass inch by inch at a high price.

II

Even the British 30th Corps was unusually reticent in the last days of February, for the ebullient disposition of its commander normally spread a sense of excitement at the dullest moments. In 30th Corps headquarters it was impossible to avoid the conclusion that "Operation Veritable", in its closing stages, had become a grim and deadly grind. The battle had never got going, and it would not get going. Three weeks of savage fighting through the mud and sodden entrails of the Reichswald forest and its neighbouring strong points had at least brought some simplicity into the pattern of the battlefield. The Canadian main axis now lay through Calcar towards Xanten, thence at the last to converge upon Wesel.

The 30th Corps main axis struck down almost due south from Cleves, through Udem, while on the extreme right the 52nd Division was to draw a wide noose round the flank and swing up the Geldern–Issum–Alpon road upon Fort Blucher and Wesel.

Studying these things it seemed that the heart of the enemy defence west of the last lay-back position must be on the road Kervenheim–Winnekendonk. Weeze and Kevelaer still held, but were no longer of great importance. But progress was dreadfully slow. On the 27th February the 52nd Division at last began to break out of the Afferden area to relieve the 51st Division. On the 1st March the Recce regiment gained a small bridgehead over the anti-tank ditch which had held their southern flank, and with that the 1st Commando Brigade, coming under command, moved south along the banks of the Maas from Afferden to Weil. It was hard going even there, and beyond Weil the enemy still held on. Perhaps that is as good a measure as any of the tenacity of the Germans with their backs to the "last ditch".

With this the Weeze–Kevelaer line shook loose, and the 53rd Division swooped down and through to link with the Americans at Geldern. The fight for the Hochwald gap was undoubtedly the last remaining heart of the matter, and still covering that heart from the full force of attack from the west were the enemy positions based on Kervenheim and Winnekendonk. The 11th Armoured Division had been slowed by heavy fire from Kervenheim in its advance on Sonsbeck, and there were no signs of enemy withdrawal as the British 3rd Division cut the Udem–Weeze road on the 27th February and faced east. The 7th Parachute Division, stiffened up by many of those who had managed to fight their way out of Goch, barred the way. Every spinney and farmhouse held enemy, every narrow stream was a lethal barrier.

III

On the morning of Wednesday, the 28th February, tactical headquarters of the 185th Infantry Brigade of the British 3rd Infantry Division, was established in an isolated farmhouse forward of the Udem–Weeze road, and some 4,000 yards short of the village of Kervenheim. The farmhouse lay sheltered under the lip of a shallow sandy bowl, and with thin rectangular belts of trees spacing the flat brown patches of arable land in the foreground. Probably because of its isolation and because at the last it had offered very little fight it had not suffered damage, except that it looked stripped, and unlived in as a farm. Three enemy tanks, seemingly undamaged, on the fringes of the woodland testified to the fact that the enemy had been surprised and overwhelmed in sleep by a strong reconnaissance patrol in the hour before dawn. A few shreds of enemy clothing and equipment lay about in the farmyard and round the tanks, but these were the only signs of struggle or flight.

Taken as an isolated incident it might have seemed to confirm the views of corps and division that nothing—or very little—was happening, or about to happen, of any note. But it would have been dangerous to read too much into the fact of a small group of enemy surprised in their sleep. For days and nights the enemy had been battered mercilessly by artillery and aircraft, denied all hope of relief, of rest, of victory, or even of escape. It was astonishing, not that some were "punch drunk", or exhausted, but that so many continued to fight with a desperate and fanatical violence in the last flare-up of their nervous energies.

The lip of the sandy bowl hid the farmhouse from the rear, and on the gentle downward slope of the land falling away behind the slight ridge a battery of bofors was already in position. Behind them the guns of a field regiment of artillery were deployed in the low scrub, and a company of machine gunners had also taken up their positions on the flanks.

At noon on the 28th February a sense of tension began to be

evident in and around the farmhouse. It heralded the approach of a zero—or H—hour. It was apparent passing through the gun lines.

In the farmhouse yard a young Guards officer stood beside his armoured scout car, waiting and poised for instant action. He searched the sky and the surrounding scrub with the air of a man striving with his senses to gain some knowledge not otherwise apparent. His driver, a corporal, shared his mood and mien.

Their brief exchanges were those of men attuned to each other. These two men had been together into and out of many battles, the eyes and ears of a squadron of tanks of the 4th Battalion the Coldstream Guards. They moved with the tactical headquarters of infantry battalions, often in dangerous isolation, spotting targets, disguised strong points, enemy armour and self-propelled guns, and strove to maintain continuous contact with their own armour. A great deal depended upon their altertness, their courage and their accuracy.

Many times they had sniffed the morning air, as they did on this morning of the 28th February, for "omens". The signs this day seemed ominous.

The officer wore the ribbon of the Military Cross. With a brief command to his driver to be ready to move upon the instant he went swiftly into the farmhouse. Three jeeps with their drivers awaited their masters, and were spaced out carefully, having discovered on many occasions the accuracy of enemy mortars. The crackle of war, of rifle, spandau and machine gun fire, was incessant, but sufficiently remote to be ignored. The more thunderous over- and undertones of artillery had become a part of the background, seeming unnoticed, as a ship's engines on a long voyage, and yet to which the ears of all are constantly tuned.

The big farmhouse kitchen, which occupied almost the entire ground floor of the building, was sparsely furnished. A large kitchen table stood off centre towards the far end of the room, and there were two smaller tables, probably with the chairs, the props of brigade. The brigadier sat at the kitchen table with the brigade major on his left, studying a map intently. The Intelligence officer sat facing the brigade major with his own map out in front of him, and his notebooks ready. The brigade major had a set of headphones and a mouthpiece on the table beside him, and the Intelligence officer had a field telephone. At a small table in the corner of the room two signals lance-corporals sat facing each other wearing headphones, their faces completely absorbed. Half a dozen officers occupied the space in the body of the kitchen, exchanging greetings and light badinage, yet attentive to the slightest gesture of the brigadier. It was almost time.

All that was known about the country ahead was on the 1/25,000 maps. Lives depended on the accuracy of maps, and the accuracy with which men read their signs. Patches of woodland filled spaces between the lines of tracks, and enclosed open tracts of arable or pasture. Here and there were farm buildings and the isolated dots marking some hamlet. Thin blue lines marked the courses of dykes or streams, and the most definite of these lines was called the Muhlen Fleuth. It was known to be twenty-four feet wide and too deep in many places for wading.

Such a stream might not appear at all on the 1/250,000 maps of corps. Such obstacles were the business of brigadiers, lieut.-colonels, and lesser commanders, looming very large in the lives and deaths of N.C.O.s and private soldiers.

"If they can get a bridgehead right off the mark the rest may be easy," said the brigadier.

The low murmur of conversation hushed upon the instant, and a burly lieut.-colonel, commanding the 1st battalion Royal Norfolk Regiment, studied the brigadier's map. "They" were the K.S.L.I. on the left, and the Warwicks on the right. The moment these two battalions secured the flanks the Norfolks would go through in the centre to assault and capture the village of Kervenheim. That was the brigade objective.

Kervenheim looked like the linch pin of the last of the enemy heavily defended positions west of the Hochwald lay-back. The area bounded by Kervenheim–Weeze–Kevelaer–Winnekendonk looked ominous. If Kervenheim went there would not be much future for the enemy in the area. The 53rd Division was on the right, and the 52nd Division on their right.

"One minute to go," said the brigadier. He leaned his left arm on the table and watched the sweep of the second hand on his wrist watch. It was exactly 1359 hours—one minute to two o'clock.

Precisely on the stroke of two o'clock an avalance of uproar engulfed the farmhouse. The bofors were firing flat from within one hundred yards. Behind them and to the flanks the whole orchestra roared out its shattering pattern, and two thousand yards ahead two battalions of infantry began to move forward from their start lines, leaning on the barrage as close up as they dared.

It was impossible for a moment or two to think under the vicious screaming din of the bofors. The lieut.-colonel of the Norfolks studied the position with the brigadier, their heads close together. Each battalion had a squadron of tanks in support, and the flails, crocodiles and A.V.s R.E. of the 79th Armoured Division.

The Warwicks came through on the telephone, going in, two hundred yards from the river, the Muhlen Fleuth. The red and blue lines, the arrows and circles, on the brigade major's map, indicating the positions of our own troops and of the enemy, at once seemed alive.

"Barrage lifts in one minute, Sir," shouted an artillery officer.

Suddenly the deluge of din gave way to the sharp intake of silence. The C.O. of the Norfolks drank a mug of tea and munched a sandwich. A tall, well built major with ginger hair came into the room, saluted smartly, his mouth immediately breaking into a wide grin.

"Good leave, Charles?" asked the brigadier.

"Grand, Sir."

The thunder of the guns began to rise again to drown for a moment the fierce mutter of the machine guns. On the headphones the fierce noises of the battle had a strange remote reality, bringing back the noises of bursting shells, a dangerous undergrowth of sounds.

At 1445 hours the Warwicks reported one company over the river, and one company at the bridging point. A.V.s R.E. and tanks were moving up.

Again the thunder of the guns rose.

"Right. Off you go, Peter!" said the brigadier.

The C.O. of the Norfolks rushed out, and was away in seconds with the young Guards officer and his armoured scout car after him, bounding, lurching, skidding over the mud tracks, towards the battle.

One thousand yards ahead the Norfolks formed, trailing off in companies skirting the woodland, stringing out in lines towards the river. The flails moved steadily over he flat open ground, their chains lashing the earth, and behind them the A.V.s R.E. bore huge fascines, and were followed by petard tanks. All the array of mechanical warfare moved steadily across the open tract of arable between the woods, the Churchill tanks of the Coldstream Guards covering the infantry.

"This is Prince Charlie six . . . . Prince Charlie six . . . . Report my signals. Over," said the scout car commander into his radio telephone.

Five hundred yards ahead bursts of flame welled up out of the earth like blood, and hovered there. A crimson mist hung over the woods, and the earth began to leap up in grey spouts from enemy shell bursts. Typhoons swooped like wild birds patterning the brazen sky with rocket trails, and out of the ditches on the edge of the wood the men of the Norfolks rose up, crouching, half running, towards the vortex.

But it was too soon. The Warwicks and the K.S.L.I. were in the midst of the enemy, and the right flank was dangerously open. Five hundred yards on the Norfolks lay again on the rim of the woods, waiting the word to go forward. It was nearly five o'clock. The C.O. had gone back for orders. Soon the sky would darken. The Norfolks lay on the edge of a wide plain of open land surrounded on three sides by woods. A troop of Churchill tanks, their besas blazing, moved on a small village half hidden in a copse which must be on the river bank. A lone tank supported a section of infantry moving in swift bounds upon a farmstead in the midst of outbuildings on the far edge of the plain.

Almost imperceptibly the battles on the flanks began to spill over and to envelop the centre. The scout car spotted the muzzle flash of a self-propelled gun threatening the lone tank and the infantry section, and at once reported. A hare sat motionless, ears flat, and small birds flew madly in zig-zags, hemmed within the invisible cage of battle. The small village, half hidden in a copse, erupted into flame, and enemy machine guns searched the woods with fire, crackling through the trees like flames fanned by the wind to consume dry bracken. The machine gun fire pressed the waiting

Norfolks close against the wet earth, urgently to dig narrow slots for shelter.

The sun was almost down, and a slender rift of gold showed in the western sky. The infantry section came running out of the farm, urging seven prisoners at the double across the open ground. Over that open ground two stretcher bearers toiled slowly with their burden of a wounded man, the sticky brown soil heavy on their boots. The high fluffing sound of enemy shells ruffled the darkening sky.

'We ought to be moving," said a tank commander. "If we're going to move."

The barrage in support of the attack of the Norfolks was due. The Typhoons and Spitfires dive bombed within four hundred yards on the right in the last flight before night.

Out of the crimson murk of smoke and flame, hedged in by spouting columns of earth, a pitiful cavalcade stumbled from the farmstead, the old and the young, a man with a dog in the lead, a woman, children, goats, geese, bewildered, overtaken by war. In this alone war had not changed. In this fashion, in all the long history of warfare, peasants had stumbled from their homes.

IV

The Norfolks lay dispersed in the woods all night in the shallow slots they had cut for themselves, two men to a slot, sitting, knees up, face to face, heads slumped forward under tin hats. In the ditches at the roadside on the edge of the open land others lay in blankets behind the bren carriers. Two hundred yards out three sections had dug in after dusk. Patrols would be out all through the night. Something had gone wrong, and nobody knew what; nor would they ever know.

Gusts of wind fanned the flames of the small burning village to moments of brilliance, and the cage of war had a more intense definition, lit with many fires, explosions, gun flashes, and the occasional Very light. The sky was restless with the drumming and shuffling of shells, and a sustained barrage was concentrated upon Weeze.

The C.O. of the Norfolks held three Order Groups in the night.

An angle trench had been dug, and in this, ankle deep in mud, under a piece of tarpaulin supported on boxes and anchored by spades, the company commanders huddled round the massive figure of the C.O. He wore a paratrooper's jacket over a thick sweater, and with a red spotted scarf round his neck. A hurricane lamp shone upon the map and the shadowed grave faces of the company commanders, their cheek bones high lighted. The C.O. had wanted a night attack, but the tank commander did not.

The battalion cooks brought up hot stew and tea in containers at about nine o'clock, and out on the edge of the plain the scout car commander directed the efforts of a tank to pull a damaged flail tank out of the ditch. An hour later a post corporal found his way to the wood with a small sack of letters, and two men sorted them by candlelight in a slot. No one would read a letter that night, and in the morning many would be dead.

The last Order Group took place under the tarpaulin soon after midnight. A decision had been reached. At a quarter to four o'clock the battalion would move over the Muhlen Fleuth and forward some one thousand yards to the rim of the woods outside Kervenheim. They would dig in and attack under a barrage at nine o'clock.

At half past three o'clock the cooks toiled forward again through the livid night with thick sweet porridge, sausages and hunks of bread, and more tea. A three-quarter moon shone brilliantly in a clear sky. The wood became inhabited with shadowy figures crawling up out of their slots, stretching aching limbs, glad of the hot breakfast.

A man said "Rabbits". It was the 1st of March. Half an hour later the leading companies began to move. The second in command, the ginger haired major with the broad grin, stood at the roadside bordering the wood. Steadily the platoons filed past, a silent procession of human pack animals, their faces framed in woollen mufflers, like visors under the tin hats. On their backs their packs, a short spade, a pick, rifles slung.

The second in command greeted each platoon commander, "'Lo, Harry, g'morning." "'Lo, Charles, g'morning."

The flames of the burning village bronzed the trail of faces as they plodded through. On the outskirts of the village in the purple-grey before dawn an old man stood with his back to the road, unmoving, his head bowed. A middle-aged woman grasped the arm of an aged woman, a bundle of skirts, a wizened shrivelled face under a thin covering of grey hair drawn taut. The two women stumbled over the fields away from the marching troops. A few yards in from the road a man buried his dead.

Beyond the river the road was open to the dark line of woods, close up on the left, and perhaps three hundred yards distant on the right. Bursts of tracer and flares shone suddenly upon a roof top in the right flanking woods, and illumined a desperate encounter. A large house stood out silhouetted in the trees, and tracer hitting the roof was ricochetting and soaring high. The crash of machine gun and small arms fire rose to a crescendo. It was ominous. It should not have been there.

One hundred yards ahead the road came under heavy fire from self-propelled guns and mortars, and the Norfolks crouched, running under cover of the armour and the bren carriers. It was not the battle of the Norfolks. Their way lay straight ahead to a line of woods marked by the burning shell of a farmhouse. They went forward in bounds of about fifty yards, strung out, a man bearing the heavy tube of a mortar sucked great gusts of the morning air into his lungs.

At five o'clock the twin beams of searchlights made artificial moonlight, forming a huge Vee in the sky, dense black between the broad incandescent bands, the outer edges fringed with purple to merge into the flames licking up from the woods, the farms, hamlets. For more than twelve hours this road, the road back, would be almost as deadly as the road forward, and over it the double decker jeeps would bear their burdens of wounded out of the battle, the R.A.M.C. men sheltering the maimed bodies with their own.

At a quarter to five o'clock a message reached battalion tactical headquarters from the Warwicks. The message reported much that was already known, and something that was not: a farmhouse and outbuildings, known as the Muserhof, on the right flank and covering the approaches to Kèrvenheim, was strongly held by enemy. The Muserhof position gave the enemy a magnificent field of fire at an oblique angle to dominate the open western approaches. It looked bad on the map.

V

Soon after five o'clock in the morning the Norfolks dug themselves in on the forward edge of the woodland belt, facing Kervenheim at a distance of about half a mile. A Company was on the right, B Company in the centre, and C Company on the left. D Company was in reserve.

Battalion headquarters made use of an old pit or cellar in the shelter of a smouldering roofless farmhouse, and reinforced it with sandbags and rubble. The rest of battalion headquarters dug in as deep as they could in the time available. The burning farmhouse had provided a beacon in the last stages of the march, and revealed the dark tunnel of trees arching over the road.

The K.S.L.I. were within fifty yards on the left and one of their patrols made immediate contact. The left flank was secure. Patrols made use of the remaining darkness to probe into the outskirts of Kervenheim, and towards the Muserhof. The moon was still up in a sky filled with scudding cloud, and the moaning of heavy shells. It was peaceful until dawn. The sunrise was very beautiful, the eastern sky filled with feathery clouds stained scarlet. The heavy clouded sky in the west was the dusky colour of ripe peaches. This was the last sight for some—at least, it was there in the sky, when the first heavy bursts of enemy mortar bombs fell in the woods, and the 88's tore out the top of a strip of woodland like a frieze. The tree bursts and the heavy mortaring were deadly, but not more deadly than the persistent accurate sniping at very short range.

It was an uncomfortable time for the Norfolks from half past six o'clock until half past eight, when the 25 pounders began to range on the target ahead. One battery, ranging short, sent three successive salvos almost on top of battalion headquarters.

The scout car had sent an urgent signal to the tank squadron, and an O.P. tank moved out forward of the wood on the right, trying to spot the muzzle flashes of the enemy self-propelled guns. It was heavy going for tanks. Two Churchills churned up the mud in a shallow dyke thirty yards behind battalion headquarters, and tore up the signal wires in their tracks when they got going. It was deadly in the open for the men laying signal wires.

From dawn onwards the R.A.M.C. men were busy bringing the wounded out of the woods, running wherever the mortar bursts were thickest, seeming themselves unaware of danger.

At twenty minutes to nine o'clock the barrage opened, and the steeple of Kervenheim church stood out dark and black above the smoke. At nine o'clock C Company went in on the left with B Company in support, and a troop of tanks. A Company attacked on the right, and with that a tornado of heavy machine gun fire ripped over the open plain out of the Muserhof and tore through the woods like the lashing of steel whips. Crawling, crouching, striving to move forward in bounds, A Company tried to worm its way right handed and onward to close the Muserhof, answering the tremendous concentration of spandaus and mortars with brens, small arms, and their own mortars. The supporting tanks of the Coldstreams could not keep with the infantry. Two tanks bogged down five hundred yards short. The last word came from the O.P. tank: "It's awfully bare . . . . " A direct hit on the tank ripped off the end of the sentence.

At eleven o'clock the remnants of A Company regained the dangerous shelter of the woods. The tank commander had been killed. A boy, red faced, and wide eyed with a kind of wonder hung with his left arm round an R.A.M.C. corporal's shoulder, trailing shattered legs. A pale-faced ginger-haired lad hung on the corporal's other shoulder, his left arm swinging loose. Slowly they came back, a steady cavalcade of wounded. Hour after hour the air bursts of the 88's, the mortars, and the heavy machine guns, lashed at the woods, and across the open ground. The armoured carriers, and the double decker jeeps, the stretcher bearers, went forward and back, steady and steadfast, and the Norfolks pressed their attacks.

On the left two companies had got into Kervenheim supported by Lt. Melikoff in his Churchill tank, and with a troop of tanks in close support. It was not just fighting in a village, but fighting in a fortress, with every house and backyard not simply a place hiding enemy, but a carefully thought out defensive position. Machine guns were mounted on every roof, and poured streams of fire from every vantage point, and these were manned by desperate men to whom the abnormal had become the only reality: there was only war, and only now.

A tremendous counter-attack drove the Norfolks out of Kervenheim within the hour, and Melikoff, wounded in the head, and his tank bazookaed, somehow managed to fight his way out. Halfway through the morning B Company had lost all its officers, and a battered remnant of the company at last regained the woodland line. It was about noon when D Company went in with the reorganized remnants of C and B Companies, and by two o'clock it was as certain as anything could be that they would hold in Kervenheim. Hidden nests of enemy seemed to be everywhere, and the fire from the Muserhof had not abated.

Nevertheless the enemy must yield to the inexorable pressure. In the rear, Brigade "Tac" moved up to the wood in which the Norfolks had spent the night. Brigade "Main" moved up to the farmstead in the sandy hollow. Divisional "Tac" moved up. The Norfolks would spend the night holding the river line through Kervenheim. The Lincolns were going through. The British 3rd Infantry Division was moving down on Winnekendonk, its right flank tied in with the 53rd Division. By nightfall on the 1st March the triangle of which Kervenheim had formed the eastern apex had fallen. Weeze and Kevelaer, and the last of the river Niers line could not be held, and indeed it must have been the confusion of enemy fighting their way back through the woods that had so disrupted the right flank of the 185th Brigade attack.

The Muserhof position finally fell to the 53rd Division, and above all to the personal courage of tank commanders and infantry. At six o'clock on the evening of the 1st March the young scout car officer and his driver stretched their weary legs for the first time in many hours. Lightly armoured and vulnerable they had worked tirelessly under fire, and had spotted the muzzle flashes of enemy self-propelled guns. The black steeple of Kervenheim church stood out black and solid above the smoke and flame of the village. There was a mist of driving rain. Sporadic fighting would go on in and around Kervenheim all through the night. From a hidden position behind the Muserhof an enemy self-propelled gun came suddenly into action to put a shell within a dozen yards of the scout car and its crew. The momentary lull of the evening was a dangerous illusion. There was no rest.

18

THE END OF "VERITABLE"

I

THE battle of Kervenheim was one of the scores of pieces which went to make up the picture of "Operation Veritable". It helped to fill in a small, but important, triangle of the struggle, and to open the way for the final phase. From the 2nd March when the last of the enemy rearguards had been forced to abandon the Kervenheim–Winnekendonk line the bridgehead began to shrink rapidly to intolerable proportions.

The fury of "Operation Blockbuster" concentrated upon the Hochwald and Balberger forests and had not diminished, but the pressure on the flanks increased alarmingly for the enemy. The 43rd Division, in contact with the Canadian 2nd Division in the Hochwald, advanced steadily, supported by flails and flame throwing crocodiles to reduce Marienbaum. On the right the enemy still clung to Sonsbeek, and the high ground to the north. On the flanks the battle for the Hochwald lay-back would be won and lost.

Between the 1st and the 4th March the battlefield was rapidly "tidied up". The 1st Commando Brigade on the extreme right flank of the 52nd Division made contact with the U.S. 17th Cavalry Recce Regiment, and the mopping up of the last of the enemy between the Maas and the Goch–Geldern road opened the way for the 52nd Division to swing eastward.

On the 4th March the 53rd Division, nearing the end of its long commitment, cleared Geldern, and moved east in solid contact with the U.S. 16th Corps on the road to Issum.

The British 3rd Infantry Division, having moved swiftly through Winnekendonk upon Kapellen, turned north-east to make contact with the Canadian 3rd Division still fighting desperately hard in the Balberger forest. Heavily cratered roads, innumerable mines, blown bridges over minor waterways, and tank obstacles, all covered by an enemy whose resolution had stiffened in the face of imminent disaster, held up the Guards Armoured Division in its efforts to go through, and exacted a heavy toll in armour and men. The whole terrain was jammed tight with enemy and obstacles, and the enemy fire power, concentrated on very narrow frontages, had become devastating. There was still no room for armour to manœuvre. No obstacles would be by-passed, and whenever armour attempted to advance alone it lost heavily. That was even more true at the end than in the beginning.

By the night of the 4th March tremendous pressure had been brought to bear upon the Hochwald and Balberger positions, but it was not until Sonsbeek fell on the 6th, and Marienbaum yielded to the 43rd Division on the left, that the last of the enemy seemed "to vanish", and the way was open between the forests. There had been no give at all, and the enemy rearguards had fought with incredible ferocity to cover the last withdrawal to the shrinking bridgehead.

The British 3rd Infantry Division, and the 11th Armoured Division, were pinched out, and the 52nd Division relieved the 53rd Division on the right. Five divisions, some of them with a frontage of little more than one thousand yards, converged upon the site of the catastrophe Hitler had not sought to evade.

Every kind of lethal obstacle filled that last narrow triangle of land, bounded by Xanten on the left, through Veen, to the Issum–Alpon road, and with its apex on Wesel. The natural defences of railway, canal, dyke and woodland, had been greatly strengthened, thick with mines and wire, with concrete emplacements and machine gun nests, and with deeply entrenched positions in the woods. The formidable defences of Xanten blocked the left flank, and Alpon, no less heavily defended, blocked the way through on the right. Veen lay at the heart, barring the way through the centre.

Behind this last enemy position, packed tight with mortars and self-propelled guns, the Wesel bridges remained open, defying all the efforts of the Allied Air Forces to destroy them. Wesel itself and the eastern and western approaches to the bridges were deluged day and night with bombs. Direct hits were reported, but still the bridges held, and some sort of traffic was maintained.

Such was the last battlefield, defended by twenty thousand paratroopers, dedicated to the last stand. As late as the 7th March no order to the enemy had been given to withdraw, and on the 8th March, when the U.S. 1st Army began to pour its troops over the Remagen bridge, the line Xanten–Veen–Alpon still held.

II

From the artillery observation posts on the ridge east of the Hochwald Gap the whole battlefield lay spread out in a magnificent and terrible panorama within the compass of the human eye. It was thus possible to watch the last act played out to its inevitable end.

From the 6th to the 10th March the battle raged with frightful intensity on a front no more than eight miles wide, the antagonists locked together at every point, almost immovable until, at the last, the tattered remnants of an army withdrew behind fanatical rear-guards.

Had the weather permitted the Allied Air Forces to play full parts in support it is difficult to imagine how any of the enemy could have survived. As it was the pounding by artillery and bombing within the confines of that narrow triangle was awe-inspiring. Through all the 6th and 7th, fighting by day and night enclosed in a diabolical inferno of fire, scarcely a yard had been gained. A tremendous assault against the western outskirts of Xanten had been repulsed and driven back. Veen with its lethal strips of forest on the left centre seemed impregnable, and on the right the 52nd Division faced formidable obstacles covering the approaches to Alpon.

It is difficult, if not impossible, to evaluate one section of that narrow battlefield against another, but Xanten was the undoubted key, for with its fall the whole of the enemy right and centre would be outflanked.

Immediately to the south of Xanten the railway lines from Cleves and Goch converged to a single track, which again split into two behind Veen, both lines joining the Geldern–Wesel line astride the

Xanten–Rheinberg road. These lines, together with a complex system of small canals, dykes and rivulets, added greatly to the defensive strength of the Veen positions.

On the British right the line of the Winnenthaler canal interlaced with the stream of the Muhohl to provide a natural defensive barrier in front of Alpon, and the whole of the right centre.

For the enemy there was nothing more to be sold for blood. This must be the end, for a break through anywhere must open the way to Wesel, and cut the last possible line of withdrawal. Thursday, the 8th March, had the feel of a day of reckoning. Left, right and centre, the 43rd, the 52nd and the 2nd, 3rd and 4th Canadian Divisions, had gathered themselves for major attacks concentrated with all their strength, and supported by an immense weight of artillery. There was the knowledge, too, that the end must be very near, that it was beyond the strength of flesh and blood to withstand so great a battering. To the 43rd and the 2nd and 3rd Canadian Divisions it seemed a very long road back to Cleves: it was longer still for the enemy, and with nothing at the end of it but death, surrender or retreat across the Rhine. At any moment the last might be impossible.

The 8th March was a day of heavy cloud masses, but with good visibility. A white smoke screen streamed across the northern flank of the battlefield to shield the 43rd Division from enemy guns beyond the Rhine. Shells from batteries of 5.5's crashed into the town of Xanten so that the dark shroud in which the town was hidden flickered incessantly with bursts of flame, and the flash of enemy fire. The lovely church and spire of Xanten, raised on a slight hill, seemed to be riding the heavy cloud banks as the smoke of battle swathed its base.

The villages of Wardt and Vynen had already fallen to the 43rd Division, and the spires of their churches stood out dark and clear against the white smoke screen. Thin lines of bushy topped poplars spaced the lush pasture lands of the valley to the fringes of the Staatforst de Hees covering Veen. In that small forest, stuffed with mines and ammunition dumps, a fanatical group of paratroopers were fighting to the last on top of a powder keg. Crocodiles, flails, tanks and men moved in eccentric fashion over that landscape like pieces moved on a board.

Behind the small forest three tall factory chimneys revealed the position of rail sidings, and in the midst of a great turbulence of smoke and flame Veen itself lay hidden at the very vortex of the tremendous struggle. Again and again the fringes of the Staatforst de Hees leapt into running flames as the crocodiles, moving with the Canadian infantry, burned and carved a way yard by yard.

The whole of the middle distance was lit hour after hour with the constant flicker and flare of running fires and explosions, and the flash of guns. At intervals farmsteads and ammunition dumps blew up in billows of heavy smoke shot through with flames, and men like ants ran and fell, moving forward and back.

Indeed from that high ridge, immune it seemed from the enemy guns concentrating all their power on the battle itself, it was easy to see everything, and yet to see nothing. There was, as always, no way of knowing the reality of the last days without going down onto that terrible stage.

By nightfall on the 8th March the 43rd Division had forced its way through to the southern half of Xanten, and hung on grimly. Nevertheless the intensity of the battle on the left did not abate. The defenders of Xanten, forced to withdraw, reinforced the defenders of Veen, and fought back with savage counter-attacks supported by cataracts of mortar fire. The Staatforst de Hees still held. Veen still defied capture.

Meanwhile on the right the 52nd Division was involved in a desperate struggle to encircle Alpon from the north. It was two o'clock on the afternoon of the 8th March when the 156th Brigade attacked in a wheeling movement to the north of the town, pivoting on the 4/5th Royal Scots Fusiliers, in an attempt to cut the lateral railway and the last line of retreat for the enemy in that quarter. The Guards in support of the left flanking battalion found the way blocked by heavy cratering, and could not keep up with the infantry. At the same time confusing reports of the American advances close up on the right flank hampered the fire plans of the gunners of the mountain division.

By dawn on the 9th the Royal Scots Fusiliers had succeeded in outflanking the town, but at a high cost. On their left the 6th Cameronians had suffered terrible casualties with two companies cut off, and a third in serious trouble. Nothing except death, it seemed, would move the enemy. At last the 6th Cameronians, their ammunition exhausted, and subjected to devastating fire from spandaus, mortars and self-propelled guns firing over open sights, were overrun. They had lost four officers and one hundred and sixty-nine men in their attempts to cut the railway line to the east of Alpon.

In the opinion of the historian of the 52nd Division the 6th Battalion Cameronians "took the brunt of the German fury in holding open one of their last lines of escape". It may be some measure of the quality of this fight to the bitter end that similar claims could be justly made for units of all the divisions involved. Even the 4th K.O.S.B. on the left of the 156th Brigade attack might have made a claim for themselves in their fight against the garrison of a castle and strong point, the Haus Loo. It was reminiscent of the Kasteel Blijenbeek at the beginning of the battle.

Haus Loo, it was claimed, was the last enemy stronghold to fall on the 10th March, but there was sporadic fighting at many points, even in the area south of Xanten, all through the 10th as the enemy rearguards strove to gain a few more hours of time to cover the withdrawal of all that remained in men and materials of General Schlemm's Parachute Army.

At last on the night of the 10th March a series of deep rumbling explosions told all those who still fought on that the Wesel bridge was blown. At twenty minutes to eleven o'clock on the morning of the 11th March an air observer confirmed that the great railway bridge had been destroyed by the enemy, and from Nijmegen to Neuss the 21st Army Group had closed the Rhine.

III

The "bag" of prisoners, equipment and materials of war, was much less than had been expected, yet the "eleventh hour" had already sounded before General Schlemm finally had permission to withdraw the 1st Parachute Army. Early in March, when the madness of continuing the fight west of the Rhine might have been apparent even to a madman, General Schlemm had appealed to his army group commander, Colonel-General Blaskowitz, for his support. It was as a result of Blaskowitz' personal intervention that an emissary from the Fuhrer's headquarters reached General Schlemm's headquarters west of the Rhine on the morning of the 9th March. This officer, a Lt.-Colonel unaccustomed to the front line realities of warfare, had been carefully subjected to a considerable "ordeal by gunfire" to ensure that his judgement of the desperate position should not be at fault. Thus it was that on the night of the 9th March the remnants of the 1st Parachute Army had begun an orderly withdrawal over the battered and much bombed concrete and steel of the Wesel railway bridge.

In the last stages of the battle the enemy had mustered more than one thousand guns, and seven hundred and seventeen mortars, to subject the Canadians and British to the heaviest volume of fire experienced in the campaign.

The battle yielded a total of 51,618 prisoners, 29,379 of them to the U.S. 9th Army, and 22,239 to the Canadians and British. They came from eighteen divisions and many hastily organized battle groups. Of these at least fourteen divisions and a high proportion of the battle groups had fought the Canadians and British in the north.

In addition it was estimated that the enemy had lost a total of 38,000 killed and wounded. The remnants of the 1st Parachute Army finally to withdraw across the Rhine had left some 90,000 men behind them in killed, wounded and prisoners.

The Allied losses had not been light. The U.S. 9th Army in its rapid advance had lost 7,300 killed and wounded, and the 1st Canadian Army 16,000 killed and wounded, two-thirds of them British.

By the fortunes of war the Canadians and the British on the left had held the hinge, as they had done in Normandy, taking the full weight of the enemy defensive battle, and opening the way for the brilliant drives of the American armour on the right. By its battle of the Rhineland the Canadian 1st Army had cleared the road to Cologne for the U.S. 1st Army.

By the fortunes of war, also, the Allied Supreme Commander's "broad front" policy, sustained from the beginning against all argument, had triumphed. By the end of March General Eisenhower had closed the Rhine over its entire length, and achieved his intention to destroy the German armies west of the Rhine. Few, I think, would deny that Adolf Hitler, refusing all the pleas of his commanders to withdraw, had been his most powerful "ally" in this achievement.

SOURCES

Report by the Supreme Commander to the Combined Chiefs of Staff on the Operations in Europe of the Allied Expeditionary Force, June 6th, 1944, to May 8th, 1945. (London: H.M.S.O., 1946.)

Operations in North-West Europe from June 6th, 1944, to May 5th, 1945, despatch submitted to the Secretary of State for War, June 1st, 1946, by Field Marshal The Viscount Montgomery of Alamein, K.G., G.C.B., D.S.O. (Supplement to the *London Gazette*, September 3rd, 1946) (No. 37711).

United States Army in World War II. The European Theatre of Operations. The Supreme Command, by Forrest C. Pogue. (Office of the Chief of Military History, Department of the Army, Washington, D.C., 1954.)

United States Army in World War II. Three Battles: Arnaville, Altuzzo, and Schmidt, by Charles B. MacDonald and Sydney T. Mathews. (Office of the Chief of Military History, Department of the Army, Washington, D.C., 1952.)

United States Army in World War II. The European Theatre of Operations. The Lorraine Campaign. (Office of Chief of Military History, Department of the Army, Washington, D.C.)

History of the Second World War, United Kingdom Military Series GRAND STRATEGY, Volume V. August, 1943—September, 1944, by John Ehrman. (London: H.M.S.O., 1956.)

GRAND STRATEGY, Volume VI. October, 1944—August, 1945, by John Ehrman. (London: H.M.S.O., 1956.)

The Second World War. Volume VI. "Triumph and Tragedy", by Sir Winston Churchill, K.G. (London: Cassell, 1954.)

The Second World War, 1939-45 by Major-General J. F. C. Fuller. (London: Eyre & Spottiswoode (Revised Edition), 1954.)

North-West Europe, 1944-45. The Achievement of Twenty-First Army Group, by John North. (London: H.M.S.O., 1953.)

The Canadian Army, 1939-45. An Official Historical Summary, by Colonel C. P. Stacey, O.B.E., A.M., Ph.D., Director, Historical Section, General Staff. (Published by authority of the Minister of National Defence, Edmond Cloutier, King's Printer, Ottawa, 1948.)

Crusade in Europe, by Dwight D. Eisenhower. (London: Heinemann, 1948.)

The White House Papers of Harry L. Hopkins, Volume II by Robert E. Sherwood. (London: Eyre & Spottiswoode, 1948.)

A Soldier's Story of the Allied Campaigns from Tunis to the Elbe, by General Omar Bradley. (London: Eyre & Spottiswoode, 1952.)

War As I Knew It, by General George S. Patton. (Boston: Houghton Mifflin, 1947.)

Top Secret, by Ralph Ingersoll. (New York: Harcourt Brace, 1946.)

The Struggle for Europe by Chester Wilmot. (London: Collins, 1952.)

Normandy to the Baltic by Field Marshal The Viscount Montgomery of Alamein, K.G., G.C.B., D.S.O. (London: Hutchinson, 1946.)

Operation Victory by Major-General Sir Francis de Guingand, K.B.E., C.B., D.S.O. (London: Hodder and Stoughton, 1947.)

The Other Side of the Hill by B. H. Liddell Hart. (London: Cassell & Co.)

The Execution of Private Slovik by William B. Huie. (London: Jarrolds.)

The Green Beret by Hilary St. George Saunders. (London: Michael Joseph, 1949.)

Borderers in Battle. The War Story of the King's Own Scottish Borderers, 1939-45. By Captain Hugh Gunning. (Martin's Printing Works, Berwick-upon-Tweed, 1948.)

Mountain and Flood, 1939-46. Divisional History of 52nd Division by George Blake. (Glasgow: Jackson Son & Co.)

Defence in the West, Milton Shulman. (Cassell, London.)

The 43rd Wessex Division at War, 1944-45 by Major-General H. Essame.

INDEX

INDEX

B

S

T

INDEX